The Great European Stage Directors

Volume 2

The Great European Stage Directors
Series Editor: Simon Shepherd

Volume 1
Antoine, Stanislavski, Saint-Denis
Edited by Peta Tait

Volume 2
Meyerhold, Piscator, Brecht
Edited by David Barnett

Volume 3
Copeau, Komisarjevsky, Guthrie
Edited by Jonathan Pitches

Volume 4
Reinhardt, Jessner, Barker
Edited by Michael Patterson

Volume 5
Grotowski, Brook, Barba
Edited by Paul Allain

Volume 6
Littlewood, Strehler, Planchon
Edited by Clare Finburgh Delijani and Peter M. Boenisch

Volume 7
Barrault, Mnouchkine, Stein
Edited by Felicia Hardison Londré

Volume 8
Bausch, Castellucci, Fabre
Edited by Luk Van den Dries and Timmy De Laet

The Great European Stage Directors

Volume 2

Meyerhold, Piscator, Brecht

Edited by David Barnett
Series Editor: Simon Shepherd

methuen | drama
LONDON · NEW YORK · OXFORD · NEW DELHI · SYDNEY

METHUEN DRAMA
Bloomsbury Publishing Plc
50 Bedford Square, London, WC1B 3DP, UK
1385 Broadway, New York, NY 10018, USA
29 Earlsfort Terrace, Dublin 2, Ireland

BLOOMSBURY, METHUEN DRAMA and the Methuen Drama logo are trademarks of
Bloomsbury Publishing Plc

First published in hardback in Great Britain 2019
Reprinted 2019
This paperback edition 2024
Reprinted 2024

A catalogue record for this book is available from the British Library.

A catalog record for this book is available from the Library of Congress.

ISBN: HB: 978-1-4742-5394-9
      HB Set: 978-1-4742-5411-3
          PB: 978-1-3504-4578-9
      PB Set: 978-1-3504-4598-7
        ePDF: 978-1-4742-5989-7
       eBook: 978-1-3504-6189-5

Series: Great Stage Directors

Typeset by Integra Software Services Pvt. Ltd.
Printed and bound in Great Britain

To find out more about our authors and books visit www.bloomsbury.com and sign up for
our newsletters.

CONTENTS

Bertolt Brecht 131

LIST OF ILLUSTRATIONS

NOTES ON CONTRIBUTORS

Minou Arjomand is Associate Professor in English at the University of Texas at Austin. Her research addresses questions about theatre, politics and the public realm: what sort of publics emerge in a theatre? And what, exactly, is political about political theatre? She is the author of *Staged: Show Trials, Political Theater, and the Aesthetics of Judgment* (2018).

David Barnett is Professor of Theatre at the University of York. He is the author of *A History of the Berliner Ensemble* (2015), *Brecht in Practice: Theatre, Theory and Performance* (2014), *Rainer Werner Fassbinder and the German Theatre* (2005) and a monograph on Heiner Müller (1998). He has written several articles and essays on German- and English-language political and postdramatic theatre. He was Principal Investigator for an AHRC-funded project, 'Brecht in Practice: Staging Drama Dialectically', which considers how Brecht's dialectical staging methodology can be applied to plays that are not written in the Brechtian tradition.

Bryan Brown is a theatre maker and Senior Lecturer of Drama at the University of Exeter. He is co-director of Maketank cultural laboratory and is currently working to reframe and rethink Russian theatre studies and its relationship to empire in the wake of the full-scale invasion of Ukraine in 2022. He is also an editorial board member of *Theatre, Dance and Performance Training* and co-curator of the journal's blog. His research interests include ensemble and collective creation practices, performer training and the laboratory theatre tradition, and the clown as an instigator of wonder. He has been a contributor to *Encountering Ensemble* (2013) and *Collective Creation in Contemporary Performance* (2013). He is the author of *A History of the Theatre Laboratory* (2019).

Meg Mumford is Senior Lecturer in Theatre and Performance Studies at UNSW Sydney, Australia. She has published widely on the work of Bertolt Brecht, and is the author of the volume on Brecht in the Routledge Performance Practitioners series (2009/2018). She has also written on Marieluise Fleisser, Pina Bausch, Australian verbatim and documentary theatre, and theatre with non-professional performers. Recent publications include: *Theatre of Real People: Diverse Encounters at Berlin's Hebbel am*

Ufer and Beyond, co-authored with Ulrike Garde (2016); and the co-edited volume *Rimini Protokoll Close-Up: Lektüren* (2014).

Olya Petrakova is a theatre maker, artistic director of Maketank cultural laboratory and Lecturer at the University of Exeter. Working with a number of displaced communities at Maketank, Olya has also founded the Devon Ukrainian Association to support Ukrainians and promote Ukrainian culture. Her research interests include creative collaborative practices, the generation of 'scenius' and the role of the director within devising processes. She has acted as consecutive oral translator for Russian artists, directors, clowns and ballet masters in Europe and USA. Her translation work has appeared in *Polish Theatre Perspectives* (2010), *Clowns: In conversation with modern masters* (2015) and *A History of the Theatre Laboratory* (2019).

Amy Skinner is Senior Lecturer in Drama and Theatre Practice in the School of the Arts at the University of Hull. Her research interests include Russian and Early Soviet theatre, theatre direction and scenography, and interdisciplinary connections between theatre, fine art and early twentieth-century physics. She is also a theatre director and designer, specializing in contemporary stagings of multi-lingual texts and plays in translation. Her work on Meyerhold includes the monograph *Meyerhold and the Cubists* (2015) and contributions to *Russians in Britain* (2012) and *Encountering Ensemble* (2013).

Klaus Wannemacher is a research associate at an institute for higher education development and a German and theatre scholar. He is writing a biography of Erwin Piscator and is author of *Erwin Piscators Theater gegen das Schweigen* (2004). His research interests include: twentieth-century theatre historiography (e.g. German post-war theatre), theatre and intermediality, theatrical adaptations and radio plays. Since 2008, he has been a board member of the International Peter Weiss Society (IPWG).

ACKNOWLEDGEMENTS

We wish to thank the following for supplying and giving the permission for the use of illustrations: Federal State Budget Institute of Culture, Moscow; Institut für Theaterwissenschaft der Freien Universität Berlin; Getty Images, ullstein bild; and the Akademie der Künste, Berlin.

Every effort has been made to trace copyright holders and to obtain their permission for the use of copyright material. The publisher apologizes for any errors or omissions in the above list and would be grateful if notified of any corrections that should be incorporated in future reprints or editions of this book.

Introduction to the Series

Simon Shepherd

The beginnings of directing

Directors have become some of the celebrities of contemporary theatre. Yet for most of its life, and across a range of practices, theatre has managed perfectly well without directors, celebrated or otherwise.

This is not to say that it has lacked direction, so to speak. Some form of directing, by actors, prompters, stage managers, designers, has always featured as an activity within theatre's processes. What was new was the concept that directing should be done by a role specifically dedicated to that purpose. Emerging around the 1890s after many centuries of theatre, it was both a historical novelty and geographically limited, to Europe and North America.

What these cultures had in common, at the start of the twentieth century, were the ideas and practices which we now call Modernism. In the arts it is associated with particular sorts of innovation made by short-lived movements such as Constructivism, Dada, Expressionism and Surrealism. But modernist thinking also influenced industrial innovation. This is seen in the creation of what F.W. Taylor called 'scientific' management, the systematization and hence separation of the role of a manager who bears responsibility for planning and oversight of the production process. As I have argued before,[1] the concept of director comes to be formulated at the same time as a managerial class is becoming defined. The value put upon the activity of management might be said to create the conditions for, and justify, the creation of a separable role of director.

This was apparent to Barker in 1911 when he observed that in Germany it was precisely the proliferation of management duties that made it impossible to combine the role of manager with that of actor. But German practice was perhaps in advance of the rest of Europe. Many of those now regarded as the founders of directing appeared to work in very similar ways to those who are not categorized as directors. Antoine ran his own company, selected the repertoire, took acting roles and directed plays, as did Stanislavski and Copeau. In this respect their practice differed little from, say, Henry Irving or Herbert Beerbohm Tree, both regarded as actor-managers.

Where the practice of the early directors seems consistently distinct throughout Europe is in its cultural, and sometimes political, positioning. Antoine, Copeau, Barker, Piscator, among others, positioned themselves against a dominant theatrical culture which they aimed to challenge and change. This positioning was an ideological project and hence brought with it an assumption of, or claim to, enlightened vision, artistic mission, the spirit of innovation. Adopting this rhetoric Antoine declared that directors had never existed before – that he was the first of a kind. When P.P. Howe wrote his 1910 book on that new organizational phenomenon the repertory theatre he distinguished the new director from the old stage manager on the grounds that, while the stage manager was adept at controlling the 'mechanical' aspects of the stage, the director was the guardian of the 'vision'.[2] This aesthetic formulation is, though, wholly cognate with management as industrially understood, as Alexander Dean makes clear. In 1926 he recommended that each company should have one person in the role of overall director because the director is not only responsible for each production but also, crucially, is 'the great connecting link between all parts of the organization'. Furthermore: 'Every organization needs a leader who has a vision; who sees a great achievement ahead.'[3] The non-mechanical visionary is also the Taylorist planner.

But some, it seems, were more visionary than others. You will have noted that none of the directors so far mentioned is North American. Yet while Antoine, Copeau and others were founding their theatres outside the mainstream, the same was happening in the United States. The Little Theatres of Chicago and New York started in 1912, the Neighbourhood Playhouse (New York), Portmanteau Theatre and Washington Square Players followed in 1915–16. Contemporary commentators such as Constance D'Arcy Mackay (1917) saw both the European and the American experiments as part of the same 'little theatre' movement.[4] Their practices look similar: founding theatres, against the dominant; culturally selecting audiences, possibly by a membership scheme; working with amateurs; performing explicitly naturalist dramatists, such as Ibsen. But while Antoine and Copeau have entered the canon of great directors, Winthrop Ames and Alice and Irene Lewisohn have not.

Reflecting on the contrast between North American and European practices, William Lyon Phelps suggested in 1920 that the United States lacked a public discourse that would take theatre as seriously as cars. His argument built on Moderwell (1914) and was taken up by Dean (1926).[5] Both saw little theatres as the mechanism for developing a larger theatre-going public, and hence were primarily interested in their success as organizational and economic entities, being much less interested in directors as artists. In Britain similar arguments proposed repertory theatre and the amateur movement as the mechanisms for building both democracy and a dramatic renaissance. Theatre, Barker argued in 1910, is a 'sociable' art. Thus North American and British discussions proposed that theatre could develop the cultural accomplishments of civil society. European discourses, meanwhile, were more interested in, and driven by, avant-gardist movements and experiment. For instance, Antoine positioned himself within an already existing public discourse about art, allying himself with the naturalist, and anti-racist, Zola; staging censored playwrights; distributing Strindberg's polemical preface to *Fröken Julie* (*Miss Julie*) – and making sure to invite reviewers to his theatre. For Piscator and Brecht the energizing link was to activists and ideas within both the political and the artistic avant-garde. The European director thus acquired the status of artistic activist, linked to and recognizable by existing networks of activists and makers, with their own mechanisms for dissemination and publicity. The European avant-garde, long celebrated as the supposed origins of performance art, was perhaps more clearly the originating moment of the theatre director.

The discursive position of European directors was consolidated by their own pronouncements and publications. Each of the early directors was adept in an established theatre craft, as were actor-managers. But when Barker, Meyerhold or Saint-Denis lectured on and wrote about the crafts of theatre, and even more when directors established regimes of training, they were showing themselves to be not just practitioners but theorists of a craft, not so much mechanics as visionaries. The early directors, and indeed directors since, claimed to understand how theatre works as an art form, and to have proposals for its future developments. In this sense they show themselves to be not only guardians of the vision of the play but also guardians of a vision of how theatre itself can and should work. The success of the claim to be visionary is evidence that what the director manages is not just the company or production but also the discourse about them.

Taken together new ideas about management, avant-garde practices and theories of theatre enabled the formulation of, and justified, a separated role of director. The role could then be seen as providing a specialism, missing hitherto, which is necessary to ensure the artistic seriousness and importance of theatre.

While the mechanism that formulated the role of director may have been discursive, its consequences were much more than that. Properly to carry out the guardianship of the vision meant taking responsibility for ensuring the aims and coherence of the processes of theatre-making. The artistic visionary slides into place as Dean's industrial manager. The discursive formulation results in actual power over other theatre workers. The director's control can determine not just that which is staged but also the hiring, if not firing, of those who stage it.

With the invention of directors a new power structure emerges. Yet it had been, and is, perfectly possible to make theatre without that role and its power structure. So there is a potential tension between the effectiveness and productivity of the crafts necessary for theatre and the new, but not demonstrably necessary, power structure that came to claim organizational authority over those crafts. This tension has made the role of director important and yet unstable, treated as celebrity and yet, after only a century, subject to questions as to whether it is actually necessary.

Those questions have been asked not least by directors themselves. Tangled up with the other issues summarized above they run through the volumes of this series. For the directors here have been selected not only because they are generally taken to be important, indeed 'great', but also because they reflect in interesting ways on the role of directing itself. Of course there are other important names, and interesting reflections, which have not made it into the selection list. Decisions such as these are usually difficult and almost always never satisfactory to everybody. But more stories are told than those of big names. The featured directors are not important because they possess some solitary essence of greatness but because they offer ways into, and are symptomatic of, a range of different practices and ideas. The discussion of each featured director frequently involves other directors, as well as designers, writers and actors with whom they worked and by whom they were influenced. For example, the authors of Volume 3 insist that we move our focus outwards from the featured male directors to attend to the women with whom they collaborated and on whom they depended.

The series begins with some of the earliest examples of the practice, but the only other chronological principle governing the distribution of directors is the decision to create two groups of volumes falling roughly either side of the midpoint of the twentieth century. What this arrangement highlights is the extent to which the practice of directing generates a system of self-reference as it rapidly developed an extensive discourse of its own very new art. Thus, for example, Volume 6 features directors who engage with, and perpetuate, the practices and legacy of Brecht.

Rather than suggesting a chronologically seamless evolution of practices the distribution of the directors across the series seeks to call attention to debate. Volume 1 deals with Naturalism, Volume 2 with critiques of Naturalism. The aim is to provoke thinking not so much about the director as an individual as about the art of directing in its different approaches and concerns. The vision of which the director is guardian and the assumptions as to what constitutes the art of directing are revealed as diverse and provisional. For some directors their creative work mainly involves the staging of their ideas about the world, for others creativity comes in the design of processes and the management of people, for yet others creativity has to do with the design and management of theatres. While Brook's philosophy of life may have constructed powerful and influential stagings, Guthrie's philosophy of life more or less invented the equally powerful, and perhaps more influential, concept of the role of artistic director.

If Volumes 1 and 2 display contrasted aesthetic approaches, Volume 3 has us focus on directors as founders and managers of companies and theatres. That topic of company formation and management returns again, in the context of the latter part of the twentieth century, in Volume 7. In a similar way Volume 4 brings together directors who may be seen as auteurs working within a modernist climate while Volume 5 gives us auteurs emerging from a post-Second World War Europe. In Volume 8, the directors are also auteurs, perhaps most powerfully so in that there is often no dramatist's text. But at the same time here the role of director begins to wobble, blurring into that of choreographer or visual artist.

In exploring the various directors, it becomes clear that, as noted above, some directors are major contributors to the discourses about directing, both reflecting on practices in general and foregrounding their own work in particular. This has an effect on their apparent status within the field. The existence of texts authored by directors often facilitates the study of those directors by others, which in turn generates more texts and elevates their apparent status, as a sort of greatness-construction machine. But there are other directors who are less textually established, perhaps because the director actively refuses to document their work, as did Planchon, or perhaps because there are cultural or geographical boundaries that English-speaking academics tend not to cross, as is the case of Strehler. Or it may be that directors have simply fallen out of theatrical or academic fashion, as, say, for Saint-Denis. That they are no longer, or ever were, serviced by the contemporary greatness-construction machine does not make these directors any less significant. Celebrity is not in itself necessarily relevant to being important.

Introduction to Volume 2

David Barnett

The three figures who are the focus of this volume of *Great Theatre Directors*, the Russian Vsevolod Meyerhold (1874–1940) and the Germans Erwin Piscator (1893–1966) and Bertolt Brecht (1898–1956), share some common interests as directors but also, of course, crafted particular ways of working and achieving certain ends. Their biographical details reflect that they were living in Europe around the same time, and, indeed, they were all working in the theatre as directors in the 1920s and 1930s. It is also difficult to ignore the effects of major historical events on the three. Meyerhold welcomed the Russian Revolution of 1917 because it promised greater social justice and offered a new model of society in which fresh theatrical experiments could be undertaken. Piscator and Brecht experienced the First World War at first hand with Piscator serving as a frontline soldier, while Brecht cleverly dodged military action by enrolling as a medical student and working as an orderly in a hospital. Both Piscator and Brecht understood the meaning of the Kaiser's abdication in 1918 and grasped the opportunities afforded and energies unleashed by their own new social order, the Weimar Republic.

That all three directors lived through times of great political tumult had an effect on the ways they understood themselves and their art. For Meyerhold, the transformation of the revolution from something liberating and exciting in the 1920s into the police state fashioned by Stalin in the 1930s proved catastrophic. The myriad artistic forms that emerged after 1917 were to be stifled and tamed by the officially imposed orthodoxy of Socialist Realism. Meyerhold continued to research and investigate the possibilities of the theatre at this time and fell foul of artistic dogma. He was accused of perpetrating Formalism, the Soviet umbrella term for any art that deviated from its norm, and was executed in 1940. Piscator and Brecht, who worked with each other at the end of the 1920s, were forced into exile in the early 1930s because their politicized art and opinions made them enemies of the state when the Nazis seized power.

The most obvious quality that unites all three directors is an emphasis on exposing and exploiting theatricality. Meyerhold began his career as an actor under Stanislavsky, but he quickly turned away from the Naturalism that was being developed at the Moscow Art Theatre in the late nineteenth and early twentieth centuries. He criticized the 'clutter' of naturalist theatre, that too much was happening on a stage that sought to reproduce the audience's experience of everyday life. In addition, he fundamentally questioned the very ends of Naturalism, believing that art could do far more than simply hold a mirror up to nature in order to reflect it back to an audience in minute detail. His experiments with Symbolist theatre at the turn of the century and its desire to look behind the veneers of social realism led him to consider the virtues of a stylized theatre, which, as Jonathan Pitches notes, had a clear and definable meaning for him. Stylization meant a reduction of complex material to its essence, the expansion of performative expression, and a close attention to rhythm.[1] Over time, Meyerhold would develop further ideas, such as a fascination with the grotesque and the development of biomechanical performance, each pointing to the theatre's unique ways of presenting material.

Piscator began directing political revues, series of sketches, to his audience, again not pretending to offer his audience slices of life but targeted material with clear themes. Over time, he identified the potential role of technology, primarily in the form of film but also, on occasion, as stage machinery, in the service of his political theatre. Film had two significant roles to play: first, it could deal with issues that went beyond the limited boundaries of the stage, bringing in larger historical forces with which to contrast or complement the scenes themselves. Second, its sheer size, projected onto large screens, had the powerful effect of intensifying the filmed material, overwhelming the audience and making the arguments more persuasive. Piscator was involved in 'turning the theatre event into a debating-chamber-cum-political-rally', as Anthony Jackson puts it.[2] In his later career, when he left Germany for the United States, returning there after the war, his interest in the possibilities of the theatre never waned, even if his politics had mellowed from militant Marxism to a more measured left-leaning humanism.

Brecht famously considered his theatre to be 'non-Aristotelian', something he expounded upon in an essay criticizing Aristotle's *Poetics* that was found in his papers after his death.[3] He objected primarily to the close identification between actor and spectator that led to the purgation of pity and terror in the latter. This, to his mind, was a politically conservative relationship because the spectator could not step back and consider the conditions or situations in which the figures on stage acted. As a result, the action gained the status of something inevitable and unchangeable.

(There were other elements present in Aristotle that Brecht found at least acceptable, such as the pleasure in both imitating reality and learning from this procedure, or locating action and not character as the soul of theatrical representation. Yet even these elements were refocused in Brecht's theoretical and practical engagement with the theatre.) Brecht proposed an approach to representation that liberated it from a purely mimetic link to everyday reality so that spectators could make judgements about social and political issues that affected them.

There is clearly a relationship between the three directors' approach to theatricality and the role of the audience, too. They all wanted to engage and activate their audiences in the face of the passivity they imputed to Naturalism. This passivity was attributed to different but related qualities in that form. To Meyerhold, the naturalist stage did the audience's work for it. That is, the naturalist director pinned down meaning and motivation so thoroughly that the audience was simply their recipient. Meyerhold proposed a mutual process of artistic enrichment: the director, together with the acting ensemble and creative team, would engage their own imaginations in order to provoke an imaginative response from the audience. To Brecht, as noted above, Naturalism connected spectator to actor too closely, robbing the spectator of a critical relationship to the material that was being presented. This position can be found in Piscator, too, yet both directors sought different responses to their non-naturalist theatres. Piscator was at first concerned with a general sense of political consciousness-raising, directed to the themes that featured in his productions. Brecht, on the other hand, sought to widen the spectators' critical faculties. While they would be invited to consider the issues of the production in question, there was a more general aim at stake, too. He wanted his audience to develop a way of seeing the material on stage and then take this mode of perception into their lives outside the theatre. They would thus be able to analyse political and social phenomena and *not* simply accept received wisdoms, 'common-sense' opinions or accepted viewpoints.

Yet although these directors lived through similar times, their artistic trajectories naturally owe much to their own sensibilities and responses to their societies and environments. Meyerhold's rebellion against Naturalism was born of a very close association with its origins in Russia, from his time at the Moscow Art Theatre. His freedom to experiment was, in part, due to the Russian theatre system that he encountered in the early 1900s. His work in the provinces was something of a double-edged sword that he was then able to wield to his advantage. On the one hand, the system insisted on a very quick turnover of productions, which valued quantity over quality. On the other, the provinces shielded Meyerhold from the metropolitan public glare and allowed him to develop his ideas more organically. The combination of swift turnaround and a degree of seclusion meant that his responses to Naturalism could explore a number of directions before he could marshal his ideas and experiment under more consistent conditions on Russia's more important stages.

Piscator and Brecht were not reacting against Naturalism in quite the same way. The German theatre system was a very different beast from the Russian one, due in part to Germany's recent history. The nation had only really existed as such since 1871 when a great patchwork of duchies, principalities and states were finally unified. Institutions like theatre and opera houses were prestigious indicators of cultural capital in each jurisdiction prior to unification. The system was decentralized and allowed for a greater variety of artistic output. During the second decade of the twentieth century, for example, Expressionism was popular, and so the two German directors were not only rejecting Naturalism but also a form of theatre that externalized the figures' inner lives, something they both found inimical to their visions of a more political theatre. The shift from a focus on character to a broader concern with the relationship between individual and society thus had a different, if related, set of stimuli from those of Meyerhold.

There is evidence that the three directors were certainly aware of each other's work, but direct influence is only clear and present in Brecht's relationship to Piscator. Meyerhold mentions Piscator's experiments with film and their effects on the actor in an important essay of 1930,[4] but Brecht, whose work in the theatre was only to find wider renown once Meyerhold was dead, appears nowhere in his writings. Piscator denied Meyerhold's influence on his theatre in his seminal book, *The Political Theatre* (1929),[5] claiming in an earlier newspaper article that he had never seen any of the Russian's productions. Piscator did, however, employ Brecht as a dramaturge and writer towards the end of the 1920s, and the two corresponded with each other from 1927 until 1949. Brecht drew strongly on Piscator's ideas for a politicized theatre, developed Piscator's concept of epic theatre beyond his conceptions, yet did not neglect to acknowledge Piscator's influence in the key theoretical work, *Buying Brass*.[6] Brecht also referenced Meyerhold in a couple of unpublished reflections on the director, one of which pithily summarized his theatre, together with those of Stanislavsky and Vakhtangov, under the heading 'bourgeois theatre is being pushed to its limits'.[7]

This volume seeks to expose the complexities of the directors' ideas and practices by drawing on the scholarship of international experts. It opens with a co-authored chapter by Bryan Brown and Olya Petrakova who examine what being a director actually meant to Meyerhold. They note that the role of director was hardly articulated in theory or practice when Meyerhold began his career, and they trace his complex understanding of the role with reference to documents that are not yet available in English and to his practice.

Amy Skinner then focuses on Meyerhold's relationship to theatrical space. She frames her arguments by understanding the director as a major reformer of the theatre and explores her themes with reference to a range of productions and his different formulations of space as way of teasing out directorial strategies. His approaches to space are not, however, limited to questions of design; rather, Skinner considers the complex relationship between performance and its reception by considering the crucial roles that audience was to play in Meyerhold's theatre.

Minou Arjomand then sets out a more chronological examination of Piscator. She opens by noting that this director is less well-known than the other two examined in this volume and speculates that this is because his more radical work ended early when he travelled to the Soviet Union in 1931, before going into exile proper with the advent of the Nazi government. She then offers a rich account of Piscator's radical innovations in the theatre that matched his political aims. She notes how he, and not Brecht, coined the term 'epic theatre', and explores the phenomenon and its connections to Piscator's notions of political theatre.

Klaus Wannemacher then picks up the story of Piscator's years in exile and his return to Germany where, initially, he was unloved and unwelcome. His successful application to run his own theatre in West Berlin, as it was then called, in the 1960s, led to his second period of distinction. The story sheds light on a career often neglected by theatre scholars and has been given a little more space than the other contributors to this volume for that reason. Wannemacher chronicles the remarkable transformation of a left-wing firebrand into a more judicious investigator of social justice and morality. The productions of the 1950s reflect Piscator's concerns regarding militarism and exploitation, yet it is in the 1960s that the director starts working closely with a new group of playwrights examining the past through document and evidence, and here one finds Piscator's final towering achievements.

Bertolt Brecht is probably the most famous and influential of the three directors in this volume, yet his work for the theatre as a director has, until recently, been less well examined than his plays and his theatre theories. In my chapter, I outline Brecht's development as a director of a politicized theatre before focusing on three productions whose direction he took over mid-rehearsal, having found their initial results lacking. The chapter thus contrasts more conventional approaches to making theatre with Brecht's own brand of realism, a term that is not to be mistaken for the kind of theatre associated with Stanislavsky [see Volume 1].

The final chapter of this volume investigates Brecht's directorial strategies for staging class and gender. Meg Mumford analyses two productions, when Brecht directed his own plays in the final decade of his life, to interrogate the ways in which he negotiated these two categories. She considers the specific means Brecht developed in theory while in exile and how he deployed them practically when he finally had access to a theatre after his return to Europe in 1947. Mumford notes that Brecht sometimes limited his own interpretive possibilities, and she points to ways in which Brecht's ideas might be developed in the theatre today.

Taken together, the chapters in this book provide both accounts of significant directorial careers and the ideas and practices that made them so important. The reader can make connections between the three directors but also appreciate how differences in their ways of thinking and working make them worth engaging with today. All are presented in a positive and critical manner, allowing readers to appreciate their achievements while remaining conscious that no-one is perfect and that activity in the theatre is always a work-in-progress.

Vsevolod Meyerhold

1

Educating the Director: Meyerhold's Pedagogy for a Theatre of Conventions

Bryan Brown and Olya Petrakova

Komissarzhevskaya called me [to work in her theatre]; [but the prospects of] St. Petersburg frightened me. Besides, she was going to task me only with directing. No matter how interesting the director's labour might be to me, the actor's work is far more interesting. In my case, directing is of interest only in so far as it raises the artistic level of the whole thing, while also helping to perfect my creative individuality [as an actor].[1]

Letter from Vsevolod Meyerhold to Anton Chekhov, 8 May 1904

Vsevolod Meyerhold embarked upon a life in the theatre because he believed in its power to express universal ideas and spiritual motifs capable of altering social relationships and challenging dominant ideologies.[2] When he began his career, that power lay almost solely with the actor. He therefore felt that his potential, the cultivation of his own creative individuality, would be realized through his work as an actor. For the young Meyerhold, there were no apparent models for what a director could be, at least not in the way this role is commonly conceived in the twenty-first century.[3] Both of his teacher-mentors, Vladimir Nemirovich-Danchenko and Konstantin Stanislavsky, were hybrid directors: playwright-director and actor-director, respectively. The director as appendage in these titles is important. At the turn of the twentieth century, the role of director was not yet fully established in European theatre.[4] Up to that point, directors (in some form and with some name, i.e. *Intendant, Regisseur, Inspector*, producer, stage manager, etc.) were perceived as an important aspect in unifying a particular production, but the art of theatre itself was still considered the domain of the leading actor(s), with the theatre's educational or intellectual provocations the domain of the playwright. At the turn of the twenty-first century, the director is now regarded worldwide as a necessity and more-than-often considered the visionary behind the success (or failure) of a production. The formulation of the director as the sole interpreter of a production became the turning point in what many theoreticians of the time considered the 'crisis of Russian theatre'.[5]

As his letter to Anton Chekhov (above) suggests, Meyerhold did not immediately grasp the innovative potential of the director, but once he did he was quick to embrace it and expand the role's territory. That expansion is the subject of this chapter and why we are introducing the term *rezhisser* to the anglophone theatrical lexicon. A Russianization of the French 'régisseur', *rezhisser* goes well beyond the original French meaning of 'the person who operationally organises the thing on the stage'.[6] As this chapter will set out, Meyerhold was instrumental in the formulation of the *rezhisser*, and his vision was one that far exceeded the general scope of the term 'director' in English-speaking theatre cultures.

Meyerhold's *rezhisser* combines three separate, but intertwined, functions: the auteur, the researcher and the pedagogue. Each of these will be discussed at greater length below, but briefly: the auteur is the author of the performance or, as we have suggested elsewhere, the visionary authority of a production *and* of an organization;[7] the researcher is charged with an in-depth study of the art of theatre, a consistent curiosity that drives the *rezhisser* towards ever-innovative productions and practices (often rooted in past traditions as well as in the synthesis with other art forms or other disciplines, such as architecture, physiology, behavioural science, etc.); and the pedagogue is committed to the teaching of one's practice in order to question its validity through dialogue with future generations. While this triadic construction of the role was developed over years, Meyerhold was engaged with all three aspects from his earliest forays into directing. Eventually, this conception of the *rezhisser* became the foundation for the professionalization of Russian theatre and remains a unique aspect of its culture.

The formal education of the director in Russia can specifically be traced to 1918, when Meyerhold was made Deputy Head of the Theatre Department of the newly formed Bolshevik government. In June of that year, together with his long-time collaborator Vladimir Soloviev, Meyerhold organized summer courses in the mastery of staging, or as they were known in Russian the *Kursy Masterstva Stsenicheskikh Postanovok* (KURMASTSEP).[8] A compilation of documents unpublished in Meyerhold's lifetime but now available in Russian, gathers lecture plans, stenographic records and student notes from nine months of Meyerhold's teaching *rezhissers*,[9] artists and actors on these early courses. Not yet translated into English and only rarely cited in scholarship, these teachings provide valuable insights into how Meyerhold envisioned professionalized training for the *rezhisser*. Moreover, the practical and 'off-the-cuff' quality of these lectures allows us to draw out specific details of the triadic nature of the role. Alongside these lectures, we shall draw upon other untranslated material to further contribute to Meyerhold's rich legacy in English. Before unpacking the triadic nature of the *rezhisser* in depth, a brief history of how Meyerhold educated himself will help illuminate how he came to conceive the *rezhisser*. Yet, to fully appreciate that conception, we need to first understand how the role of the director in Russia was conceived before him.

The journey to the *rezhisser*

Up until the twentieth century, a live performance in Russia was overseen by the prompter. The prompter was not only there to give lines to the actors when forgotten but knew the dramaturgical arc of the play and, therefore, could steer the actors towards its overall purpose. Similar to the conductor of an orchestra, the prompter understood the entire arc, tones, moods and tempos of a performance's score, but was also able to feed improvisational lines to actors when a scene suddenly went off-course. Alongside the prompter was the *Inspector*. This position was a combination of stage manager, censor and administrator. Eventually this role came to be called the *rezhisser* from the German use of the French term *régisseur*. However, its new name did not radically alter the ways in which it operated. In other words, the name did not yet reveal the depth of its function. Primarily, the *Inspector*'s role consisted of 'demonstrating entrances and exits, arranging stage pictures, and instructing the stage crew'.[10]

In 1826, as the term was being introduced, the leading actress of Russia, Vera Semenova, called for the *rezhisser* to be more like a conductor and work to harmonize the actors. Semenova felt constrained by her colleagues' unwillingness to work as an ensemble and support each other in the discovery of more expressive forms of acting.

Seventy years later, the problems Semenova identified had only become worse. The leading actor of the day, Alexander Lensky outlined the relationship between the financial decline in theatre and the quality of acting.[11] An actor whose work greatly inspired both Stanislavsky and Meyerhold, Lensky put forward the idea that companies should be headed by a director-artist (*rezhisser-khudozhnik*). Lensky's choice of phrase is particularly striking a hundred years on as it has become central to the Russian conception of the *rezhisser*. The term *khudozhnik* means 'artist', but is primarily used for fine artists, painters in particular. However, at the time, Lensky used *khudozhnik* more broadly to mean a creative person, in other words, a *Regisseur* that was not simply an *Inspector* who told the actors where to go or what their lines were. He envisioned someone who could work with, and train, actors. Konstantin Stanislavsky and Vladimir Nemirovich-Danchenko, the co-founders of the Moscow Art Theatre (MAT), fitted this description well.

Both of these men were integral to Vsevolod Meyerhold's own education as a *rezhisser* and his later formulation of the position. As a student of Nemirovich-Danchenko, he learned the art of dramatic literature, the value of text and how to approach the stage with an informed sense of the character as a whole, rather than the dominant practice of approaching a role from the actor's own personality or 'emploi'.[12] These lessons were deepened in Meyerhold's experiences as a founding member of MAT and augmented under the direction of Stanislavsky. However, Stanislavsky admittedly did not like directing[13] and is perhaps best seen, then, as an actor-trainer who lived to explore the imaginative and improvisational possibilities of the art of acting [see Volume 1].

In its first four years, the Art Theatre had set the standard for a new theatre based on ensemble and naturalistic staging practices. But this new standard was already being criticized, from within and without. Inspired in part by Alexander Pushkin (1799–1837), the defining poet of Russian literature, Meyerhold advocated for a new type of theatre, one that was conscious of its artifice and could use that consciousness *and* artifice to make socially and spiritually relevant commentary. Similarly, symbolist writer Valery Briusov attacked MAT's overly detailed and naturalistic productions. He called for a return to 'the deliberate conventionalization of the ancient theatre',[14] which allowed for a more imaginative participation by the audience. With the term 'conventionalization', Briusov echoed Pushkin from a century before. Both writers used the term *uslovnost'* to describe the type of theatre that focused on the meaning-making relationship between the stage and the audience.

Although all theatre is based on often implicit conventions, a 'theatre of conventions' is our terminology for the Russian *uslovnyi teatr*. There are multiple translations for this term and its adjectival noun *uslovnost'*. Edward Braun chooses to translate it as 'stylized theatre', but in so doing conflates *uslovnost'* and *stilizatsiia*, both terms used by Meyerhold for different purposes.[15] Marjorie Hoover uses 'conditional', but prefers 'conscious theatre'. Laurence Senelick and Dassia Posner opt for 'conventionalization', which seems to us the most appropriate. Posner elaborates:

> Conventionalization is a conscious, overt application of theatrical conventions that are defined by each individual director or production in an eternal quest for new ways of making meaning together with an audience. Rather than being a specific style, conventionalization is a structural philosophy of theater-making *that generates expectations, surprise, and thought by rejuvenating and reapplying how theatrical conventions are used.*[16]

Convention, which may sound conservative or backward-looking, attains the opposite meaning in this usage.

In the summer of 1902, frustrated with the repertoire and seeking a theatre of conventions, Meyerhold and a handful of other MAT actors struck out on their own. The Association of New Drama (as this new actors' cooperative came to be called) created over 170 productions in fewer than four seasons. This was Meyerhold's baptism of fire in his own education as a director. Meyerhold was lead actor, director, primary designer and occasional translator/adaptor. New performances were mounted every other night. At first, Meyerhold claimed to be 'slavishly imitating'[17] Stanislavsky and the Moscow Art Theatre. Yet even from the beginning, Meyerhold was stretching his own artistic muscles. For example, while he primarily used MAT's *mise en scène* for the opening performance of *Three Sisters*, he radically altered the portrayal of Andrei, making him more contained and still. This was the beginning of Meyerhold's theatre of mood (a theatre based on atmosphere generated by the rhythmic poetry of an actor's delivery rather than the naturalistic *mise en scène*) and his later immobile theatre (the presentation of tragedy not through extreme reactions but through quiet, still, static forms), both of which Meyerhold developed with his provincial stagings of symbolist and other dramas.[18] These required completely new processes and conceptions of what theatre and its functions might be. Moreover, he tested himself as an author through his translations and adaptations of German-language playscripts, of which the first successful one was *Acrobats* by Franz von Schönthan. This production of January 1903 began to explore territory Meyerhold would later develop into an entire aesthetic of the grotesque, a style of performance that artfully mixes popular art forms with the philosophical leanings of a more refined theatre.

It is worth pausing here to note, in a volume that positions Meyerhold side by side with two of Germany's leading twentieth-century directors, that besides his German ancestry, Meyerhold spoke and wrote German fluently. While Meyerhold's theatrical practice is deeply embedded within a Russian context, there remains a tendency in scholarship to overlook Meyerhold's voracious engagement with German literature and art.

Wagner in particular was an enormous influence on Meyerhold. Wagner conceived of music as 'the manifestation of the deepest vision of the essence of the world'.[19] Meyerhold's sense of musicality and its central place in performance was directly informed by this thinking. Rhythm and tone as embodied experiences provide an actor with confidence, and they can be used as points of contact (generally referred to as mutuality in contemporary performer training) as well as specific markers for the actors during performance.[20] They are also primary stimuli for exciting the senses of the audience. Similarly, Meyerhold's experiments with silence, gesture and physicality as theatre's primary expressive means for 'fathom[ing] the complex soul of humanity'[21] were informed by Wagner's theory of a total work of art reflecting the universal drama.

After two seasons of provincial repertory work, word of Meyerhold's choice of plays and staging experimentations reached Vera Komissarzhevskaya, one of St Petersburg's leading actresses who had plans for her own theatre. Radically in an age of leading ladies, Komissarzhevskaya was eager for her theatre to strike out in bold new directions, to discover a theatre that would only 'speak of the eternal'.[22] She seems to have genuinely wanted Meyerhold to develop the *rezhisser* as part of a collaboration capable of innovating new forms and conceptions of performance, albeit with her remaining the leading actress and head of the theatre. However, as gleaned from the letter to Chekhov, Meyerhold initially rejected Komissarzhevskaya's offer.

Yet this was 1904, the year in which the notion of the director broke free from its status of appendage to the job of playwright or actor, and became, at least in the mind of Meyerhold, what Simon Shepherd has called 'a discrete practice in its own right'.[23] There is no one eureka moment, but over the course of the year, Meyerhold glimpsed that his creative individuality was being realized through his focus on the *mise en scène*, rhythm, tones and colours of the entire performance. 'Creative individuality' is our term for the mixture of two Russian words: *lichnost'* (personhood) and *mirovozzrenie* (outlook on the world). A complex notion, it is, at its core, the unique perception and approaches to artistic practice of an individual, often referred to as one's own voice. In Meyerhold's Russia, culture was 'the creative experience of life, and creativity [was perceived] as the spiritual self-determination of personality [*lichnost'*]'.[24] In discovering his creative individuality more powerfully through a focus on the whole production, Meyerhold found his own abilities to organize the performance stronger by dint of being fully outside it, rather than leading the performance from within as featured actor. This change was not a rejection of acting, for Meyerhold continued to act for at least a decade (albeit more seldom) and maintained throughout his career that the essence of theatre was the actor. Rather, it was an understanding that for a truly new theatre to appear, a new mode of working was necessary and that new way of working required a new position. While the historians' privileged sight allows us to place these changes in a much longer period of growth, all of this focus on the new was directly in line with the spirit of the times.

In 1904, Vyacheslav Ivanov published his thoughts on a new theatre that would embrace the ritualistic aspects of the medieval mystery play and restore the poet's relationship to the masses. Ivanov was inspired in large part by Wagner and Nietzsche, both of whom were influences on Meyerhold and The Association of New Drama's literary manager Alexei Remizov. The relationship between Meyerhold and Remizov was a fertile and important one for both men. A bookish revolutionary, Remizov introduced Meyerhold to Marxist ideology and together they translated Albert Rode's book *Hauptmann and Nietzsche*. With such a mixture of Marxism, Nietzscheanism and Symbolism, the two men inspired each other to further their own ideas of revolution and theatre. Meyerhold went so far as to say that he had been reborn through his meeting Remizov.[25] For Remizov, the new theatre was to become a mystical mass in which '[b]oth actor and spectator, as one being, an illuminatus, will be submerged in a single action, a single feeling'.[26] As Edward Braun has argued, such a theatre had the 'aims of repairing the separation of the intelligentsia from the people and of turning the theatre into a means of transforming society'.[27] This new mystical theatre demanded that the *rezhisser* act as the conduit between two ensembles: the actors and the spectators.[28] For Meyerhold's own education, this conception of the *rezhisser* as conduit or organizer of the new mass combined aesthetic value with social context. His search for new repertoire and new stagings became a search for a theatre that could speak to the contemporary social issues without presenting the morals of the performance simplistically.

In 1905, Meyerhold and Stanislavsky began to develop such a theatre in Moscow. Eventually settling on the name Theatre-Studio, the enterprise was conceived as 'a theatre of searches', and Meyerhold was given nearly complete freedom as director of the institution.[29] The Theatre-Studio was the first organization in which Meyerhold was not contracted to act. All of his attention was therefore placed on the new role of the *rezhisser*. This meant he was able to develop the notion of a key idea for each production leading him towards his later role of 'author of the spectacle'.[30] Meyerhold also collaborated with visual artists on the creation of non-naturalistic scenic environments capable of evoking the moods of the dramatic texts the Theatre-Studio was attempting to stage. This experience proved how important the *rezhisser-khudoznhik* relationship was for a theatre of conventions. Without the pressure of acting himself in Theatre-Studio productions, Meyerhold was further able to focus on training the young actors. He began to develop new modes of how to work with actors in the use of their bodies and vocal tones to serve the theatre of conventions, and implemented group exploration of an author's stylistic oeuvre. This was the first time Meyerhold had the opportunity to focus specifically on training a company for performance of non-naturalistic texts and forging new staging techniques. Importantly, this was not just Meyerhold's imposition of his own forms onto actors. His work with the Theatre-Studio was in fact, as Kathryn Mederos Syssoyeva has argued, the beginning of collective creation processes in the Russian theatre laboratory tradition.[31] This collaborative pedagogy was foundational to Meyerhold's career and informed his complex understanding of the *rezhisser*.

While tremendous strides were made in the brief six months of the Theatre-Studio's existence, finances, revolution and aesthetic differences led to its close. Meyerhold was again without a permanent theatre and forced to return to the provinces. Yet, he continued to experiment with the performers' relationship to the audience. Many of the productions dispensed completely with the trappings of the naturalistic set: performed without a curtain, without any decor at all, with only fabrics draped variously to give impressions of moods and atmospheres. Besides these relatively innovative, for that time period, set designs, the forestage became a prominent location for experimentation. Exploration of the forestage would represent a major part of Meyerhold's education as a director and a central component of his training of actors, allowing for more associative psychological relationships to arise between audience and performer. As the following chapter by Amy Skinner will address, questions of the forestage led Meyerhold to question the roles and functions of space entirely.

He also continued the Theatre-Studio's work with actors approaching text as a musical score and embodying their physical performance as rhythmical movement through space. Thus in Schnitzler's *Cry of Life* (1906), the actors were directed to treat every movement as a dance. This conscious stylization was an attempt to play with oriental staging conventions (as understood by Meyerhold at the time) and was a further experimentation towards the creation of a theatre of conventions. Additionally, Meyerhold developed this experimentation through an exploration of colour as an associative play on larger character themes. In Ibsen's *Ghosts* (1906), for example, the character of the maid Regina had only a small apron to designate her position, while the rest of her costume was bright, burning red to indicate her own passionate nature (and perhaps Oswald's love for her), and Oswald was dressed entirely in black as the syphilitic painter.

After much activity in the provinces, Meyerhold accepted the post of *rezhisser* at Komissarshevskaya's theatre in 1906, having been offered a contract for a second time. St Petersburg, the capital of Russia at that time, was a hotbed of artistic, intellectual and political revolutionary thought that further propelled Meyerhold's ideas of theatre and the role of the *rezhisser*. Driven by vibrant discussions held within small, often secret circles,[32] theatre in Russia was undergoing a sea change. One of these influential circles was a veritable cult of the German-language writer E.T.A. Hoffmann. From a deep engagement with the fantasist, composer and caricaturist, Meyerhold developed many of his conceptions about the role of the *rezhisser* and its power to effect a revolutionary change in the individual's and society's perception of life. As Posner argues, 'Hoffmann symbolized the Russian theatricalist revolt against naturalism, the rebellion against nineteenth century acting and production clichés at imperial and commercial theaters, and the search for conventions that would celebrate theater's inherent theatricality'.[33]

In 1908, Meyerhold assumed the name of Dr Dapertutto (Dr Everywhere) from a short story by Hoffmann to experiment more fully with conventions and audience imagination through the creation of cabaret or small-form theatre. This section of his career marks another important part of his education as it provided him with an outlet to work on short performances in intimate spaces. Hitherto, the majority of his work had taken place in large theatres. It was in this period of cabaret exploration that Meyerhold fully realized the power of the theatre of conventions. (Experimentation in episodic conventions and dramaturgy would later lead to Meyerhold's theories of montage.) But the most fertile soil for this period of Meyerhold's life was Dr Dapertutto's Studio.[34] Here Meyerhold gathered a cohort of fellow teacher-researchers capable of instructing and exploring a wealth of theatre history, conventions and training regimes. These included the *commedia dell'arte*, movement and spatial composition, improvisation, rhythmic and musical training, and the development of the grotesque as a renewed theatrical convention.

Part research laboratory and part school, Dr Dapertutto's Studio transitioned in 1918, in the wake of the Russian Revolution, into a new existence as KURMASTSEP. Fifteen years on from his directorial debut in 1903, Meyerhold was now ready to begin educating other *rezhissers*.

The *rezhisser* unpacked

When Meyerhold and Soloviev established the first professional training programme for the *rezhisser* in Russia, their foundational principle was that 'the theatre has to create its own [artistic] masters'[35] capable of thinking theatrically. In other words, these were masters of their craft, thoroughly versed in 'theatrical laws, theatrical demands and theatrical problems'.[36] In Meyerhold's understanding, such masters would be capable of using the theatre's conventions to frame a performance in such a way that the audience was enticed and empowered to become the final co-creator of each performance.

To train these masters, KURMASTSEP was organized around the dual education of *rezhissers* and artists together. This was Meyerhold's answer to Lensky's *rezhisser-khudozhnik*. Given the distinct histories of theatre and visual art, Meyerhold recognized that one individual was rarely a specialist in both aspects. It is therefore extremely uncommon for a *rezhisser* to be a visual artist or for a visual artist to be capable of working with actors. Thus the education of young *rezhissers* into the processes and thinking of artists, and of artists into the history, processes and thinking of a *rezhisser* was considered necessary to effectively acquire the mastery of staging. However, a foundational principle of the courses was that the collective art form of the theatre must 'be concentrated in a single pair of hands; at the theatre there should be one will – otherwise it can become cacophony'.[37] KURMASTSEP, then, marked the rise of the '*rezhisser*-master [as he or she who unites] the collective of scenic creators participating in a performance (the actors, the playwright, the scenographer, the technicians, etc.) for the sake of carrying out one artistic idea'.[38] The formulation of that one artistic idea was the primary drive of the first aspect of the *rezhisser*'s triadic construction.

The auteur

An import of French New Wave cinema terminology into theatrical practice, the term auteur usefully describes the first aspect of Meyerhold's conception of the *rezhisser* as author of the production: organizing, shaping and envisioning the conventions, rhythms, moods, tones, colours, compositions and dramatic arc of the performance. Auteur theory developed from Alexandre Astruc's formulation of the *caméra-stylo* (camera-pen) which asserts that cinema is its own means of expression, comparable to painting or literature, a medium in which the film director uses the camera like a pen to become the author of the artistic product.[39] Astruc was essentially making the same argument KURMASTSEP had made thirty years previously when Meyerhold and Soloviev asserted that 'the theatre encompasses all other artforms' and 'the *rezhisser* is the author of the production'.[40] However, there is a fundamental difference between cinematic auteur theory and the way in which Meyerhold envisioned the *rezhisser* as auteur: for cinema, the term is used to describe 'those directors who adapt/interfere with/deconstruct the playwright's original script or construct their own, having developed a unique style, a trademark that characterizes their work'.[41] The theatre of conventions, on the other hand, demands a *rezhisser* who is adaptable and flexible to the needs of each source material, cultural context and audience. The notion of a trademark is anathema to such a *rezhisser*.

Inspired by E.T.A. Hoffmann's style for writing 'in the manner of', the *rezhisser*, as conceived by Meyerhold, creates productions 'in the manner of' a source material. A writer of immense creativity, Hoffmann borrowed language and techniques from music, painting and theatre to frame his stories in such a way that attention is called to the artifice while the boundaries of the real and the fantastic are simultaneously blurred. Hoffmann's unique style, his 'manner of working "in the manner of", where one is deeply inspired by, yet does not directly imitate another', exemplified the Russian conception of creative individuality.[42] In each process of adaptation, the artist is allowing the source material to work on her or his fantasy, produce new images and creations that then populate the new work. Fantasizing, then, is the auteur's primary work. It is the principal means by which the central thought of a production is discovered, but the Russian use of the term fantasy is particular, as Posner observes:

> While the word 'fantasy' in modern English is often associated with 'caprice' or 'whim', sometimes in a binary contrast with a pragmatic focus on reality, the German and Russian refer first and foremost to the artist's ability to create. In [the pre-eminent Russian lexographer Vladimir] Dal's *Explanatory Dictionary*, the primary definition of *fantaziia* is 'the imagination, the mind's inventive force; the creative force of the artist, the distinctive force of creation', though appropriately in a Hoffmannian context, the word also prompts associations with 'fancy, whimsy; unrealizable delirium, unbridled thoughts', and, in music, 'a free composition, based on its own caprice, without rules'.[43]

The imaginative capability, or the capacity for fantasy, is for Meyerhold the fundamental skill of the *rezhisser*. Meyerhold advised young *rezhissers* to train their imagination by 'reading particular literature that incorporates the theatrical element [...] for example, [the works] of the fantasy writer E.T.A. Hoffman, of Edgar Allan Poe, and of Dostoevsky. For these and similar works give your imagination a chance to grow wings'.[44] At this early stage, Meyerhold encouraged the wings of imagination to fly where they may:

> The one devoted to art will notice that when it comes to the work of others, one very quickly develops a habit of reading with a wandering mind. The first page is read ordinarily, rather attentively, but going further, on the second, on the third, on the fourth page, what's noticed is a flooding of imagination with one's own images that distract the attention. As a result, it often happens that it becomes necessary to stop reading other people's work already by the fifth page in order to write one's own composition. The artistically minded reader has received a series of kicks leading him towards his own creativity.[45]

The source material at this stage is a prompt. One which must be treated with respect, but which serves primarily as a means for concocting one's own images and impressions. However, this is a training tool, a first step in the auteur's work. However useful this type of reading is for developing one's imagination, once the *rezhisser* is approaching material that will be staged, he or she must practice restraint. For fantasy is both, to paraphrase Dal, 'the distinctive creative force of the artist' and 'unrealizable delirium'. The auteur must therefore place creative restrictions upon her or his fantasy.

While Meyerhold was adamant that 'the *rezhisser* is the author of the production,' he was equally resolute that 'the playwright is the author of the play'.[46] In other words, the auteur cannot alter the source material only to serve a delirious sense of originality. For Meyerhold, the auteur's ability to reveal her or his creative individuality while maintaining a collaborative relationship with the author of the source material is exemplified by Pushkin:

> Instead of allowing himself to be guided by his own experience, by his sufficient stock of knowledge which, undoubtedly, Pushkin had, to construct the language of characters in a tragedy, instead of affording himself this liberty, he placed upon himself various restrictions. Pushkin read the Russian historical chronicles, and on the pages of these chronicles he perceived clearly a system of structuring the historical ways of thinking and speaking, such original ones that, while reading the chronicles, it was as if he was following his own plan and fell in love with what he was detecting. He also studied Shakespearean theatre, and he took on Shakespeare's manner to represent the characters, but without imitating in a literal sense, of course. It was as if he 'stayed in the atmosphere' of a dramaturgical structure, establishing it for his drama, but while following it, he composed his characters in an 'extraordinary' fashion. [...] He

looked for an approach that didn't exist before. It was not a scheme to be original, but an obligation to himself to not fall into triteness, into what's already been established; and he ended up following his own approach. He did it in such a way that wasn't done before him; of course, not in the sense that if people walk on their feet, then they should be flipped on their head.[47]

The example of Pushkin shows how the *rezhisser* mines the past to learn the techniques and useful constraints of the medium. Yet, in keeping with the purpose of KURMASTSEP to educate *rezhissers* in the laws of theatre, Meyerhold importantly advocated for a non-literary reading of the source material and other texts. He instructed his students to 'single out from the work that which is related to thinking not with ideas, but with images, that relates to art and is capable of making you yourselves construct your imaginative world'.[48] In so doing, Meyerhold was not encouraging his students away from thought but, rather, imploring young auteurs to not be excessively intellectual, for theatre as a total work of art operates on the audience's imaginations which are complex networks of physiological and conceptual processes. Not everything in the theatre can be easily put into words, nor should it be. As Meyerhold noted:

> Theatre does not exist to say anything, because theatre does not exist for the expression of this or that thought which, with the same success, could be put into words. Theatre and the stage have their own special aims, their own distinct tasks, and everything that we see here comes to a particular sequencing, a particular rhythm which stirs in our soul a very special music accessible only to the ones who experience it directly.[49]

The first access point to that special music is the *rezhisser*'s explication (*eksplikatsiya*), a term Meyerhold developed and that is now embedded in the lexicon of Russian cinema and theatre, needing no explanation and considered a given part of every *rezhisser*'s pre-production work. For non-Russians, the explication is best described as the overall design and plan of the production, similar to German director Max Reinhardt's *Regiebuch*[50] [see **Volume 4**] or the cinema director's combination of a shooting script and storyboards. In the 1918–19 lectures, Meyerhold highlighted how the explication (then called the 'scenic statement') was a collaborative process between the *rezhisser* and the artist-designer. This is necessary because of the specialized skills of each. However, the goal of KURMASTSEP was to merge those skills through a shared understanding of theatrical principles, effectively channelling one's fantasy through a theatrical prism. Practically, Meyerhold himself went through two stages of work: the first was his own deep engagement with the source material at the end of which he created his explication, the second was the refinement of that explication through collaboration with artists, actors and musicians.

An explication is, therefore, a unique creation, one that inevitably must come from the *rezhisser*'s own creative individuality. As Meyerhold stated in a lecture to regional *rezhissers* in 1935:

> [I]f I describe to you how I work, could you say: 'Ah, I will also work that way?'. No, this would be wrong. Similar to memory, what we have at our disposal are the apparatus of hearing and seeing. The way I work depends on my entire physical make-up. If my seeing apparatus is more developed, then that determines a lot in my work. I need only look at what's written, and immediately it starts to play in my mind. I see the production before I hear it. But for those who have a better developed hearing apparatus, everything is reversed.[51]

Despite the rightful differences in *rezhissers*' perceptions and approaches, an explication must contain a central thought from which everything else unfolds. One of Meyerhold's students and later actor-collaborator, Erast Garin, regularly referred to the central thought as the key to the production.[52] While perhaps an overused term, here 'key' has three important associations for Meyerhold's theatre and the work of the auteur: it is a material object that can unlock something, thus revealing what has remained hidden, solving problems of the play and production; it is a musical system that allows all players to harmonize; and in Russian (*kluch*), it means a spring or source from which nourishment flows. Identifying the central thought or key is both a verbal and visual task: the explication combines both the key idea and the key image (*obraz spektaklya*).

The key idea most often takes the form of an underlying theme such as the passion and demonic power sitting just below the romantic, opulent surface of *Masquerade* (1917), or the importance of property for bourgeois morality in *Magnanimous Cuckold* (1922).[53] While Meyerhold's productions were grounded in a sociocultural context, the notion of the key helped him banish what he considered the unnecessary portrayal of everyday life. This was not simply a critique of Naturalism but all theatrical art that presents the universal drama or poetic aspects of the soul in mercantile or blatantly domestic terms. Therefore, the key is often the discovery of a hidden layer within the source material, and in keeping with historical comparisons of the role of the director as an orchestral conductor, the key is often a contrapuntal solution.

Finding the key is a subjective task fuelled by one's experiences of reading and the fantasies provoked. In considering *Crime and Punishment*, for example, Meyerhold urged his students to cut through the meticulous details of Dostoevsky's seeming realism by observing the piece as a whole. In so doing he instructed:

> Having read such writing and trying to restore it in your imagination, you shouldn't repeat the thoughts of the author in the particular order that

they were stated. For the task here is not the scrupulous restoration of details. The task here is rather that, having forgotten all the details, try to imagine the general arrangement and the course of action, what is called mise en scène.[54] You need to try to imagine only the general arrangement of scenes, of staging the whole scenic material. Also it is necessary to accustom oneself to clearly imagine this arrangement, snatching out from a story only the most interesting, only the most essential to you personally. [...] How the literary work will be used for one's own directorial needs – that is up to your discretion. It will be different for everyone.[55]

This work may lead the auteur to the creation of a key image. Consider this example: after reading Daphne du Maurier's *The Birds*, Alfred Hitchcock was struck by the image of the bird attacks and little else. From this he and screenwriter Evan Hunter constructed an entirely new story.[56] This was a radical adaptation, one that epitomizes the cinema auteur. Despite perceptions of Meyerhold as the 'author of the production' running roughshod over the playwright,[57] he emphasized to his students the difficulty of alteration and the inviolability of the author's thinking. 'It is possible to alter, and you have the right to do so, if', Meyerhold stressed, 'the main thought of the author remains'.[58]

Perhaps the best example of how an explication operates can be seen in Meyerhold's 1926 production of *The Government Inspector* (*Revisor*). After nearly a decade of engaging with the original material, Meyerhold distilled Gogol's text to its most simple, direct and banal essence: a farce in which the characters have only the basest 'physiological' and 'gastronomic' desires.[59] These desires must continually be satiated and from this arose the key image of a revolving door, which then developed into the stage design of fifteen doors and acting platforms on trucks. Meyerhold arrived at this explication through the incorporation of Gogol's original material for the play that was initially banned by the censor.

In doing so, Meyerhold may have used a radical process for generating another aspect of his explication, the adapted script. When working on *Masquerade*, Meyerhold acted out the entire script as he envisioned it with an assistant in front of him. The assistant arranged the characters' lines on pieces of paper and laid them out sequentially on the floor. Meyerhold then further rearranged the script to create the new adaptation, drawing the *mise en scène* on pages in-between.[60] He called this process recomposition, which effectively nods to the importance of both musical and literary techniques for Meyerhold's vision of a theatre of conventions. While Meyerhold's process of recomposition perfectly fits the previous definition of the auteur as the one who 'adapt[s]/interfere[s] with/deconstruct[s] the playwright's original', all of his additions to *The Government Inspector* – Khelstakov's double, text from Gogol's *Dead Souls*, etc. – aided the mysterious, transformative power of the production which was wholly in keeping with Gogol's fantastic and grotesque style. Importantly, once in the rehearsal room, Meyerhold would attempt to forget the work he had done on the adaptation, allowing for new configurations to reveal themselves.

The auteur's work begins alone with her or his fantasy which is then shaped into an explication combining a key idea and a key image. In creating an explication the auteur is answering the deeper personal question of 'Why am I staging this material?'. But the answers are not codified. The explication is brought to the first production meetings to inspire and drive the *rezhisser*'s collaborators to their own research and creative individuality. For Meyerhold this sharing was always a celebration. His rehearsals and lectures were known for their joviality and mischievous humour. The following tongue-in-cheek commentary provides insight into this process:

> I believe it is necessary to bang the actors on the head with your explication right from the start. Otherwise the desire won't be kindled in them, the penchant to gain an insight, to learn something, won't come about. It is necessary to bang them on the head right away, and the more the better. They will scamper. They will come out of their calm pig-like state. They will run to the libraries. They will hear some word, and this word will make them scamper from library to library. Thus, the explication carries an enormous importance. But, at every stage it is necessary to give an explication, as horizons extend, something gets defined, the plan widens in general … You go through a corridor, then into a closet, end up in the basement, find yourself on the porch, and then you break directly into the sky, shooting to the stars. At each stage, it is necessary to bang [your colleagues] with the explication. Enormously important.[61]

The urge to run to the library is part of a feedback loop Meyerhold envisioned as research, and this was so essential that it is the second aspect of the triadic construction of the *rezhisser*.

The researcher

In her book *The Director's Craft*, English director Katie Mitchell claims lineage to the Russian *rezhisser* and recommends research as a type of fact-finding mission that 'will help the actors to say and do everything they have to say and do in the action of the play'.[62] While she stresses the point that research is not meant to support a historical reconstruction of the playtext, Mitchell clearly shows her affinity for the practices of the Moscow Art Theatre, practices which, following the Meiningen Theatre, prioritized detailed historical research as dramaturgical preparation. This near archaeological approach, not unlike the cinema auteur's trademark, leads far too often to the creation of one specific convention: Naturalism.

Meyerhold conceived of research differently: as a practical means of educating the *rezhisser* in how to create a new theatre of conventions. This included a comprehensive understanding of historical theatrical epochs and styles (Japanese kabuki and noh, Chinese opera, medieval mystery plays, Spanish golden age, Elizabethan, French farce, etc.) as well as the techniques and laws of other fine arts (painting, architecture, music, poetry and sculpture). If the auteur is at essence asking the question 'why?', the researcher asks 'how?'. Therefore, central to the education of the *rezhisser* is the development of critical research skills. Such skills include analysis, reflexivity, source acquisition, practical application, etc. and enable the *rezhisser* to grasp the techniques and principles that inform the processes of staging, but of equal import, they also develop her or his creative individuality.

This complex training begins simply: by experiencing original works of art. Meyerhold argued:

> It is necessary to accustom oneself to visit museums without any preconceived idea, without any firm intention to put what's seen into one's own theatrical work. It is simply essential to do the following: saturate yourself with artistic impressions and train your eye to notice the harmony of lines and colours. I said already, that in all arts we deal with the organization of material elements. Visits to museums, plazas, foreign countries, remarkable cities, Venice, for example, will put you at a great advantage in that respect – your eye will unwittingly adjust to the understanding of that which escapes your attention in the daily environment, when you live in only one place. This is how you very simply open for yourselves new areas of art.[63]

This approach to learning is both technical and subjective. 'Don't go and see these works of art alone,' Meyerhold insisted, 'what's needed is consultation with people who understand the art'.[64] Through conversation with experts, the *rezhisser* learns how to analyse and comprehend the terminology and techniques of various artistic disciplines. At the same time, by training oneself to 'simply distinguish that this building is singing [to me], while this one does not speak to my eye, my imagination',[65] the *rezhisser* learns how to reflect upon the visceral, experiential impact of an artwork. In so doing, the *rezhisser* begins to understand what sort of effect colour, lines, shape, rhythm, etc. have upon the spectator *and* begins to cultivate her or his own artistic perspective and outlook on the world.

There are multiple ways in which this education can then be applied to the theatre. One example is that of composition: in his early stagings in St Petersburg, Meyerhold used paintings as visual references for his *mise en scène*. In *Sister Beatrice* (1907), he instructed his actors to literally recreate famous Pre-Raphaelite and early Renaissance paintings. This direct lifting served the purpose of extending the reach of Maeterlinck's symbolist drama, but such obvious *tableaux vivants* were not repeated in future productions. However, understanding the principles and techniques of composition, including lighting, allowed Meyerhold to collaborate with the progressive visual artists of his day, including

Kazimir Malevich, Lyubov Popova, Varvara Stepanova and El Lissitzky, and create entirely new sets that existed as stage-machines: sets that were conceived as independent works of art and constructed to manipulate, and be manipulated by, the performers. Actors no longer played in front of, or around, these sets but played *with* them. By 1926, Meyerhold was a scenographer in his own right, devising the highly kinetic and cinematic staging of *The Government Inspector's* truck-stage himself.[66] Working from Albrecht Dürer's painting *Jesus Among the Doctors*, Meyerhold also used sharp lighting to highlight the 'compositional units' of objects and hands throughout the production building towards the striking conclusion of 'frozen figures' at the performance's finale; thus he demonstrated how space and image create an 'organic unity' capable of evoking dramatic associations in the audience.[67]

Just as he exhorted his pupils to visit museums and study architecture, Meyerhold encouraged them to listen to music, particularly symphonies, to comprehend how the various instruments, such as characters, play specific parts and contribute to the whole. Students were instructed to be attentive to how the rhythmic changes and different tempos allow for the development of multiple themes. 'The solution adopted for the composition of a piece of music can often help you find the principles for the construction of a production,' Meyerhold advised.[68] Such musical solutions were not just applied to text, as in the timbres, tones and delivery of the actor's words, but equally to the creation of the stage compositions. *Mise en scènes* were also to be fundamentally informed by compositional principles, so much so that Meyerhold 'treated mise-en-scene as visible music'.[69] Music creates atmosphere, mood, feeling and most importantly, effectively organizes time. It is the unifying element of the entire production.

The analogy of a symphony to theatre works the other way around as well. Robertson notes: 'Meyerhold believed that the secret of acting lay in the cohesive unity provided by the ensemble of actors, each one playing a part like instruments in the performance of music.'[70] Acting is an essential area of research for any *rezhisser*. To usefully direct actors in specific conventions, a *rezhisser* must first understand what the fundamentals of acting are and then how to channel and apply them within various conventions. Meyerhold's performer training regime, known as biomechanics, is the culmination of his comprehensive understanding of these factors.[71] The term 'biomechanics' is mentioned for the first time in 1919 as part of the KURMASTSEP protocols, but it was a new name given to a process of training and working with the actor that Meyerhold began to formulate in Dr Dapertutto's Studio.

Founded on in-depth historical research into the theatre of conventions, Dr Dapertutto's Studio traced the theatre's roots to the improvisational and transactional relationships between actor and audience that comprise all folk theatre traditions. In their quest to retheatricalize the theatre, Meyerhold and his colleagues researched the masks and routines capable of being recombined in various new configurations:

All of *balagan* is full of original rituals.[72] [...] Those who mastered
balagan knew and understood the theatrical form perfectly. In commedia
dell'arte it was known that without 'thingies' [Meyerhold's colloquialism
for antics, routines, devices], the theatre is not interesting. In Japan, to
deepen the impression of the action, it was common for the stagehands
– at the most intense moment of a scene – to bring out rugs of bright
colours in order to tease the public, as is done in Spain, when bulls are
teased in *corridas*. In China, a special orchestra exists in every theatre, to
beat the drums and strike the gongs. All of this sends the audience into
such excitement that it says to itself 'damn it, afterall, everything on stage
is real!' [...] Theatre is inconceivable without the antics inherent in it.
Moliere and Shakespeare are true theatrical authors because they knew
this.[73]

While well grounded in theatre history, Dr Dapertutto's Studio was also a
practical research laboratory. Much of the actor's training was dedicated to
reconstructing the physical and verbal routines of *commedia dell'arte* and
other theatrical traditions. However, this was not reconstruction in order
to faithfully reproduce previous theatrical styles or modes of performance.
Rather, it was to understand the building blocks of theatre, specifically the
tools that allow actors to connect to an audience while remaining committed
to the dramaturgy of a performance. Through this research, Meyerhold was
also excavating the components of *mise en scène* and asking the essential
rezhisser-as-researcher question of 'how?' – how to keep provoking,
surprising and engaging the audience?

Meyerhold's 'thingies' are the conventions that structure *mise en scènes*
and affect the associations of an audience. In the 1920s this research
would develop into a theory of montage constructed in large part through
dialogue with Meyerhold's collaborator at the time Sergei Eisenstein.
A major component of film theory, montage in Meyerhold's theatre was
comprised of rhythmic and visual contrasts purposefully used to provoke
strong associations in the imagination of the spectator. These associations
compound to generate the production's meaning in the mind of the
spectator furthering the conception that a Meyerhold production was not
just an 'interpret[ation of] the world, but a contribut[ion] towards changing
it'.[74] Understanding how the conventions of theatre work on the associative
mind of the spectator is part of the research for the *rezhisser*, as Meyerhold
stated:

Mise en scènes* work on the audience's associative abilities. To read the
mind of the audience, to be able to predict particular associations: this
is the task of the theatre. The thinking apparatus of the audience is even
more complex than the thinking apparatus there, on the stage. There it is
the thought of one person, while here we have a thousand people sitting,
moreover they are all absolutely different. [...] Disparate associations

are happening, an ocean of disparate associations, an ocean of disparate impressions, and we must know how to wake up the thoughts of the audience, so that the old professor starts to work differently, so that the housekeeper prepares food in a different fashion. What appears then is a new cultivating task for the theatre.[75]

Research for Meyerhold, then, was not about building up facts for the surety of the actors (and director) in the rehearsal room. Rather, it was a practical way to discover new, unique, innovative modes of thinking with an audience.

No analysis of the *rezhisser*-as-researcher would be complete, however, without a mention of how deeply Meyerhold incorporated the term 'research' into his theatrical practice. In the plan for the second year of KURMASTSEP, a scientific component was added to the original course on theatre history and practical staging technique. This move coincided with a larger discursive shift happening in Soviet Russia whereby a scientific research methodology was idealized and incorporated into as many aspects of social organization as possible, specifically in educational institutions. By 1930, Meyerhold's own theatre was given the appellation of Scientific Research Laboratory or *nauchno-issledovatel'skii laboratorii* (NIL). This was not, however, a purely formal or bureaucratic move. Research was so engrained within Meyerhold's picture of a theatre of conventions and the role of the *rezhisser* that his colleague Vladimir Soloviev described Meyerhold's theatre as a 'theatre laboratory whose aim was to scientifically research the entire history of theatre, in order to prepare materials which could be used by future theatre directors with their students'.[76] This meant that alongside a theatre of productions, a school and a laboratory for the discovery of new forms, the State Theatre of Vs. Meyerhold housed a number of research laboratories as well as a comprehensive library/archive.

One of these research laboratories was The Notational Laboratory conceived and supervised by Leonid Varpakhovsky whose aim was to discover a way to notate acting scores, a modification of an idea previously begun by the composer Mikhail Gnesin at Dr Dapertutto's Studio. Some of the materials Varpakhovsky laboured over were Meyerhold's own idiosyncratic scores for productions – his re-compositions extended into a type of musical stave with his own personal musical symbols.

Another research laboratory was focused on audience response. The theatre of conventions was based upon the audience–actor relationship. Meyerhold had been trying to systematically capture what audiences thought about a performance since at least his 1918 production of *Mystery-Bouffe*. These early attempts were simple surveys, but as Meyerhold had an increasingly larger organization behind him, he encouraged a much more systematic study. Part of this process included the production of a detailed record of the performance called the 'chronometage', which measured not only the duration of the show but individual movements and speeches of

actors. Alongside this, researchers noted each time the performance elicited
a reaction from a member of the audience, such as sighing, hooting, leaving,
throwing objects, etc.[77]

Finally, throughout his life Meyerhold worked very closely with leading
scholars and historians of theatre. Alongside KURMASTSEP, he organized
the beginning of a professional union of theatre makers. Its members were
rezhissers, artist-designers and academic-historians. Meyerhold firmly
believed that a robust exchange with academics fuelled artistic practice,
helping to analyse it and push it further towards new conventions and
new potentials. This belief in the interplay between artistic and historical/
theoretical practices has been described as a 'theater producing itself as it
produces its own *theory*'.[78] The education of collaborators and the desire
to formalize such training was added to the cyclical process of research
leading to the creation of productions, sparking new questions, leading back
to research and further new practices. Meyerhold's theatre of conventions
was built, discovered, reconstructed and birthed through historical research
put into practice, and one of the best ways to do so was through teaching.

The pedagogue

Teaching for Meyerhold, like the majority of his activities, served multiple
purposes. In his quest for new forms of theatre, Meyerhold needed
collaborators. Those collaborators needed to be educated with a proper
understanding of the theatre of conventions. Therefore, pedagogy was the
practical task of training new actors, designers, musicians, *rezhissers* and even
critics. This started with a comprehensive collective training in the history
of theatre alongside practical experience of the art of the actor. Meyerhold
was adamant that in their first year of study, students should not specialize
in one area but receive a general education all together. This structure was
institutionalized in Russian theatre education, meaning that *rezhissers* and
actors receive the same training in the first year. When Meyerhold was given
control of the State Higher Directing Workshops (GVYRM) he changed
the name to the State Higher Theatre Workshops (GVYTM) to reflect the
emphasis on shared training practices.

Former GVYTM student and later lead actor in Meyerhold's theatre,
Erast Garin has highlighted how Meyerhold's pedagogy was Socratic in
style. Just as Meyerhold left no major methodological publication, such
as a book on biomechanics, his teaching did not consist solely of his own
proclamations or detailed theories delivered to students to memorize and
emulate. Rather, as one participant in KURMASTSEP noted:

KURMASTSEP formed a kind of brotherhood of like-minded
apprentices. [...] Lectures were not considered the principal mode of
study. Predominant were discussions, conversations about plays, books,

sketches, presentations by teachers and students of all kinds of concepts followed by all-encompassing discussions, with equal participation from teachers and students. It was expected that each person contribute their share towards the conceived project. Woe to the one who wanted to hide behind the stockade of critical speech, not offering any positive proposals. Meyerhold would say to them: 'Explain how to make it; make it visible with your own hands by drawing, creating the ground plan, or the maquette, or something similar.'[79]

This approach to teaching reflects Meyerhold's ardent belief that culture was the spiritual creative work of human beings. The primary task of pedagogy for him was to guide students towards their own creative individuality. His main pedagogical method for doing this was experiential, learning through doing. That doing could be organized in two forms: imitation and experimentation.

When Meyerhold began directing, he consciously imitated the Moscow Art Theatre, despite wanting to find his own voice and create a new kind of theatre. This was a traditional approach to learning rooted in the guild system of a master-apprentice relationship. In Russian, the artisanal guild workshop is called a *masterskaya*. When he created KURMASTSEP and its sibling institution, the School for Actors' Mastery, Meyerhold was instrumental in reintroducing the term *masterskaya* to theatrical training (the 'workshop' in the above translations of GVRYM and GVYTM is *masterskaya*). In doing so, he created a system unlike most Western academies or professional training institutions where an individual's personal artistic practice and style is the foundation of the pedagogy. This structure emulated that of the Russian fine art academies which had been based on the personal 'pedagogic power of the master' since the Academy of Arts was established in 1757. What this pedagogy implies is that students in such programmes in Russia are to imitate their masters. However, Meyerhold was clear about the role of imitation:

> Take Lermontov, he began by picking up a small notebook and simply copied into it the poems that he liked. He would copy down Pushkin or other poets, and then one day he recklessly began copying Pushkin's 'The Prisoner of the Caucasus', and unwittingly, imperceptibly he began to enter his own verses there, and in the end he wrote his own 'The Prisoner of the Caucasus'. [...] His aspiration was to find his voice, and by strongly imitating Pushkin, Lermontov found his creative individuality. I believe that every *rezhisser*, no matter what, must be looking for their own creative individuality, to find their own walk, not reminiscent of anyone else's, they have to create their own.[80]

For Meyerhold, teaching from a personal pedagogic power of the master was the same as how he operated practically as a *rezhisser*. Because he was a highly competent actor, able to do the more extreme biomechanical exercises well into his fifties, Meyerhold often demonstrated what and how he wanted his actors to perform. Essentially he created the composition and the actor's score and then performed it for them. However, similar to a musical score given to a master musician, Meyerhold expected his performers (or students) to find their unique voice within it. As actor Mikhail Sadovsky recalled:

> Meyerhold's demonstrations at rehearsals always put us in awe, but they did not clamp the actor – the opposite, they gave her or him wings. Actors received these demonstrations with gratitude and excitement; they developed them with their creative initiative, enriched them with their mastery and individuality.[81]

Imitation in Meyerhold's conceptualization then cannot easily be divorced from experimentation. This is because that which is imitated must be filled with one's own individuality, which requires one to experiment with new ways of playing the score, coming up with one's own unique solutions.

One of Meyerhold's modes of positioning experimentation within his pedagogy was to test his own research. In his efforts to develop a physical and rhythmic approach to actor training, Meyerhold had his *rezhisser*-students learn, and immediately teach, biomechanics. Underpinning Meyerhold's desire for experimentation was an attempt to formalize theatrical training. Partly, as mentioned above, this was a methodological approach that was in keeping with the scientific discourse of its time (the revolutionary fervour to scientifically organize labour and the new man, for instance), partly it was the desire to dispel the myths of theatrical processes and root them in the artisanal craft tradition.

In another lecture to the summer courses of 1918, Meyerhold prioritized fantasy over talent. His purpose in many of these initial lectures was to dispel the myth of talent as the source of creative individuality. The tendency for young theatre-makers in the St Petersburg summer courses to idolize talent as an innate ability, and therefore as something untrainable, corresponds to what Shepherd has identified as the belief in personal temperament as the defining aspect of a theatre director.[82] To counter such excessive veneration of seemingly god-given individual traits, Meyerhold aimed to inspire his students towards the practical training of fantasy:

> Beside technique, what is present in this work is the element of composing, and precisely this element is considered crucial. When we talk about composing, we talk about imagination. We are not talking about talent, but about imagination and how it needs to be trained. [...] To think up a joke, to compose some invention is already an expression of your ingenuity, your ability to fantasize. And this ability, this power to imagine, instead of talent, is what's necessary to develop in oneself, to train and cultivate it in every possible way.[83]

Meyerhold wanted to formalize theatrical craft in order to dispel myths that had accrued around it, particularly the notion of an actor as some sort of shaman capable of mysterious and unique transformations, completely and utterly untrainable, or that talent, rather than rigorous and curious learning, was solely behind the vision of the *rezhisser*.

Meyerhold's approach to training the *rezhisser* was thorough and exacting. He made sure his students learned theatre history in order to practically explore various conventions. He trained them as actors in order to have them better understand the fundamentals of theatre and to, in turn, work with and train their actors. He taught them fine art so they could devise innovative staging designs. And of course literature and music were essential to the programme, yet Meyerhold's own pedagogy was never fixed:

> Stanislavsky often changed and modified his formulations, I do the same. [...] It is by this virtue that art is so wonderful, as you catch yourself at every stage as a student. I am amused when I am called Master, as I am aware that I still lack a great deal, that I need to travel to Norway, for instance, as I've never been there before; aware that this wasn't seen, that wasn't read. I catch myself realizing that every premiere is a new exam, every time I bring about something completely new which causes me to tremble and shake. In this lies the beauty of art, in its continuous change.[84]

If the auteur is 'why?', the researcher 'how?', then the pedagogue, for Meyerhold, is 'what?' – 'what do I know?' and 'what of what I know is relevant for a new generation?'. Teaching was an essential component of the reflexivity Meyerhold valued so highly, to understand how much of the craft one has learned as well as to assess how much of that craft is still valid.

In twenty-first-century Russia, the pedagogic power of the master is so deeply ingrained in the culture that one is not truly considered a *rezhisser* until one has students. True to Meyerhold's pedagogical philosophy of open enquiry, this pedagogical imperative allows *rezhissers* to continue exploring their own practice, rather than resting on the success of particular productions or the creation of one aesthetic style or trademark. Of course, this does not mean that the majority of *rezhissers* in Russia are consistently innovating and challenging theatrical knowledge. In large part, the Soviet Union's theatrical Renaissance ended with the full implementation of Stalin's policy of Cultural Revolution in the early 1930s. Yet experimentation continues today within a largely imitative culture, and new theatres are born from the leading training institutions, such as Sergei Zhenovach's Studio of Theatre Art or the Laboratory of Dmitry Krymov.[85] The pedagogy of these practitioners echoes Meyerhold's as summarized in an April 1917 speech to Dr Dapertutto's Studio:

I am not a teacher; I am an explorer of new shores on the ocean of theatre. Commedia dell'arte is an island for recreation. I am not an organizer; I have a lot of initiative, achievements, successes, but no established position, no attachment to one, and this is my strength. So my task is to swim further and further, to take off, rather than dwell on the same coast. Always – investigations and searches – since 1905 I cannot find my shore. I declare that the studio is not a school: it is a brotherhood of those who are unhappy with the contemporary theatre, of the builders of the new theatre, of the seekers of the new technique. Myself, I am just an elder brother, a wiser and more intense one. And among you, brothers, I am looking for cleverer ones than me, for more daring scouts.[86]

The legacy of the *rezhisser*

Vsevolod Meyerhold is considered one of the twentieth century's great theatrical innovators because of his radical and rigorous enquires into the nature of theatre, its history and its conventions. From that sense of enquiry came a complete and utter re-evalution of the organization of theatre, one that led to the formulation of the *rezhisser* and its triadic construction.

The auteur, researcher and pedagogue are not independent, compartmentalized aspects operating at specific times throughout a *rezhisser*'s career. Rather, the triadic nature works together in the reciprocal processes of teaching, researching and crafting a unique vision for the theatre. Meyerhold's seminal productions *Don Juan* (1910, based on the play by Moliere), *Masquerade, Magnanimous Cuckold, The Forest* (1924, based on the play by Alexander Ostrovsky), *The Mandate* (1925 by Nikolai Erdman) and *The Government Inspector* were only possible because of the collaborative interplay between these three aspects.

Teaching in a variety of settings, but particularly in Dr Dapertutto's Studio, GVYTM and his own theatre, allowed Meyerhold to cultivate new collaborators in his theatre of conventions, primarily new actors capable of executing his vision for the theatre. The grace, agility, musicality and tragicomedy of these innovative productions (such as the biomechanical exercises of *Magnanimous Cuckold*, the clowning of *The Forest*, the complexity of skills required to perform the intricate score of *The Government Inspector* while on the sloping, moving platforms) was only possible through Meyerhold's patience, curiosity and desire to be a research-led pedagogue.

His theatrical vision was equally informed by his exhaustive research. The designs and final texts of *Masquerade* and *The Government Inspector* both required nearly a decade of research into epochs, styles and the oeuvres of each author. Similarly, his ongoing research into the conventions of theatre allowed Meyerhold to not only generate an entirely new theatrical language (the grotesque) but to have acute influence on the creation of an entirely new medium (cinema) through his development of montage with pioneering Russian filmmakers, such as Lev Kuleshov, Sergei Eisenstein and Sergei Yutkevich.[87] Meyerhold's research into the devices of *balagan* fused with his knowledge of art history to create purposeful set design that heightened the impact of a production. *The Mandate*, in particular, incorporated furniture as another player in the production and a revolving stage to create a surprising and insightful ending.[88] *Don Juan* and *The Forest* further played with conventions, particularly research into masks, to emphasize how historical playwrights (Moliere and Ostrovsky, respectively) were capable of speaking to a modern audience.[89]

Finally, Meyerhold's directorial vision was born in all of the pre-production fantasizing and recomposition work of the auteur. The boldness to restructure and rewrite a playwright's original text defined Meyerhold's formulation of the *rezhisser* as the fulfilment of one's creative individuality. This important cultural and spiritual work not only produces one's own unique voice but hones it to speak back to collective or social concerns, thus providing new opportunities for meaning making and possible change. *The Government Inspector* was the pinnacle of Meyerhold's creativity as 'author of the production' and perhaps nowhere was his daring more evident than in the final salvo to the bourgeois audience: after a four-hour performance that illuminated the rampant injustice in their society the audience was left to realize in their own time that they were applauding a stage full of mannequins.

Such audaciousness and innovation was Meyerhold's fledgling call to a life in the theatre, and despite initial reservations he found himself radically altering the theatre of Russia and, in turn, the thinking and philosophies driving Russian society, through his acceptance and formulation of the position of the *rezhisser*.

2

Directing Theatrical Space: Meyerhold's Reconstruction of the Theatre

Amy Skinner

> The author and the director regard all the work which they carry out on a production simply as preparation of the ground on which those two vital theatrical forces, the actor and the spectator, will work daily in the course of the performance. The author and the director provide no more than the framework, and it must not cramp or hinder the actor and the spectator, but encourage them to work harmoniously together.

Vsevolod Meyerhold, Rekonstruktsia teatra (The Reconstruction of the Theatre, 1930)[1]

The directorial career of Vsevolod Emilevich Meyerhold spanned four decades and was set against a backdrop of communist revolution, international conflict and political persecution. Driven by his desire for a theatre that would encourage the actor and spectator to 'work harmoniously together', Meyerhold's *oeuvre* combined production practice with a rigorous approach to theatre pedagogy and an extensive output of theoretical lectures and publications. He developed a distinctive theatrical aesthetic, embedded within the formal innovations of the Russian avant-garde and influenced by historical theatre practice, as well as a vast range of literary, musical, visual arts, philosophical and scientific reference points. In the mid-1920s, Meyerhold was arguably one of the most significant theatre directors in the Western world, with a reputation extending beyond the USSR, propagated by foreign visitors to his theatre and European tours, for example, his company's combined tour of Paris and Berlin in April 1930.[2]

By 1930, however, Meyerhold's reputation in Russia was becoming increasingly precarious: his status as the champion of the post-revolutionary theatre was in jeopardy and his communist credo questioned. He had thrown his support behind the Bolshevik regime from its inception: Meyerhold considered the 1917 Revolution to be his 'second birth' and was one of a small group of attendees at the meeting for artists organized by the Bolshevik government soon after their rise to power.[3] In 1918, he took up a government post, serving as head of TEO, the Theatre Department at NARKOMPROS, the People's Commissariat for Education. Here, he turned his attention towards theatrical reform intended to echo the wider sociopolitical changes of the new regime, calling for an 'October in the Theatre', an allusion to the 1917 October Revolution.[4] The avant-garde experimentation which had characterized Meyerhold's pre-revolutionary theatre was refocused towards developing new theatrical forms for the new Soviet era, and, during the 1920s, the emergence of a broad range of artistic innovations left relatively unhampered by government intervention suggested a convergence between these new performance styles and communist politics. Ultimately, however, it was Meyerhold's interest in form and formal innovation that led to his eventual fall from grace.

Meyerhold's experiments sought to uncover a theatrical form which would express, serve and challenge Soviet society. As Soviet arts policy developed, emphasis was placed on communist commitment as expressed primarily through content, with opportunities for formal innovation becoming increasingly constrained and, ultimately, dangerous. The official doctrine of Socialist Realism, introduced at the 1934 Soviet Writers' Congress, restricted the sort of writing considered appropriate within the Soviet Union, emphasizing an exaggerated realism that glorified the achievements of the Soviet state and its heroes. From the 1930s, non-compliance to Socialist Realist tenets resulted in severe, even fatal, consequences.[5] 'Formalism', that is, the favouring of form over content particularly as associated with the artists of the avant-garde, became the ultimate aesthetic 'crime' in that it was seen to place the artist and his or her interests over those of the working people. Repeatedly levelled at Meyerhold, charges of Formalism suggested that the director was more interested in formal experimentation than in government-approved artistic content. Meyerhold's significant public profile, and his refusal to restrict his theatrical practice to government-endorsed texts or theatre styles, resulted in a steadily increasing ostracization and condemnation of the director and his practice. In 1938, as a result of these increasing tensions between Meyerhold and the Soviet government, his theatre company was liquidated and, less than a year later, Meyerhold was arrested. On 2 February 1940, the former hero of the Soviet theatre was executed by firing squad, his remains placed in a mass grave and all public affiliation with his name forbidden.[6]

Despite the increasingly difficult circumstances of Meyerhold's final decade, his writing during this period offers significant insight into his directorial aesthetic. In 1930, he published 'The Reconstruction of the Theatre', an article based on three lectures given during 1929 that called for a radical reworking of Russian theatre practice. The 'reconstruction' of the title encompasses both a literal reconfiguration of the theatre building and a reconceptualization of how theatre can serve the needs of both the Soviet government and the Soviet spectator. At the centre of the article is Meyerhold's call for a harmonious and creative relationship between the actor and the spectator, seen as the most salient quality of the theatre that he seeks to build. In its, sometimes confrontational, responses to government policy, Meyerhold's writing also hints at the professional, political and personal crisis that the director was about to encounter. In his commentary on the article, Edward Braun notes the significant changes that Russian artists faced the year that Meyerhold gave his lectures:

> 1929 was the first year of Stalin's first Five Year Plan; with the launching of this shock programme of industrialization and agricultural collectivization, the relative tolerance of the NEP [New Economic Policy] period was succeeded by a ruthless onslaught on the surviving dissident elements in Soviet society. The arts were called upon to participate in this campaign.[7]

The product of twenty-eight years of directing experience and more than 270 productions, 'The Reconstruction of the Theatre' contains the reflections of a mature and experienced practitioner. By the 1930s, Meyerhold's extensive output had led to the consolidation of key ideas in his theatre making, and these are embedded as themes in his article. One such theme, to date under-discussed in the analysis of Meyerhold's practice, but vital in the realization of his work, is the role played by theatrical space and stage shape. This life-long area of exploration emerged repeatedly in his productions, and in 'The Reconstruction of the Theatre', Meyerhold explicitly associates the configuration of the playing space with his overall intentions as a director.

The goal of this chapter is to consider Meyerhold's engagement with theatrical space as a central facet of his directorial approach that developed across his career. There has been much analysis of Meyerhold's collaboration with designers and the features of individual stage designs in his theatre.[8] The emphasis here is less on individual designs or design practice, and more on scenographic questions of theatrical space and shape; specifically, how Meyerhold used stage shape and *mise en scène* to engage with the different orders of space that exist in a theatrical context, from the architectural space of the theatre building to the fictional spaces constructed through the play's narrative. In order to explore Meyerhold's use of theatrical space, this chapter identifies two spatial themes in his practice. Beginning with an overview of Meyerhold's approaches to directing and design, I then consider how space is constructed to develop specific actor–audience relationships ('relational space') and how the director constructs theatrical worlds in which the relationship between the real and the fictional hinges on the invitation to the spectator to generate their own ideas of space ('imagined space'). Ultimately, it emerges that the conceptualization of space in Meyerhold's theatre informed the director's understanding of both the performer and the spectator: space became the foundation for Meyerhold's 'two vital theatrical forces' to 'work daily in the course of the performance'.

My argument is developed with reference to a range of productions from across Meyerhold's career. These productions have been selected because they clearly highlight the director's diverse uses of space and because they are well-documented and accessible in English language sources, allowing for cross-referencing by readers.[9] Transliteration of Russian titles is made according to the Library of Congress System (2012), although common names are rendered in their most recognizable English form.

The body in space: Meyerhold's approach to direction and design

Meyerhold's work as a director was defined by two main aesthetic concerns: the configuration of the stage space and the craft of the actor. Viewing the actor as 'the principal element in the theatre',[10] Meyerhold consistently explored approaches to acting technique and actor training. Vitally, though, how his understanding of the actor was realized in performance was closely connected to Meyerhold's work on stage space. His directorial aesthetic was profoundly visual, emphasizing the structural elements of the *mise en scène* and creating stage images that drew the spectator's eye, communicating beyond the narrative of the play text. Meyerhold's concern for the visual was manifest in his working practice with stage designers. Alla Mikhailova notes the significance that Meyerhold's relationships with visual artists had on his development as a director:

> [The] decisive influence on Meyerhold's progress as a stage director was undoubtedly exerted by artist-designers. This may have been due to his keen visual perception: he used to say that vision was his greatest natural endowment, that he was able to see a play in his mind's eye before he could hear it.[11]

Meyerhold's ability to visualize the stage space sat in tension with his lack of skill as a visual artist. Although his ideal working model was that of Edward Gordon Craig[12] – as both director and designer – Meyerhold's shortcomings with the sketchpad meant that he relied on collaboration to realize his 'keen visual perception' on stage. In some instances, this meant work with some of Russia's leading visual artists (Alexander Golovin, Liubov Popova or Alexander Rodchenko, for example). These relationships, alongside his passionate interest in fine art, brought new visual languages into his theatres. For other productions, Meyerhold worked with a 'designer-realiser', whose role was to enact the director's design plan.[13] This approach centralized the design elements of Meyerhold's work, bringing all scenographic decisions under his control. In effect, either through collaboration with visual artists or with the 'designer-realiser', Meyerhold can be seen as a scenographer-director, who intentionally and consciously brought design into the director's purview and for whom theatrical space and visual *mise en scène* were central concerns.

The relationship between the actor and the performance space, either held in tension or merged in unity, formed the foundation of Meyerhold's strikingly visual aesthetic. Questions around how the body relates to onstage space emerged in his writing as early as 1906. Reflecting on the Moscow Art Theatre's 1903 version of *Julius Caesar*, he queried the use of a painted backdrop for the otherwise realist production:

> The hills on the battlefield [...] may be constructed so that they decrease in size towards the horizon, but why don't the characters become smaller, too, as they move away from us towards the hills?[14]

Although Meyerhold's complaint concerns what he perceived as the implausibility of Stanislavskian Naturalism [see Volume 1], it focuses on the disjuncture between the performer and the setting. The resolution of this tension between actor and space became a theme in Meyerhold's directorial practice. After spending his early years as a director 'slavishly imitating Stanislavsky',[15] under whom he had worked as an actor at the Moscow Art Theatre, Meyerhold quickly turned towards symbolism as an alternative aesthetic. Between 1906 and 1907, his symbolist experiments centred on Georg Fuchs's model of the relief stage, which comprised a narrow strip of downstage space located close to the audience. This reduced playing space drew attention to the actor's body, forced out in relief against non-representational painted backdrops. The tension between the ethereal painted cloths and the resolutely physical and three-dimensional actor's body formed the basis of Meyerhold's symbolist aesthetic. Reflecting on this work, Meyerhold notes the necessity of tension between the different theatrical elements, referring to the example of Wagner's *Gesamtkunstwerk* (total work of art):

> The theatre is constantly revealing a lack of harmony amongst those engaged in presenting their collective creative work to the public. One never sees an ideal blend of author, director, actor, designer, composer and property-master. For this reason, Wagner's notion of a synthesis of the arts seems to me impossible.[16]

Meyerhold's solution to the impossibility of synthesis was to exploit the differences between the three-dimensional actor and the restricted, painterly stage space, creating a *mise en scène* that, drawing on Fuchs' model, was founded on tensions.

The use of the relief stage in its purest form was to be short-lived in Meyerhold's theatre. This restriction of the stage space suited his symbolist experiments, in which the actors' bodies were used to form static tableaux. From 1906, however, Meyerhold began to turn his attention away from symbolism towards Russian folk theatre, the *balagan* (fairground booth), and the Italian *commedia dell'arte*. These performance styles called for a new form of acting, drawing on the *cabotin*, a figure Meyerhold describes as 'a strolling player [...] a kinsman to the mime, the *histrion*, and the juggler' who 'keeps alive the tradition of the true art of acting'.[17] Meyerhold's reform of acting brought him back to questions of the *Gesamtkunstwerk*: writing in 1910, he notes that a new style in acting is key to facilitating Wagner's model:

> The artistic synthesis which Wagner adopted as the basis for his reform of the music drama will continue to evolve. Great architects, designers, conductors and directors will combine their innovations to realize it in the theatre of the future. But there can be no complete synthesis before the advent of *the new actor* [emphasis in the original].[18]

Meyerhold's new actor was unsuited to the confines of the relief stage: the *cabotin*, an actor-acrobat, required a much less restricted performance space. Finding both an ideal new form of acting and a suitable space to facilitate it continued to occupy Meyerhold's attention into the 1920s. Russia's 1917 Revolutions prompted a new conceptualization of the actor in Meyerhold's theatre, and by 1922, he had formalized a post-revolutionary training model, biomechanics,[19] and forged a new visual arts relationship with the constructivists – artists whose primary concern was with the utility of the artwork. For the constructivists, it was qualities of the artist's materials and the social role of the artwork that gave visual arts practice its meaning.[20] Liubov Popova's constructivist-influenced structure for Meyerhold's production of Fernand Crommelynck's *Velikodushnyi rogonosets* (*The Magnanimous Cuckold*, 1922) provided the Meyerholdian actor-acrobats with a 'spring-board' to explore their biomechanical training in performance, a space in which the physical potential of the performer's body could find full expression through jumping, climbing and sliding across the stage.[21]

In *The Magnanimous Cuckold*, Meyerhold and Popova created a performance aesthetic that suggests a unified relationship between the performer's body and the onstage environment. Not only did the construction allow the actor to explore their skills as a physical performer, it also facilitated the creation of a *mise en scène* in which the forms of the set and the actor's body could blend: the line of an actor's arm is extended through a parallel trajectory in the setting; the performers create echoes of lines across multiple bodies on different levels of the set; the shadow on the back wall blends the actor and the setting together into a seamless whole.[22] Meyerhold's developing understanding of the relationship between the body and space, facilitated by his collaboration with designers and the evolution of his actor training system, had led him by 1930 to a belief in the potential of an onstage synthesis. In 'The Reconstruction of the Theatre', he returns to the theme of the *Gesamtskunstwerk*, noting that:

> There was a time when Wagner's idea of a new theatre which would be a dramatic synthesis of words, music, lighting, rhythmical movement and all the magic of the plastic parts was regarded as purely utopian. Now we can see that this is exactly what a production should be.[23]

In terms of the style of the performance and the *mise en scène*, how the human body relates to its spatial context was a building block of Meyerholdian direction. Anne Ubersfeld calls the interaction between the actor and the stage space the 'three-dimensional relationship' of theatre.[24] The question of three-dimensional form was particularly significant in Meyerhold's practice. Through biomechanical training, the actor learnt to orientate the body in space through a series of exercises that require shifting through different planes, angles and directions. During the mid- to late-1920s, in parallel to the use of biomechanics as a training tool, Meyerhold repeatedly turned towards a motif of curved stage space to emphasize the three-dimensional nature of the performance environment. Meyerhold's *mise en scène* had featured curved lines since the 1910s: Konstantin Rudnitsky, for example, notes the 'intoxicating refrains of Meyerhold's circular stagings' in his work on Mikhail Lermontov's *Maskarad (Masquerade)*, premiered 25 February 1917 at the Alexandrinsky theatre.[25] Rudnitsky's choice of words captures both the play's content and Meyerhold's production: *Masquerade* tells the story of a man, Arbenin, who becomes convinced that his beautiful, and loyal, wife Nina is unfaithful, ultimately murdering her and being driven mad by his own guilt. Meyerhold's production emphasized the inevitability of Arbenin's fate, a man controlled by external forces including the mysterious character of the Stranger, who manipulated circumstances to convince Arbenin of Nina's transgressions. In Meyerhold's production, it was not only the curvature of the stage that was 'intoxicating', but the whole of Arbenin's world.

From 1924 onwards, curvature became a regular and defining feature of the director's *mise en scène*. The visual idiom of a number of key Meyerhold productions in the mid-1920s was largely based around curved lines. In Alexander Ostrovksy's *Les (The Forest,* 1924), Meyerhold enclosed the playing space with a large, curved platform, sweeping from upstage left to downstage right, serving as a spatial metaphor for the journey of the two itinerant players that he used to structure the production. For Alexei

Faiko's *Uchitel' Bubus* (*Bubus the Teacher*, 1925), the stage was framed with a curved curtain of hanging bamboo poles, between which the actors could enter and exit. In Nikolai Erdman's *Mandat* (*The Mandate*, 1925), the curve was even more pervasive, as the main facet of the design was a series of concentric revolving stages at the centre of the playing space. The significance of the curved spaces was cemented in Meyerhold's unrealized production of Sergei Tretyakov's *Khochu rebenka* (*I Want a Child*). Working with artist El Lissitzky between 1929 and 1930, Meyerhold conceived a performance space wholly defined by curvature, with two superimposed circular stages at the centre and the audience divided into two groups, facing one another in curved seating blocks on an adaptation of the thrust staging model (see Figure 2.1). The curvature of the space is particularly highlighted by the banner of text that marches around the edge of the auditorium: *Zdorovyi rebenok – budushchii stroitel' sotsializma!*, or 'a healthy child is the future builder of socialism!' As Figure 2.1 demonstrates, the repetition of this text around the theatre encourages the reading of the space as circular, expanding the curved spatial idiom beyond the shape of the stage into the shape of the auditorium as a whole.

The use of curved space creates a setting which emphasizes three-dimensionality. Unlike the narrow strip of stage proposed by Fuchs, which echoed the principles of *bas-relief* art, the curved space is sculptural and

FIGURE 2.1 *Set model for Meyerhold's planned production of* I Want a Child *(Federal State Budget Institute of Culture 'A. A. Bakhrushin State Central Theatre Museum', Moscow).*

tangible, drawing attention to its own existence in depth.[26] For Meyerhold, the question of tangible space provides a direct link between visual aesthetics, the performer and the spectator:

> We have only to talk to the latest followers of Picasso and Tatlin to know at once that we are dealing with kindred spirits … We are building just as they are building … For us the art of manufacturing is more important than any tediously pretty patterns and colours. What do we want with pleasing effects? What the *modern* spectator wants is the placard, the juxtaposition of the surfaces and shapes of *tangible materials*! [emphasis in the original].[27]

The influence of cubist and constructivist understandings of space on Meyerhold's work led to a desire for a stage space that was tangible not only for the actor but also for the spectator. The use of a sculptural curved space invited the spectator to consider the objects and bodies presented on stage as three-dimensional, physically realized entities. Considering a performer located within a curved space, where the trajectory of the lines of the setting encircles them, the spectator had the opportunity to understand the actor's body as existing in three-dimensions and to imagine the other sides that are momentarily not visible to them. The body, and the space in which it was located, became tangible, something which could – potentially – be touched. Understanding the performance space as three-dimensional can be read as a vital stage in Meyerhold's activation of the spectator. In the proscenium arch model, the literal framing of the performance space implies a parallel between the stage and the framed painting, keeping the viewer at a distance and encouraging observation rather than active involvement. This is a point that may apply in general, yet theatre history shows that the proscenium arch did not in itself prevent disquiet, protests and, on occasion, riots. The use of curved spaces in Meyerhold's theatre subverted the model of the proscenium arch as a barrier, arguably bringing into the spectator's consciousness both the three-dimensional nature of theatre and the parallels between their own three-dimensional body and the embodied performer on stage. It is this parallel that locates the consideration of Meyerhold's theatrical space as a tool for constructing the spectator's active, locational and imaginative responses to his productions.

Locating the audience: Meyerhold's relational space

In her taxonomy of spatial function for performance, Gay McAuley considers the theatre building to be the 'first spatial fact' of the 'social reality of the theatre experience'.[28] This building, which as McAuley notes can be a space either dedicated to or adapted for theatrical use, provides the context for the social and spatial interactions that will occur during the performance. McAuley further subdivides this 'theatre space' according to its function for the different participants in the theatre event:

> [The theatre space] is a place of employment for some, a place of entertainment and cultural enrichment for others. The two groups have their designated areas within the space that is, in traditional theatres, quite rigidly demarcated and conceptualized in terms of front and back ('front of house' and 'backstage'). For the spectators theatre is a social event, their reception of the performance is part of a social experience, the areas within the theatre space to which they have access, which can be called *audience space*, facilitate (or discourage) types of social behaviour and social interaction [emphasis in the original].[29]

For McAuley, audience space is partnered with practitioner space, that is, the space which is the province of the 'theatre workers'. Although she places the auditorium into the category of audience space and the stage into practitioner space, McAuley also identifies a third spatial typology, where spectator and practitioner come together:

> It will be noticed that I have so far put stage and auditorium into two different categories, practitioner space and audience space respectively, but there is a third domain within the theatre space, the place constituted by the coming together of the other two. Overriding yet subsuming the division, the divided yet nevertheless unitary space in which the two constitutive groups (performers and spectators) meet and work together to create the performance experience, is the privileged domain that I shall call the *performance space* [emphasis in the original].[30]

McAuley's categories of audience, practitioner and performance space, as represented through the relationship between stage and auditorium, provide a framework for considering the first of Meyerhold's uses of theatrical space: that is, relational space, or space used to produce the interaction between actor and spectator. How to facilitate the audience's engagement with what McAuley calls the 'performance experience' was a fundamental question in Meyerhold's theatre. Meyerhold's rejection of the the spectator as onlooker had its roots in his disillusionment with Naturalism, a theatrical form in which he believed nothing was 'left unsaid', hindering the spectator's opportunities to make an active, cognitive contribution to the performance.[31] For Meyerhold, this need for active spectatorship was at the heart of the theatrical experience, and the act of engaging with the 'unsaid' was, to his mind, the very quality which '[drew] so many people to the theatre'.[32] The early Soviet era reinforced the need for an active spectator, giving a new sociopolitical impetus to

Meyerhold's theatrical theorizing. In 'The Reconstruction of the Theatre', he writes:

> We produce every play on the assumption that it will be still unfinished when it appears on stage. We do this consciously because we realize that the crucial revision of a production is that which is made by the spectator.[33]

The role of the spectator in the performance experience was reflected in Meyerhold's manipulation of the relationship between audience and practitioner space. As McAuley observes, the form of the audience space shapes social behaviour and interaction. In Meyerhold's theatre, it was the location of the stage or playing area in relation to the auditorium that not only facilitated interaction between spectator and performer, but also laid the foundation for the spectator's cognitive and imaginative responses to the performance experience.

The spatial layout of the stage and auditorium is a clear starting point for considering audience, practitioner and performance space in Meyerhold's work. During his career, Meyerhold worked at more than thirty performance venues.[34] These included tours of provincial theatres and non-theatrical settings (such as living rooms and school halls), as well as established venues, including the Komissarzhevskaya, Alexandrinksy and Marinsky Theatres in St Petersburg, and the Moscow Art Theatre Studio on Povarskaya Street.[35] In 1922, he found a permanent home and his own theatre company at Moscow's former Zon Theatre. Leach recounts Meyerhold's typically military approach to claiming this space, using his students from the State Higher Theatre Workshop (GVYTM):

> In April, Meyerhold led his students in a commando-style raid on the theatre [which then housed the failing Nezlobin Theatre Company] – typically enough, he divided them into brigades, assigned each brigade to an area of the theatre and had the whole place cleared from top to bottom. Everything – flats, scenery, props, curtains and all – was chucked out into the yard. When the dust settled there was an empty theatre which was to encompass Meyerhold's work for the next ten years.[36]

As Leach goes on to note, this was the end of the Nezlobin company ('their scenery and costumes had all been destroyed'), and Meyerhold's theatre would not only take on the Zon space but also the acronym TIM (*Teatr imeni Vs. Meierkhol'da*, or Meyerhold Theatre). In 1926, on gaining State subsidy, TIM became GosTIM (*Gosudarstvennyi Teatr imeni Vs. Meierkhol'da*, or State Meyerhold Theatre). In 1931, the former Zon building was closed for renovation, and Meyerhold worked with architects Mikhail Barkhin and Sergei Vakhtangov to develop a new theatre space that met his exact requirements. The project was ultimately aborted when GosTIM was liquidated in 1938, although the three extant variants of the architects' designs give some indication of Meyerhold's intentions for the space.[37] Meyerhold's plans for his new building are arguably some of the clearest indications of his developing theatrical approach towards the end of his life, and are closely affiliated with the ideas he discusses in 'The Reconstruction of the Theatre'. Barkhin and Vakhtangov's proposed theatre was a radical reworking of theatrical space and a reframing of the stage and auditorium. In contrast, the theatres in which Meyerhold produced the majority of his practice between 1905 and 1931, were predominantly what McAuley calls 'traditional' theatre spaces, comprising an end-on stage configuration, 'rigidly demarcated' with the playing space located at one end of the auditorium and the spectators facing the stage.

Meyerhold's objection to this rigid demarcation is clearly reflected throughout his career. In 'The Reconstruction of the Theatre', he discusses this stage-auditorium configuration as an ideological device, associated with pre-revolutionary imperialist Russia. He claims that the layout fosters an audience of onlookers, unsuited to Soviet theatre, who are so separated from the action on stage that they become entirely disengaged from the performance experience:

> Obviously it is our intention to build new theatres and to vacate those which we inherited from the age of imperialism, nobility and private ownership. In those days they built box-stages designed to foster illusion, stages for plays during which the spectator could relax, take a nap, flirt with the ladies, or exchange gossip.[38]

Meyerhold's connection of the box stage with the imperialist theatre was borne out in his own experiences of directing at the Alexandrinsky, one of Russia's subsidized imperial theatres, where he was employed between 1907 and 1917. Built in 1832, and designed by Italian architect Carlo Rossi in the Empire style, the Alexandrinsky seats approximately 1,300 spectators across its five circle auditorium.[39] For his production of Molière's *Don Zhuan* (*Don Juan*), premiered 9 November 1910 at that theatre, Meyerhold and his designer Alexander Golovin tackled the dividing line between the stage and auditorium by adding a curved proscenium, or apron, to the stage, seeking to bridge the gap between spectator and actor that resulted from the size of the venue and the depth of the playing space, as well as the end-on configuration. Moliere's play concerns the comeuppance of the womanizer Don Juan, who has offended heaven with a string of proposals and false marriages. The influence of the *commedia dell'arte* on the text is reflected in the inclusion of asides, particularly from the character of Sganarelle, Don Juan's servant. The forestage configuration allowed Meyerhold to locate Konstantin Varmalov, playing Sganarelle, close to the audience, facilitating the interaction that the writing style implied.[40] Reflecting on *Don Juan*, he claims that this innovation is rooted in Molière's own attitudes as a playwright:

> The academic theatre of the Renaissance failed to take advantage of the projecting forestage, keeping actor and audience at a mutually respectful distance. Sometimes, the front rows of the orchestra stalls were moved right back to the middle of the parterre, sometimes even further. How could Molière accept this segregation of actor and public? [...] How could the waves of accusatory monologue of an author outraged by the banning of *Tartuffe* reach the spectator from such a distance? Surely the actor's ability and freedom of gesture were hemmed in by the wings?[41]

In his reflections on *Don Juan*, Meyerhold triangulates the relationship between theatrical space, spectator engagement and the actor's potential playing style, arguing that the form of the stage space is central to achieving the playwright's goals.[42] To this end, Meyerhold's production incorporated a series of design-led innovations intended to forge connections between audience and practitioner space. The proscenium became the main playing area for the production: Konstantin Rudnitsky notes that in the plans discussed with Golovin in 1909, Meyerhold

> stressed particularly that the players would act *only* on the proscenium, and only for the final scene did he indicate a spot at a relative depth, at the border between the proscenium and the rear plane [a space he had reserved for painterly backdrops, the 'artists' canvases'].'[43]

In addition, he ensured that the houselights remained on during the performance, not only bringing the presence of the auditorium into the actors' consciousness but also allowing the spectators to see one another. The theatre's footlights, perhaps the most physical manifestation of the barrier between stage and auditorium, were removed. There was no curtain, as this impeded the audience's opportunities to engage with the atmosphere of the production from its very start, as Meyerhold notes:

> Curtain art is received casually, weakly, since the viewer has come to see what is concealed behind the curtain. After the curtain is raised, some time is required for the viewer to assimilate all the charms of the environment surrounding the players in the play. It is another matter with a stage open from beginning to end: by the time the actor appears on the stage, the viewer has already managed to 'breathe in the air of the period'.[44]

Finally, design features on stage echoed features of the Alexandrinsky's auditorium, highlighting audience and practitioner spaces as part of a single visual idiom: chandeliers, for example, hung over the playing space and echoed the house lighting. This had the effect of locating the era of Molière's play (which Meyerhold conceived of as an atmosphere rather than a literal representation) but also implicated the spectators in the development of the action onstage, establishing a parallel between the playing and watching spaces.

These innovations continued to influence Meyerhold's theatre after the 1917 Revolutions. In his production of Emile Verhaeren's *Zori* (*The Dawn*), premiered on 7 November 1920 at the RSFSR Theatre Number 1 in Moscow, Meyerhold and his designer Vladimir Dmitriev introduced a curved staircase between the stage and the orchestra pit in order to provide a space for the chorus, which mimicked the forestage at the Alexandrinsky.[45] Critic K. Famarin's review of the production highlights the similarities in staging to his earlier work:

> No footlights. In the full sense of the word ... *The Dawn* is staged on the principle of stage platform. The plane of the stage boards is used and nothing more. The lights are on full in the auditorium. The actors not only play in the area where the footlights used to be, but descend a wide staircase into the space that previously was occupied by the orchestra.[46]

Meyerhold saw the use of the proscenium post-1917 as a sociopolitical tool for bringing performer and spectator together, writing that 'the proscenium is far more than just a technical refinement: it is the first step towards the unification of the stage and auditorium'.[47] The justification for Meyerhold's aesthetic may have shifted from the aims of the playwright towards a Soviet sociopolitical rhetoric, but the scenographic devices remained the same. In his production of Alexander Sukhovo-Kobylin's *Smert' Tarelkina* (*The Death of Tarelkin*) premiered on 24 November 1922 at the former Zon, some of the playfulness that Meyerhold saw in Molière's theatre was incorporated in a far more physical interaction between the actor and spectator taking place during the interval, as Leach describes:

> Meyerhold was considerably exercised by the question of the interval, which he called a 'reef' upon which the production might flounder. So, in *The Death of Tarelkin* in 1922, he filled it by bringing students into the auditorium, some of whom played catch between the stalls and the circle, while others lowered on strings from the ceiling apples for the spectators to take and eat, and signs with legends such as 'Death to the Tarelkins! Make way for the Meyerholds!'[48]

Although it appears that Meyerhold was striving to overcome a boundary between the stage and auditorium, neither the interactive playfulness of *The Death of Tarelkin* nor the scenographic devices that defined his work on *Don Juan* or *The Dawn* suggest that he was interested in the total erasure of this divide. Meyerhold's staging choices might imply a 'unification' of actor and spectator, but he maintained a separate audience and practitioner space throughout his productions. Although Meyerhold is clear in 'The Reconstruction of the Theatre' that his theatre spaces had been restricted by a lack of funding, the maintenance of a separate stage and auditorium was not necessarily simply a concession to buildings unsuited to his goals.[49] The possibility of this divide as a deliberate aesthetic choice is confirmed by the plans for the new Meyerhold Theatre. The second and third variants of Barkhin and Vakhtangov's designs show two round playing spaces located at the centre of a raked amphitheatre-style auditorium (see Figure 2.2). Mimicking the Greek model, roughly half of the larger stage and nearly two-thirds of the smaller stage are surrounded by spectators. The back third of the larger stage is adjacent to a wall inset with a series of doors leading

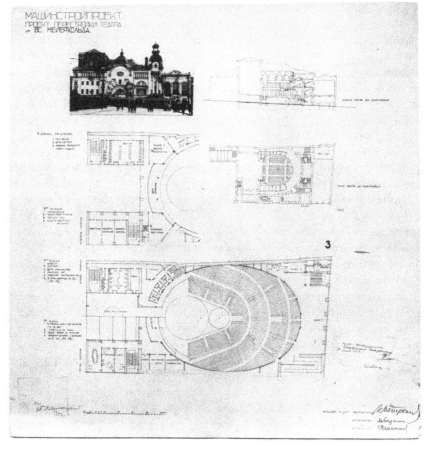

FIGURE 2.2 *Second and third variants of the design for the new Meyerhold Theatre, showing the raked auditorium (Federal State Budget Institute of Culture 'A. A. Bakhrushin State Central Theatre Museum', Moscow).*

to the performers' dressing rooms. The effect was, as Leach notes, intended to 'unsettle the customary spectator-object relationship' and the end-on configuration is certainly gone.[50] The audience and practitioner spaces, however, remain separate.

Maintaining separate places for the actor and the audience became a persistent theme in Meyerhold's use of space. Gail Lenhoff notes that:

> When one views [Meyerhold's] work as a whole [...] his forays into the audience are seen to be largely perfunctory. In the end, we must conclude that Meyerhold's work is centered on the stage.[51]

Lenhoff suggests that Meyerhold's attention was on other matters (the reform of acting style and new approaches to the text, for example) rather than on the reconfiguration of the stage and auditorium.[52] However, Meyerhold's refusal to abandon separate acting and performing spaces could also imply an ideological decision. The separate spaces allowed Meyerhold to construct a visual metaphor for the relative roles of the performer and spectator. In practice, Meyerhold's work suggested that the actor and the spectator are two separate groups of bodies whose relationship relies on alternating moments of similarity and difference, and this attitude was embedded in the layout of the theatre building. The separate location of the audience indicated the nature of the spectators' role at the Meyerhold Theatre: they shared the theatre space with the actors, but their function was different; they were separate but still integral to the realization of the experience. In Meyerhold's words, their role was that of co-creators, participants in the 'corporate creative act of the performance.'[53]

The realization of these moments of similarity and difference between performers and spectators can be seen in how Meyerhold exploited the tension between the stage and auditorium to imply different models of actor–audience relationship. The play during the interval in *The Death of Tarelkin*, for example, can be read as a moment of similarity through identification, when the actors and spectators temporarily became one group, united in the enacting of a specific task (playing catch with a ball, or passing on an apple): as the performers entered the auditorium, the boundary between the audience and practitioner spaces was temporarily transgressed. The echoing of design features between the stage and auditorium in *Don Juan* was a form of mirroring, in which the auditorium and the stage shared a visual aesthetic that implied a different sort of similarity between the two spaces. The implications of the mirror as a space of reflection (that is, intellectual self-examination) was not facilitated through the blurring of boundaries seen in *Tarelkin* but through the conscious separation of actor and audience. A mirror cannot function without spatial separation: the viewers must be able to separate themselves from the 'other' of their reflection in order to (intellectually) reflect. As such, the separation of spaces not only facilitated the spectator's understanding of their literal and metaphorical place within the performance but also allowed Meyerhold flexibility in how he constructed interactions between the two groups, constantly shifting and unsettling the spectator–performer relationship.

As such, the spectator's role in Meyerhold's theatre became one of continual reorientation and renegotiation. The location of the audience space within the theatre acted as a metaphor for the sorts of interactions that can exist between the stage and auditorium, models of separation, transgression and mirroring. In the constant renegotiation of the terms of their interaction with the stage, Meyerhold's spectators were cast as active and creative contributors to the performance experience, involved in a dialogue with both the performance and the theatre-maker. The implications of this are significant, particularly in light of Meyerhold's sociopolitical context. Restrictions placed on the arts by initiatives like Socialist Realism demonstrates the perceived power of theatre by the Soviet government: the theatrical experience was seen as a training ground for the negotiation of everyday life under the Soviet regime. Just as Meyerhold's actor training system intended to produce a new Soviet actor to parallel the new Soviet Man, spectatorship at the Meyerhold theatre can also be seen to target a new sort of viewer and a new sort of thinker, able to deal with shifting contexts as part of a collective: an idea that could be both extremely useful, and extremely dangerous, for those in power.

Relating the real and the fictional: Meyerhold's imagined space

In his 1907 article 'First Attempts at a Stylized Theatre', Meyerhold identifies 'four basic theatrical elements': the author, the director, the actor and the spectator.[54] Meyerhold uses these elements to model two different approaches to the role of the director. The first is the Theatre Triangle, in which the work of the actor and playwright are filtered through the director to the audience; the second is the Theatre of the Straight Line, in which the emphasis travels from playwright, to director, then to actor and finally to spectator, a cumulative process in which the production emerges through the incorporation of each participant. Meyerhold's intention, in his exploration of these models of working practice, is to facilitate 'creative freedom' for the actor and spectator.[55] In his preferred working model, the Theatre of the Straight Line, he notes that:

> The director, having absorbed the author's conception, conveys his own creation (now a blend of the author and the director) to the actor. The actor, having assimilated the author's conception via the director, stands face to face with the spectator (with director and author behind him), and

freely reveals his soul to him, thus intensifying the fundamental theatrical relationship of performer and spectator [emphasis in the original].[56]

The benefit of this approach, in Meyerhold's words, is that it 'leaves [the actor and spectator] both free, and forces the spectator to create instead of merely looking on (for a start, by stimulating his imagination)'.[57] Meyerhold's statement implies an interesting demotion of the status of the director, particularly in light of his reputation as a theatrical auteur, or even directorial dictator (for example, as suggested by Norris Houghton).[58] In reality, Meyerhold's aesthetic vision suffused his practice, and his creative (re)interpretation, for example of the play text, was a significant element in the development of his productions. In his Theatre of the Straight Line, Meyerhold places the actor and spectator at the centre of the theatrical experience, suggesting that the director's role is the creative facilitation of this relationship, through the lens of his or her own aesthetic conception of the performance event. Meyerhold picks up again on this theme of the spectator's imagination in 'The Reconstruction of the Theatre', outlining the complexity of imaginative engagement for the Soviet spectator. Here, he suggests that theatre in a Soviet context has a dual role: to engage the spectator in political debate (that is, intellectual engagement) and to facilitate responses to characters, situations and narrative – a specifically theatrical and emotional form of engagement:

> This ability to start the spectator's brain working is just one of theatre's properties. But it has another, quite different property: it can stimulate the spectator's emotions and steer him through a complex labyrinth of emotions.[59]

In a stance that seems to challenge directly the emerging didacticism in Soviet theatre, Meyerhold advocates for a theatrical form that moves beyond straightforward conclusions through imaginative engagement with specifically theatrical devices:

> Since a dramatic performance depends on laws peculiar to the theatre, it is not enough for it to appeal purely to a spectator's intellect. A play must do more than prompt an idea or depict events in such a way as to invite automatic conclusions. Actors do not perform simply to demonstrate the idea of the author, the director or themselves; their struggles, the whole dramatic conflict has a far higher aim than the mere exposition of thesis and antithesis. It is not for that the public goes to the theatre.[60]

For Meyerhold, engagement with the fictional world of the play text, represented by the 'dramatic situations and characters' in the performance, facilitates sociopolitical debate among the spectators: the ultimate goal of his post-revolutionary theatre.[61] The process of shaping the spectator's imaginative response through the performance experience became a key factor in his directorial practice.

Writing in 1936, six years after Meyerhold's 'The Reconstruction of the Theatre', and influenced by the Prague School of Czech Structuralism, Karel Brušák suggests a model for the 'imagined action space' that resonates with Meyerhold's calls for an active and imaginative spectator. This is space that, in Brušák's words:

> form[s] a kind of twin to the dramatic space. This twin is, however, not identical. It only exists in the imagination of the spectator, and it does not possess all the elements of the dramatic space. But it is a space where action indispensable for the development of the drama takes place.[62]

In effect, this is 'other' space, related to the onstage action, imagined by the spectator as the result of signification that occurs in the playing space. McAuley suggests a more nuanced reading of imagined space in the context of what she calls the 'physical/fictional relationship', incorporating the relationships between the physical stage space, the presentational space ('the physical use of this stage space in any given performance') and the fictional place ('the place or places presented, represented or evoked offstage and on').[63] How Meyerhold negotiated the relationship between the physical and the fictional indicates that his use of imagined spaces was closely associated with his desire to activate the spectator's imagination.

The function of the physical/fictional relationship in Meyerhold's theatre can particularly be seen in his use of kinetic scenography, a recurring device in his practice which allowed him to disrupt any sense of fictional spatial unity in his productions. In Meyerholdian theatre, these kinetic scenographic devices had a primary function in constructing and controlling the rhythm of his productions. For Meyerhold, rhythm was more than a structural device; instead, it underwrote the dramaturgical development of each performance. As early as 1908, in his essay 'The Naturalistic Theatre and the Theatre of Mood', Meyerhold explored the potential of rhythm in constructing relationships between the spectator, character and narrative through close analysis of Act 3 of Chekhov's *Vishnevyi sad* (*The Cherry Orchard*):

> The author intended the act's *leitmotiv* to be Ranevskaya's premonition of the approaching storm (the sale of the cherry orchard). Everyone else is behaving as though stupefied: they are dancing happily to the monotonous tinkling of the Jewish band [...] They do not realise that the ground on which they are dancing is subsiding under their feet. Ranevskaya alone foresees the disaster; she rushes back and forth, then briefly halts the revolving wheel, the nightmare dance of the puppet show.[64]

Although Meyerhold's tone overtly references the Symbolist movement which influenced him during this period of his career, it is the director's interest in rhythm that is most clearly manifest in his analysis of the play text. Meyerhold suggests that this sequence, in which the sale of the orchard takes place, functions through the playwright's construction of various on-stage rhythms which provide the basis for the dramaturgy: a party hosted on the family estate, where a Jewish band plays and the characters flirt, dance and perform conjuring tricks, is set against the barely concealed panic of the estate's owner, Liubov Ranevskaya. The chaotic party provides a visual, external manifestation of Ranveksaya's inner rhythm, communicating aspects of characterization to the spectator. Meyerhold's clear connection between the rhythm of the sequence and its potential visual manifestation through staging and *mise en scène* suggests that the director's understanding of the rhythmic was not only musical (the '*leitmotiv*') but also closely related to uses of the term in visual art, where line, shape and trajectory combine to create the rhythm of the canvas.

Meyerhold's understanding of rhythm as spatial was reflected in his use of kinetic scenography to establish and maintain pace during a performance. Meyerhold used moving settings in order to shift rapidly from one fictional place to another: this is seen, for example, in his use of curtains in *Masquerade* (which interrupted the action in order to isolate characters on the proscenium, allowing for large-scale set changes to take place that did not interrupt the production's rhythm), in the revolving stages of *The Mandate* and perhaps in its most sophisticated version in his work on Nikolai Gogol's *Revizor* (*The Government Inspector*). The kinetic elements used in this production, arguably Meyerhold's masterpiece, had a function which moved beyond the rhythmic towards a more fundamental disruption of spatial unity, indicating a sophisticated use of scenographic devices to manifest a series of different orders of imagined space during the performance.

The Government Inspector premiered at GosTIM on 9 December 1926. In Gogol's play, conman Khlestakov exploits a corrupt Russian town who are expecting an inspection from central government. Mistaken for the inspector, Khlestakov is wined and dined, accepts bribes and seduces both the Mayor's wife and daughter. An intercepted letter, opened after Khlestakov's departure, exposes him as a fraud – at the very moment that the arrival of the real inspector is announced. In Meyerhold's production, the director, working alongside Victor Kiselev as designer-realiser, constructed a scenographic idiom that had three features:

1   a curved back wall, inset with a series of doors
2   small wheeled trucks, featuring realist decor, on which ten of the production's fifteen episodes were played[65]
3   the physical stage space into which these trucks were temporarily placed. This space was identifiable in its physical features as nothing more or less than the stage at GosTIM.

Meyerhold considered the use of trucks in *The Government Inspector* to be a significant development in the future of theatrical staging. In 'The Reconstruction of the Theatre', he calls for a reconceptualization of theatrical space according to these principles:

> We must destroy the box-stage once and for all, for only then can we hope to achieve a truly dynamic spectacle. By making the stage machinery sufficiently flexible to present a series of rapidly changing scenes, we shall be able to abolish the tedious unity of place and the compression of the action into four or five unwieldy acts. The new stage will have no proscenium arch and will be equipped with a series of platforms which can be moved horizontally and vertically to facilitate transformation scenes and the manipulation of kinetic constructions.[66]

For Meyerhold, the kineticism of the trucks went beyond simply embedding movement into the production's scenography: these moving platforms 'abolish the tedious unity of place', allowing the director freedom in his representation of place and location.[67] Through the agency of the platform stages, Meyerhold constructed an imagined or fictional space that played with on- and offstage boundaries. One of the most striking features of the *mise en scène* for *The Government Inspector* was the motif of restricted space. The trucks that formed the main playing space measured just 3.5 by 4.25 metres, and their spatial restriction was reinforced by the highly populated tableaux that the director created and the close attention to naturalistic detail in the trucks' settings, crowded with period furniture, fabrics and props, and described by A.A. Gvozdev as looking 'like a staging by the Moscow Art Theatre' (see Figure 2.3).[68] The highly populated tableaux created a very clear distinction in the *mise en scène*, between the busyness of the trucks and the stage space that surrounded them. In other words, to draw on a term used by Brušák, the trucks' primary mode of functioning was through delineation, a device which 'pre-conditioned the spectator to presume [the] continuation [of the onstage space] beyond its limits'.[69] The discontinuity of the detailed naturalistic settings on Meyerhold's trucks was vital in the function of this delineation: these were not whole rooms but fragments of rooms, room-pieces cut out from a larger fictional place that was not visually manifest on stage.[70] The creation of this fictional place, as with the discontinuity of any stage set, was placed in the hands of the spectator, who had the opportunity to generate an imagined space in which the action continued outside of the staged environment.

For Brušák, this imagined space must be actualized through the action. In *The Government Inspector*, however, delineation operated as a form of actualization in itself; that is, that the delineation of the trucks is enough of a sign to the spectator to prompt an engagement with an imagined space beyond. This was in part due to the relationship between the trucks and the wider stage space. The full stage space, without trucks, was used on two

FIGURE 2.3 *Meyerhold's production of* The Government Inspector, *1926 (Federal State Budget Institute of Culture 'A. A. Bakhrushin State Central Theatre Museum', Moscow).*

occasions in the production, for sequences with a predominantly fantastical or nightmare motif: the episode 'Bribes', in which Gogol's bribery scene (where a queue of officials take it in turns to try to bribe Khlestakov) was reworked as the conman's drunken nightmare; and the final moments of the production, when Khlestakov's deception is uncovered and, in Meyerhold's production, the mayor descended into madness and was restrained with a straightjacket. Both of these sequences dealt with the characters' mental state, either through Khlestakov's drunken and greedy dream or the mayor's collapse, details added to the production by Meyerhold. Meyerhold's recasting of elements of Gogol's play as fantasy (for example, turning the bribery scene into a dream), suggests that Meyerhold developed an association between the full stage space without the trucks and moments when the production engaged with the imagination or fantasy of the characters.

For the majority of the production's fifteen episodes, however, the trucks were used. Placed downstage centre, their sharp edges begged to be extended, inviting the spectator to generate imagined settings to fill the wider stage space. It is the placement of this imagined space that was particularly significant in Meyerhold's production: rather than considering how the fictional place of the trucks might extend offstage, as in Brušák's model of delineation, the spectator was invited to consider how it could extend through the onstage vacuum that Meyerhold created in the wider stage space. The process of generating imaginary action space was embodied within the scenographic idiom: Meyerhold had created an onstage setting that could function as if it were offstage space through the clear delineation of the trucks.

As an upstage boundary for the performance space as a whole, Meyerhold constructed the curved back wall. Describing the wall, he requested that 'a polished surface [...] be selected, such as will be associated with the era of the 1830s to 1840s' and that 'eleven doors open out of these polished surfaces', forming an upstage border for the playing space.[71] For Brušák, the door is an essential onstage signifier, used to invite the spectator into a relationship with the imaginary action space. Writing about Gogol's play specifically, Brušák explicitly locates the imagined space implied by the text as lying 'behind a closed door'.[72] Doors became a complex signifying element in Meyerhold's interpretation of *The Government Inspector*. Perhaps the most straightforward use of a door, echoing Brušák's 'closed door' to his imaginary action space, was seen in the entrance of the comic pairing Dobchinsky and Bobchinsky in the episode 'After Penza'. During this episode, Dobchinsky and Bobchinsky have been listening outside the door to the action on stage, and, when the door opened, in a set-piece of Meyerholdian comic-acrobatics, they fell through it and down the stairs into the room. Implicitly, this closed door opened onto an extension of the onstage fictional place: Bobchinsky and Dobchinsky were, quite simply, outside.

Other doors, however, fulfilled more complex functions. One example is the wardrobe door in the episode 'Filled with the Tend'rest Love', a sequence in which Meyerhold sought to showcase the character of Anna Andreevna, the mayor's wife. Prompted by a line in the text suggesting her vanity, Meyerhold's episode explored Anna's self-image as seductress, as a large group of soldiers appeared through her wardrobe door whilst she dressed, presenting her with gifts, and one even shooting himself after her rejection. The status of the door here was more ambiguous, both opening onto an extension of fictional place (Anna's wardrobe) but also, metaphorically, to the internalized place of the character's psyche. Behind the door lay Anna's fantasies and, as the spectator cannot believe that her wardrobe is *really* filled with soldiers, the nature of the imagined space shifted from narrative-driven (in which the obvious conclusion would be that Anna's wardrobe is filled with clothes, especially as the spectator has just seen her dress), to character-driven (the space is filled with Anna's desires). This shift implied that scenographic and staging choices can engender multiple and different qualities of imagined space, or space imagined from multiple perspectives. The spectator was invited, in 'Filled with the Tend'rest Love', to imagine space *as if* they were Anna, to share momentarily in her fantasy, glancing behind the closed door of the individual character.

It was the entrance of the wheeled trucks through the upstage doors, however, that most clearly differentiated the quality of the imagined space created onstage from that visualized as offstage: if the onstage imagined space contained an extension of the fictional place on the trucks, the offstage imagined space was responsible for their very existence: it appeared to generate the restricted settings that emerged through the central doors. Although Meyerhold's choice of era for the production was vague (the 1830s–1840s), it was quite clearly historicized, and as a result, the space that generated the trucks was, in effect, the past. The doors opened to admit another Russia, fragments of which were being released for the consideration of the contemporary, Soviet, spectator. In this sense, the imagined spaces were both differentiated and shared: as each individual was invited to generate their own imagined spaces, the context of that generation was collective, rooted in a shared sense of history. In other words, the spaces are shared not in terms of their content but in terms of their context and in terms of the imaginative process with which each spectator was engaged.

Shifting spaces: Meyerhold's scenographic spectatorship

As Meyerhold notes in 'The Reconstruction of the Theatre', the creation of the production occurs not in the rehearsal room but on the stage, in a process of daily work that takes place between the actor and the spectator at each performance. Meyerhold's experiments with theatrical space formed the foundation of that process, building relationships between stage and auditorium, and inviting imaginative spectatorial engagement. Meyerhold facilitated the creative act of spectatorship through the configuration of the stage space, creating a model of spectatorship that was fundamentally underwritten by scenographic choices.

In both his relational and imagined uses of theatrical space, Meyerhold's practice was characterized by multiplicity. The articulation of stage and auditorium spaces allowed the director to create multiple relationships between the actor and spectator, constantly shifting between models of identification and separation. The combination of onstage and offstage imagined spaces facilitated multiple modes of engagement with the play text and the context of its performance. Meyerhold's spectator was consistently asked to manage multiple and shifting frames of experience, and the director was, in effect, directing spectators as well as actors: the spectator was subject to a similar process of reorientation that the biomechanical actors experienced as their bodies shifted through space in the training room. Meyerhold's emphasis on spectatorship as a creative act, rather than as an act of reception by an onlooker, was fundamentally empowering for the spectator: his imaginative, spatially-aware and embodied form of scenographic spectatorship was complex and intellectually challenging, and in direct conflict with the requirements of the Socialist Realist theatre endorsed by the Soviet authorities during the last decade of his career.

Space was at the heart of Meyerholdian theatre. By moving the focus of my analysis away from stage designs and artist collaborations per se, either considered in isolation or grouped according to aesthetic influence (Symbolist, Constructivist and so forth), models of theatrical space in Meyerhold's theatre can be used to consider the on-going themes that emerge across his diverse career. These themes transcend individual productions and his associations with individual designers, and become central elements in his aesthetic approach as a director. They are specifically directorial contributions to the developing understanding of space in twentieth-century theatre. Through his consistent experiments with space, Meyerhold blurred the roles of director and designer in theatre making, claiming questions of scenographic exploration as a directorial act. The consideration of his work with relational and imagined space highlights how the exploration of theatrical space underlay all aspects of Meyerhold's direction and was foundational in how he conceptualized other elements of the theatrical event, including acting, actor training and, perhaps most significantly, spectatorship.

Erwin Piscator

3

Erwin Piscator: Staging Politics in the Weimar Republic

Minou Arjomand

Erwin Piscator was a key figure in the development of twentieth-century theatre. His ideas about political theatre inspired generations of playwrights, actors and directors, and he was a mentor to a remarkably diverse range of theatre professionals, such as Bertolt Brecht, Tennessee Williams, Judith Malina, Marlon Brando, Harry Belafonte and many others. He also innovated in the field of theatre machinery using film and projections in radical new ways. But for all this, Piscator is less well-known than his contemporaries Bertolt Brecht and Vsevolod Meyerhold. We can speculate as to why this is the case: perhaps it was because he did not develop his own theories and techniques of acting as the other two directors did. As all of Piscator's work was so collaborative, it can be challenging to point to his specific contributions, and this has led scholars to undervalue his achievement. Piscator's lack of recognition may also be in part because his exile from Germany occurred at the high point of his career, and it was not until the end of his life that he once again became the artistic director of his own theatre. Whatever the reasons for his neglect, Piscator's career helps us think through the relationship between theatre and politics, and, as I will show, better understand the possibilities of political theatre today. Piscator's work and writings also provide crucial insights into the historical avant-garde movements in Germany between the two world wars.

This chapter will focus primarily on Piscator's work in Germany up until he left in 1931 in order to shoot a film in the Soviet Union. This stay turned out to be the beginning of a long exile after the National Socialists seized power in 1933. (The next chapter in this volume deals with his career from 1931 onwards.) In order to explore who Piscator was, what social and political forces helped to shape his theatre, and why his work is still important today, this chapter is divided into an introduction and three further analytical sections. The introduction contextualizes the first half of Piscator's career within the tumultuous and violent period of the First World War and the Weimar Republic. In this section, we will see how Piscator's work related to changes in the urban landscape, political upheaval and contemporaneous artistic movements. Understanding Piscator's work in relation to his historical context is essential because his ethos of making theatre was based on engagement with pressing political questions. The following three sections each take different approaches to answering a deceptively simple question: what is political theatre?

Historical context

Erwin Piscator was born in 1893 and grew up in the small town of Marburg, Germany. His family had close ties to the German Protestant tradition, stretching back to his forefather, Johannes Piscator, an important early seventeenth-century theologian. Piscator's father had hopes that he would become a minister, but to Erwin, 'a different pulpit seemed more important'.[1] From a young age, Piscator rejected his Calvinist father's conviction that worldly inequality was god-given, and instead saw injustice as something that human society creates and that people can alter.[2] All the same, Piscator never disavowed the values that he saw in the 'true Christianity' of his grandparents and uncle: 'forgiveness of the mistakes of others, understanding, goodness, tolerance.'[3] The playwright Rolf Hochhuth describes Piscator as

> the last surviving champion of the truly clean, sermon-on-the-mount type of socialism of the twenties [...] like his famous forebear [...] he is a theologian, a man of Christian nature – but as his God, like the God of many others, died in Flanders or before Verdun, his stirring Ethos is firmly surrounded in this earth.[4]

Instead of looking to the church or to the Bible as a source of morality, Piscator hoped to create a theatre that would better the world.

When the First World War broke out, Piscator was studying at the University of Munich and working as an apprentice actor at the Hoftheater (Court Theatre).[5] Across Germany the news of the war was greeted with widespread enthusiasm, but Piscator describes feeling distanced from the displays of patriotism and militarism surrounding him.[6] He was conscripted into the army and sent to the Western Front just before the start of the

Second Battle of Ypres (1915), in which the Germans used mass quantities of poison gas for the first time.[7] In his book, *Das Politische Theater* (The Political Theatre), Piscator writes that it was his experience as a soldier that first spurred his commitment to political theatre. He describes how his company arrived at the Western Front and was sent to clamber over decaying bodies to fill out the trenches. As grenades fell around the men, their commanding officer shouted to spread out and burrow into the ground. Piscator scrambled to dig but was not as able as the other men. His commanding officer screamed at him: 'Get on with it, damn you!' to which Piscator responded frantically: 'I can't'. The officer demanded to know Piscator's profession. Aware of how trivial it would sound in the midst of corpses and heavy artillery, Piscator told the officer that he was an actor. According to Piscator, at that moment, his shame of his profession exceeded even his fear of the incoming grenades. From that day forward, Piscator tried to create theatre that had no shame about fighting on the front lines of political struggles.[8]

After two years in the trenches, Piscator began to work as an actor in a theatre troupe made up of soldiers that gave performances along the front lines. Their repertoire was composed of light-hearted comedies, a stark contrast to the battlefields around them. Piscator writes that instead of engaging with current events and the experience of war, this theatre was 'degraded into vulgar trash' and used like cheap liquor for the soldiers to briefly anesthetize themselves.[9] Piscator's experience of war shaped his ideas about art's purpose. Piscator writes that after 1919, he was no longer interested in art as an end in itself but believed that it needed to become 'activist, combative, political'.[10]

When Piscator left the army and returned to his family home, everything seemed at once the same and different. All of the furniture was the same, his school books were still there, everything was in its place, except, he writes, 'the foundation of bourgeois security had fallen out from under them'.[11] Piscator moved to Berlin to be at the centre of the rapid and radical changes that Germany and Europe as a whole were undergoing. In Russia, the October Revolution of 1917 brought the Bolshevik Party, led by Lenin, to power. One year later, inspired by those events and sensing imminent defeat in the First World War, sailors in the German Navy began a revolt that grew into a full-fledged revolution, now known as the November Revolution of 1918. The first phase of the revolution led to the abdication of Emperor Wilhelm II, Germany's declaration of unconditional surrender and the creation of a parliamentary democracy in Germany led by the Social Democratic Party (SPD). For members of left-wing groups such as the Spartacus League (which later became the Communist Party of Germany), the SPD did not do enough to overthrow the ruling elites and stamp out nationalist militarism. Just months after the November Revolution, the Spartacus League attempted their own revolution, the January Revolution. This revolution was a failure, and the League's leaders Rosa Luxemburg and Karl Liebknecht were both murdered by paramilitary groups. Piscator was in Berlin during the January Revolution and describes the time as one of energy and civic participation as well as violence: 'Wild confusion in the streets. Debating clubs on every street corner. Massive demonstrations of workers and fellow travelers'.[12]

In Berlin, Piscator became friends with a group of artists connected to movements such as Dada, Expressionism, the Bauhaus and New Objectivity, including John Heartfield, George Grosz, Walter Mehring and Raoul Hausmann. Each of these movements took a very different approach to art-making. Expressionists saw art as way to externalize the depth of human emotion, a position which the artists of New Objectivity rejected, calling instead for art that would reflect social reality, however ugly. The Bauhaus movement sought to break down the boundaries between ideas of high art and artisan craft, while the Dadaists used bitter satire and absurdist performance to challenge the very idea of what art is. What all of these men had in common despite their different artistic approaches was a shared commitment to leftist politics. Together they tried to tease out how art could become part of the class struggle, and after the murder of Liebknecht and Luxemburg, they joined the Communist Party of Germany.[13] Piscator went on to collaborate with Heartfield and Grosz as designers for his productions, and he staged two plays by Mehring, *Der Kaufmann von Berlin* (The Merchant of Berlin, 1929) and *The Golden Doors* (1943).

Along with the radical political changes, Berlin was experiencing tremendous shifts in social and cultural norms. Traditional bourgeois gender roles were beginning to change. During the First World War, women entered the work force in large numbers. The absence of men during and after the war created an opening for women to enter universities and white-collar professions.[14] Increased independence for women was also connected to greater access to birth control and reforms in abortion law, the subject of Piscator's production *§218*, to which we will return in the next section. Women's entry into the workforce also had a dark side: following the mass casualties of the First World War, destitute women were driven into prostitution, becoming a common feature in the visual representations of Berlin nightlife by painters like Otto Dix and Ernst Ludwig Kirchner. Berlin was also a hub for queer life, as chronicled most famously in Christopher Isherwood's *Berlin Stories*.[15]

Berlin had it all: on the one hand, it was a cosmopolitan hub for art and culture, a space for sexual liberation and experimentation, and a place of relative freedom for socially marginalized people. On the other hand, it was a city with desperate poverty and deep resentments, perpetually on the verge of violence and revolution. The tension stemming from these contradictory social relations in the Weimar Republic was exacerbated by extreme economic insecurity. In order to finance the First World War, Germany relied on selling war bonds and printing money. These policies, combined with the punitive conditions of the Treaty of Versailles, plunged Germany into great economic difficulty. In the period 1922–3, Germans experienced rapid hyperinflation that rendered currency almost worthless. To give a sense of the scale of this inflation: in 1914, a loaf of bread cost less than one Reichsmark. By the summer of 1923, the price had shot up to 1,200 Reichsmarks. Just a few months later, in November 1923, a loaf of bread cost 428 billion Reichsmarks.[16] Although hyperinflation was brought under control in 1923, it had a devastating effect, particularly on the middle class.[17] This economic uncertainly in turn primed the ground for the rise of the radical right as well as interest in the German Communist Party. The Nazi Party was founded in 1920 and in November 1923, at the height of hyperinflation, Hitler led a failed attempt at a coup in Munich, now known as the Beer Hall Putsch. Throughout the 1920s, politics in the Weimar Republic became increasingly polarized. In 1932, the last free election before the Nazi seizure of power saw the Nazi Party win the highest number of seats in the Reichstag (196), while the Communist Party took 100, coming in third after the SPD.

As the Nazi Party grew in power, it propagated hatred and anti-Semitism, blaming Jews for the economic crisis. In the late 1920s, rumours began to spread that Piscator's real name was Samuel Fischer and that he was an *Ostjude* (Eastern Jew), a pejorative term for Jewish immigrants from Eastern Europe.[18] These rumours reveal the paranoia furthered by the Nazi Party about Jews, immigrants and leftists, who were often seen as one and the same. The rise of Nazi ideology led Piscator to think about politics in new ways. Throughout most of the 1920s, he focused on the politics of class struggle and economic inequality, but from the late 1920s on, he became increasingly concerned with anti-Semitism. Piscator's concern with this theme marked the beginning of his turn away from the Communist Party. The ideology of the Communist Party emphasized that Fascism and Nazism were simply the apex of capitalism in general. Piscator, by contrast, saw early on that anti-Semitism was central to the Third Reich in a way that could not be fully explained by economics or class struggle. The failure of communist ideology to account for anti-Semitism shook Piscator's faith in the party even before the Stalinist purges of the 1930s, which shook the faith of many party members and fellow travellers. Piscator's concern with anti-Semitism in particular, and bigotry in general, strongly informed his later work in New York and post-war West Germany.[19]

Throughout an era of political tumult and uncertainty, Piscator's theatre productions sought to engage directly in reshaping social, economic and political relations. In one of his early writings, Karl Marx noted that until now: 'The philosophers have only *interpreted* the world, in various ways; the point, however, is to *change* it.'[20] This famous line also applies to Piscator's theatre and its rejection of styles that dominated late nineteenth- and early twentieth-century theatre. Each of these movements seeks to give an interpretation of the world, either by mimicking the routines of bourgeois life (Realism), revealing the scientific or deterministic mechanisms at work in human relations (Naturalism), conjuring elements and states beyond our immediate perception (Symbolism), or externalizing the inner life of an individual (Expressionism). For Piscator these types of theatre, different as they are, still shared the fundamental quality of merely interpreting the world instead of actively changing it. But changing the world is a big task; how can theatre become a site for this sort of political change? How can actions on a stage affect the world outside the theatre's walls?

The following three sections each focus on different, but intertwined, aspects of how Piscator sought to use theatre to change the world. The first section examines audience reception and Piscator's attempts to make audience members active participants in his productions. This aim challenged the prevailing understanding of theatre as a place to present literary works for the consumption by and appreciation of middle-class audiences. The second section considers how and why Piscator rejected this sort of literary theatre and replaced it with a theatre in which the staging and the atmosphere of the performance were more important than the pre-existing dramatic text. In the third section, we turn to Piscator's use and his understanding of the function of technology, and his incorporation of multiple media and documentary materials into his productions. Finally, I will conclude with some questions that Piscator's early career leaves us with today.

The political audience

What does it mean for theatre to be political? Today, we are accustomed to a very broad understanding of what is political: the feminist mantra that 'the personal is the political' has helped us see just how much political ideology and inequality can reach into our private lives as individuals. By this understanding, there are many turn of the century plays that we might term 'political', ranging from the social satires of Oscar Wilde to the realist works of Ibsen and Chekhov. But when Piscator called his type of theatre 'The Political Theatre', he had something more specific in mind. For him, political theatre meant theatre that directly engaged with current political debates, not only by thematizing them on stage but also by taking the more radical step of leading the audience in immediate political action in the form of community meetings, protests and rallies.

The most important element of political theatre, for Piscator, was the relationship between the audience and the actions on stage. During the Weimar Republic, Piscator wanted to create a theatre for working-class audiences that reflected their lived experiences *and* that encouraged their participation in revolutionary politics. The first theatre that he founded in Berlin, called the Proletarian Theatre, was a world away from the luxurious Munich Court Theatre where he interned in his student days. The company did not have access to a stage or professional actors, but instead produced plays with amateur actors in the meeting halls of working-class neighbourhoods.[21] Tickets to their performances were inexpensive, even for low-wage workers, and were distributed for free to the unemployed.[22] The Proletarian Theatre had close affinities to several different theatre movements. Its mission and staging style was most influenced by Agitprop theatre, which developed during the Russian Revolution. Agitprop (which conflates agitation and propaganda) developed as a way to spread the message of the Communist Party to workers and peasants (many of them illiterate) across the vast territory of the former Russian Empire. Agitprop theatre companies created touring productions like the *Living Newspaper*, in which they would present important news items as well as information about social issues for audiences in a direct and factual manner (of course, with the ideological slant of the party informing those facts). This style of presenting current news and issues spread to leftist theatre makers in Germany and even in the United States, where the director Hallie Flanagan led a series of *Living Newspaper* productions focused on issues like housing, sexually transmitted diseases and unionization. Like Agitprop, Piscator's Proletarian Theatre featured short scenes with hyperbolic, and sometimes allegorical, characters, who offered simple and clear arguments for joining the class struggle.

It addition to Agitprop, Piscator borrowed freely from many genres of both high and popular art. Like the Dada movement, the Proletarian Theatre tried to blur the boundaries between art and life, and to challenge the idea that artistic institutions could or should remain distinct from the fray of politics. As Peter Bürger argues, this idea of blurring the boundaries between art and life is characteristic of the historical avant-garde.[23] Like the Dadaists, as well as Meyerhold in Russia, Piscator turned to popular art forms such as acrobatics, puppet shows and circuses in his work. He was also influenced by the cabaret culture of Weimar Berlin and created political 'revues' that included music and multiple, loosely connected numbers instead of a traditional dramatic arc with acts and scenes.[24] By adopting popular forms, Piscator implicitly rejected the mode of audience reception typical of high art theatre in his time. Realist and naturalist theatre was created for an audience of individuals, sitting in the dark and each singularly experiencing the play. The audience is supposed to pay attention to what is happening on stage, and not to other audience members, while the actors are supposed to act as though the audience were not there at all, creating a 'fourth wall' between themselves and the audience. By contrast, the audiences at circuses or cabarets are expected to be active – moving around the space, interacting with each other and responding vocally to the actors.

Over the course of the 1920s, Piscator developed his own particular form of theatre, which he called 'epic theatre'. Nowadays, 'epic theatre' is associated almost exclusively with Brecht, yet it was Piscator who pioneered the practical and theoretical exploration of the term. It is no coincidence, however, that Brecht and Piscator both called their new forms of theatre 'epic theatre'. Brecht was five years younger than Piscator and was beginning his career when Piscator was already an established (albeit controversial) figure in Berlin. Brecht became part of Piscator's dramaturgical collective between 1927 and 1928, working on productions including *Die Abenteuer des braven Soldaten Schwejk* (The Adventures of the Good Soldier Schweik).[25] Brecht and Piscator were both committed to the cause of proletarian revolution. They also both believed that this revolution required new forms of theatre that incorporated elements drawn from the theatre of classical antiquity (a chorus, a narrator commenting on actions) and from popular entertainments (songs and musical interludes).[26] The term 'epic theatre' itself combines two different genres that Aristotle defines in the *Poetics*: the epic and the dramatic. Instead of letting audiences settle into one mode of reception, combining the epic and dramatic challenged audiences to think about the contradictions between styles and modes of reception. Bringing these two modes of reception together was Brecht and Piscator's way of activating the audience and encouraging them to think and act. For these theatre-makers, conventional techniques of realist theatre were dangerous because their portrayal of the world also implicitly presented the world as something that audience members did not have the power to change. Brecht and Piscator rejected the passive audiences that would quietly absorb the values and morals of melodrama and realist theatre, and instead envisioned an active, critical audience that would learn to challenge the existing political order. For all of their similarities, though, Brecht and Piscator imagined the relationship between the audience and the stage in very different ways. Brecht writes that their two versions of epic theatre developed simultaneously but with different emphases: Brecht focused on acting style and Piscator focused on stage design and technologies.[27] While Brecht's techniques were designed to create a critical distance between the audience and the staged events, Piscator sought to incorporate audiences into the action, creating a 'Total Theatre' in which there was no separation between audience and stage.

According to Piscator, the new genre of epic theatre was born of an impromptu moment of collective improvisation. The Proletarian Theatre was performing a play called *Der Krüppel* (The Cripple) at various meeting halls in working-class neighbourhoods in Berlin. Piscator played the title role. At one performance, John Heartfield, who had designed the backdrop for the production, arrived late. Heartfield burst into the hall with the backdrop under his arm in the middle of the first act and shouted: 'Stop, Erwin, stop! I'm here!' As the audience turned to look at Heartfield, Piscator set aside his role as the 'cripple' for a moment, stood up and yelled: 'Where have you been all this time? We waited almost half an hour for you and then we had to start without your backdrop'.[28] With the audience watching, Heartfield and Piscator began to argue. Heartfield blamed Piscator for not sending a car and described how he had had to run through the streets because nobody was willing to transport him with the large curtain. Piscator interrupted him, telling him that the show must go on, but Heartfield insisted that they hang his backdrop before continuing the performance. So, Piscator put it to a vote among the audience members. An overwhelming majority voted for hanging the backdrop, which they did before starting the play again from the beginning. This, Piscator tells us in *Das Politische Theater*, was the beginning of epic theatre.[29]

This little story offers great insight into how Piscator understood the role of the audience in epic theatre. We can start with the location itself: a meeting hall in a working-class neighbourhood. Piscator wanted to foster class-consciousness and solidarity among the proletariat. For him, it was important that these events were accessible to members of the public and that they offered a way for audiences to participate. In this first instance of epic theatre, the audience vote came about as an accident, but in later productions, Piscator made the audience a key part of the performance in a variety of ways. In his production of Carl Credé's play *§218* (1929), advocating the legalization of abortion, Piscator planted actors in the audience to speak about abortion from different professional perspectives. The production toured throughout Germany, and whenever possible, Piscator would engage local doctors to speak.[30] In this production, the experts themselves delivered documentary evidence. He raised the house lights and opened the discussion to the audience in general, leading one reviewer to call the performance the first time 'the ending of a play corresponded to a public meeting'.[31] Piscator used the technique of having actors emerge from among the audience in other plays as well. In the *Revue Roter Rummel* (Red Rabble Revue), commissioned by the Communist Party of Germany, Piscator and his collaborators structured the entire performance as an argument between two figures – an Unemployed Man and a Master Butcher – who were initially seated among the audience and appeared to emerge out of it (again, breaking the boundary between the audience and the stage). Each of the vaudeville-style numbers in the *Revue* responded back to the argument between these two figures. The whole performance, then, was staged as though it were prompted by and responded to a debate between members of the audience.[32]

Although Piscator's career in Berlin began with small-scale productions, he soon gained access to the resources of professional theatres, starting with the Central-Theater and then the Volksbühne, and finally his own companies, the Piscator-Bühne (Piscator Stage) and Piscator-Kollektiv (Piscator Collective) that performed at two different theatres in Berlin and went on two national tours between 1927 and 1931. The idea of the Volksbühne, which literally means the 'People's Stage,' corresponded to Piscator's understanding of theatre as a public forum. Berlin's Volksbühne was founded in 1890 by workers groups, unions and leftist intellectuals who wanted to create a theatre that was affordable for workers. The workers would pay a low subscription price and each member was guaranteed a seat for each performance in any given season. Piscator describes the Volksbühne as the first time that workers as 'a large organized mass' were recognized as consumers of art.[33] In its early days, the Volksbühne focused on naturalist dramas about the plight of marginalized members of society like Gerhardt

Hauptmann's plays *Vor Sonnenaufgang* (Before Dawn) and *Die Weber* (The Weavers). Piscator saw this focus as a first step toward political theatre but an inadequate one for the current day. Naturalism, he writes, was not revolutionary because 'it never got past stating the problem'.[34] Throughout the Volksbühne's history, there was debate over what sort of theatre should be performed: whether the goal was to expose workers to the classics or whether to use the Volksbühne as a tool in propagating class struggle. (As we will see in the following chapter, the mission of the Volksbühne stayed with Piscator throughout his career.) By the time that Piscator began to work at the Volksbühne, though, it had moved away from some of its earlier political ambitions and had become a relatively apolitical theatre, staging classics like Shakespeare and Schiller. Piscator's work at the Volksbühne marked a radical departure from the sort of theatre that had hitherto been performed at large institutional theatres, and it proved highly contentious. Piscator's controversial (and expensive) productions resulted in his being fired from the Volksbühne in 1927 (see below), although this was not the end of his relationship with the institution. As we will see in the following chapter, Piscator eventually returned to the Volksbühne: in 1962, Piscator was appointed its director and in 1965 presided over the seventy-fifth anniversary of its founding.

From dramatic works to performance events

Piscator's first stint at the Volksbühne only lasted three years (1924–7), in part because he had a fundamentally different understanding of the theatre's function from the Volksbühne's leadership. Putting the audience and political agitation front and centre, as his work in the 1920s did, required a new understanding of the dramatic text's role in the theatre event. In Piscator's time (and perhaps still today), we may often think about plays when we think of theatrical works: Shakespeare's *Hamlet*, Ibsen's *A Doll's House*, or even Brecht's *The Good Person of Szechuan*. But for Piscator, the text was not the most important aspect of a theatre production. He saw theatre as an *event* rather than as the staging of (canonical) literary works. In Piscator's productions, the director and dramaturges were more important than the playwright; the literary text was no longer the focal point of the production.

The Weimar Republic was a key moment in the development of what Germans call *Regietheater* (director's theatre), a theatre in which the director shapes the performance's overall meaning and vision. Alongside Piscator, the directors Max Reinhardt and Leopold Jessner were also developing this concept of director's theatre, though without Piscator's political aims. In *Das politische Theater*, Piscator comes right out and says that the author's intentions should not determine how a play is performed, and even that plays should be cut or expanded to strengthen their revolutionary power: 'the conservative personality cult of the artist need not concern us', he writes.[35]

Here, Piscator connects adherence to authorial intention with the veneration of individual artistic geniuses like Goethe or Lessing. This veneration, for Piscator, is part of the value system of a bourgeois society that focuses on individualism and individual greatness instead of understanding that theatre always develops through collaboration.

For Piscator, one way to reject the conservative cult of the artist was to collaboratively develop new plays instead of recognized classics. During his work in the Weimar Republic, Piscator staged only two plays by canonical authors (Schiller and Strindberg). In his production of *Die Räuber* (The Robbers) at the Prussian State Theatre (1926), Piscator made extensive cuts to the play and rewrote significant scenes. He costumed one of the characters as the Russian revolutionary Leon Trotsky, and played the 'Internationale' during his death scene. He even scrambled the order of scenes in the play and had multiple scenes play out simultaneously on stage, so that it was almost impossible to distinguish what the actors were saying.[36] Schiller, certainly, was not there to object, but Piscator also used the same process with contemporary plays, at times working with the playwright, and at other times expressly against the playwright's wishes and intentions.[37] In his production of Ehm Welk's play *Gewitter über Gottland* (Storm over Gotland), set in 1400, Piscator had his main character wear a mask of Lenin, while film footage of Moscow and Shanghai appeared over the set. Changes like these got Piscator into trouble with some playwrights and institutions: his production of *Die Räuber* had to close after criticism from the Prussian State Assembly and his loose interpretation of Welk's play was what led to his dismissal from the Volksbühne.[38] This interpretation presented a challenge not only to Welk's intentions for the play, but also to copyright law and the concept of intellectual property that is central to how art circulates in a capitalist economy.

After leaving the Volksbühne, Piscator began the first of his own companies, called the Piscator-Bühne (Piscator Stage). The structure of the company reflected Piscator's rejection of literary theatre. Rather than hiring individual dramaturges to work on productions, as was the norm, this new company had a 'dramaturgical collective' devoted to writing, editing and developing the plays (Brecht was one member of this collective).[39] Instead of staging plays written by one single author, they concentrated on developing performances in which the written word was only one, often subordinate, component of the production. This working process was similar to what we today call devised theatre: work created through the rehearsal process itself by an ensemble of collaborators. Piscator thought of his productions as part of an ongoing process: he did not create final works, but rather works-in-progress, each building on the last one and looking toward the next.[40] In doing so, he presented the art-making process as one of continual negotiation, collaboration and innovation.

If Piscator dethroned the literary elements of theatre, what took their place? To answer this question, one first has to consider how audiences experience theatre and how they determine the meaning of what they see. The Theatre Studies scholar Erika Fischer-Lichte argues that all performances feature two different yet complementary systems of meaning.[41] The first is semiotic (i.e. sign-based). Understanding the semiotic meaning of a performance involves interpreting the signs and symbols on stage; for example, understanding that the actor holding a skull on stage represents Hamlet and decoding the skull itself as a symbol of mortality. Understanding the semiotic meaning of a play is thus primarily an intellectual exercise, one that often involves previous knowledge of the play and/or the theatre, and the cultural traditions of the context in which it is staged. However, the intellectual element is not always conscious: equating an actor wearing a dinner suit and a top hat with a member of the upper classes is hardly a great intellectual leap. The second system of meaning is phenomenal (i.e. perception-based). The phenomenal meaning of the performance includes the elements that cannot simply be read as signs and articulated in words, for example, the atmosphere in the room, the way the audience gains or loses energy during the performance, the particular charisma, actions, delivery and presence of an actor. Fischer-Lichte argues that all performances include both of these systems of meaning, but different techniques of staging can emphasize one type of meaning over the other. When Piscator underplayed the literary elements of his theatre, he shifted emphasis from semiotic to phenomenal meaning, emphasizing in particular the energy and feelings of solidarity that audiences might experience.

In Piscator's large-scale productions, there was not the same possibility for audience discussion as in his smaller touring productions. Instead of creating class-consciousness through discussion, the larger productions built on the energy and spectacle created by new technologies to fuse audiences into a collective. Perhaps the best example of this type of work is the production, *Trotz Alledem!* (In Spite of it All!), staged as part of a Communist Party convention in Berlin. Throughout the production, the actors on stage addressed the audience directly, encouraging them to become part of the performance. The audience was also invited to interact with each other and to experience the performance as a collective, instead of as individuals. Piscator describes the performance as successful because

> the masses took over the stage direction. The people who filled the house had for the most part been actively involved in the period, and what we were showing them was in a true sense their own fate, their own tragedy being acted out before their eyes. Theatre had become reality, and soon it was not a case of the stage confronting the audience, but one big assembly, one big battlefield, one massive demonstration. It was this unity that proved that evening that political theatre could be effective agitation.[42]

In this description, we see that *Trotz Alledem!* conveyed semiotic meaning: the audiences understood the films and action on stage as a representation of recent history and current events. But Piscator's main emphasis was on the phenomenal experience of the performance. The audience was not sitting quietly and thinking about the relationships between stage and reality, instead they were creating the performance through their own engagement and participation. According to Piscator, the performance did not stop at *representing* class struggle, it *was* class struggle: the theatre was a meeting hall, a battlefield and a demonstration all at once. In his essay 'Bühne der Gegenwart und Zukunft' (Stage of the Present and Future), Piscator writes that the experience of the performance changed the way audience members related to one another: 'A thousand people who fill a theatre are no longer just a sum of individuals, but a new being, gifted with special emotions, impulses, and nerves'.[43] This collective consciousness is achieved by pulling the audience into the action taking place on stage. As Piscator notes:

> The lifting of the boundary between the stage and the audience, the pulling of each individual spectator into the action fuses the audience completely into a mass, for whom collectivism does not remain a learned concept, but an experienced truth.[44]

While Piscator may well be over-exaggerating the success of his own production in this passage, his description is useful because it shows what his measures for success were. He was not celebrating because the audience understood the author's meaning. For him, the performance's success depended on the collective energies of the people present. He describes the meaning of this event as taking shape during the performance and being inextricably linked to the social and historical context, and to the individuals who were in the room during the performance.

Trotz Alledem! shows what Piscator hoped to achieve in his epic theatre of the 1920s, and it can also help us further differentiate Piscator's concept of epic theatre from Brecht's. Unlike Piscator, Brecht was primarily a playwright and a poet. As radical as Brecht's theatre was, Brecht never challenged the primacy of the text in his theatre. While Brecht sought to create an active audience, the audience's role – even in his 'learning plays', in which the boundary between stage and auditorium was to be abolished – was carefully scripted. The key terms Brecht uses to describe his epic theatre, such as distance and making the familiar strange (*Verfremdung*), imagine a radically different sort of audience than the tumultuous audience who 'took over the stage direction' of *Trotz Alledem!*[45] While Brecht wanted to create a critical distance between the audience members and the action on stage (and even between the actors themselves and the roles they played), Piscator wanted to collapse this distance. Brecht's epic theatre is directed at the cool-headed, smoking spectator who judges the events onstage for her or himself. *Trotz Alledem!*, by contrast, tries to create a collective out of the audience. Piscator encourages the audience to identify directly with the characters on stage ('it was their fate, their own tragedy') and to connect with their new 'emotions, impulses, and nerves' as a collective.

Media and technology

In his attempts to draw the audience into the production and to create collective revolutionary energy, Piscator turned to new technologies and massive, multi-level sets. Piscator's emphasis on technology was not only about style and effects; it was a key part of making audiences a part of the performance. Piscator's most ambitious project, which was never finished, was for a '*Totaltheater*' (Total Theatre). The architecture of the *Totaltheater* was meant to eliminate the boundary between audience and stage, drawing the audience into the action. Designed by the Bauhaus architect Walter Gropius, the *Totaltheater* would feature a moveable auditorium that could be reconfigured during the performance, for example, suddenly transforming the space from a proscenium to an arena layout. The plans for the *Totaltheater* included at least fifteen film projectors that were designed to immerse the entire auditorium in film.[46]

Theatre, by definition, is always created through multiple media and multiple forms of art. In the German context, there is a long tradition of theatre artists reflecting on this unique element of theatre stretching back to the great founding figures of German theatre, Goethe and Lessing. In the late nineteenth century, the composer Richard Wagner sought to create a *Gesamtkunstwerk* (total work of art) that would unite all of the arts (poetry, music, visual arts, dance and architecture). Although Piscator certainly rejected Wagner's nationalist politics, there is, nevertheless, a certain affinity between Wagner's idea of a Total Work of Art and Piscator and Gropius' plans for a Total Theatre. Both would fully immerse spectators in a performance through the employment of cutting-edge technology and the simultaneous use of multiple media. Where Piscator breaks strongly with the German tradition of theatre and opera as an intermedial art form is in the type of media that he chose. Whereas Goethe and Wagner viewed theatre as a composite of different forms of art (painting, poetry, etc.), Piscator's theatre was composed of mechanically reproducible forms of media, some quite new (film, projections, sound recordings) and some of them very old (posters, leaflets, programme books). All of these media served the core purpose of Piscator's epic theatre, as he puts it, 'the extension of the action and the clarification of the background to the action, that is to say [...] a continuation of the play beyond the dramatic framework'.[47] While the live actors on stage represented the dramatic action of the play, the other media provided information about the historical background and contemporary political situation that contextualized and 'clarified' the play. In other words, the media that Piscator incorporated into his productions were not typically seen as artistic media, but rather as sources of information. He used film, projections and posters as pieces of evidence for the political claims of the play. At the same time, though, he presented these media in aesthetically compelling and formally innovative ways, blurring the boundary between artistic and non-artistic media, and between theatre and reality. Brecht describes the criticism Piscator received for being 'the first person to think it necessary to provide *evidence* in the theatre. He projected authentic documents on to large screens. Many people immediately accused him of breaking the rules of art. Art had to construct its own realm, they said'.[48]

In *Das politische Theater*, Piscator writes that he experimented with new media in order to create a form of documentary theatre based in evidence and documentation. Piscator writes that his goal in *Trotz Alledem!* was 'not the propagation of a view of life through formal clichés and billboard slogans, but the presentation of solid proof that our philosophy and all that can be deduced from it is the one and only valid approach for our time'.[49] Here, we see Piscator at his most ideologically dogmatic. While Brecht nudged audiences toward a particular interpretation of the world, Piscator went much further in declaring that theatre could definitively prove that the philosophy of the Communist Party was the *only* valid world view. For Piscator, theatre could offer this sort of 'proof' by using documentary evidence. Piscator was not the first person to incorporate documentary materials into theatre; the German playwright Georg Büchner, for example, used transcripts of speeches given during the French Revolution in his play *Dantons Tod* (Danton's Death). But Piscator was the first director to create theatre wholly out of documentary materials from multiple media. Piscator's onstage 'evidence' included written documents and posters, films taken from newsreels, projections and photographs of historical figures. He even went so far as to include a parade of actual mutilated war veterans in *Die Abenteuer des braven Soldaten Schwejk* as proof of the war's brutality.[50] When the former Emperor Wilhelm II sued Piscator for libel because of his portrayal in *Rasputin*, Piscator had the actor who was supposed to play the role of Wilhelm read the court order forbidding the performance in place of his lines.[51]

Trotz Alledem! was Piscator's first production in which 'the text and staging were based solely on political documents'.[52] The entire production was created through a montage of speeches, essays, newspaper clippings, calls to action, fliers, and photographs and films of the First World War, the October Revolution and historical figures. Even the title itself is a quotation from Karl Liebknecht. The production featured three different films that expanded on the action taking place on stage by showing documentary footage that revealed the consequences of those actions. The use of film here is similar to the use of film in Meyerhold's production *Earth Rampant* (1923) in that both incorporate documentary film as a form of commentary on the actions taking place on stage. Instead of immersing the audience in the dramatic action, these films served an epic function of leading audiences to reflect on the actions.[53]

Of all of the documentary elements, Piscator saw film as the most powerful way to convey the horror of war.[54] Piscator argues that film could better portray the scale of carnage and devastation of the war than actors on stage. He writes that these documentary films 'brutally demonstrated the horror of war: flame-thrower attacks, piles of mutilated bodies, burning cities', all images that could not be replicated on stage or effectively described in words.[55] Strikingly, he notes that the film had such a strong impact on audiences because war films were not yet popular at the time he staged *Trotz Alledem!* and audiences were seeing this type of footage for the first time. The effect that these films had was emotional and even physical, conveying horror that went beyond an intellectual understanding of the devastation of the war. We might ask whether including footage like this in theatre today, when audiences are accustomed to seeing graphic videos of violence on a daily basis, could still have a similar effect. In a media-saturated world, this is unlikely.

Piscator also used film in *Trotz Alledem!* to expand the dramatic action on stage by showing the consequences of the actions taking place on screen. For example, one scene of *Trotz Alledem!* portrayed the Social Democrats approving a war bond, and immediately after there is a film showing Germany mobilizing for war and the first casualties.[56] The film here served two purposes at once: it targeted the emotions of the audience ('shaking them'), while it also appealed to the audience's rational judgement by presenting evidence for the production's interpretation of events.

Between 1925 and 1931, Piscator used film segments in fifteen different productions. These films were projected in a number of ways: onto screens above and to the sides of the playing area, directly onto the playing area, and/or onto a scrim in front of the playing area. Some of these films were pre-existing documentary films, while others were filmed specifically for the productions. Piscator differentiated between three types of film used in his productions: teaching films (focused on conveying objective facts), dramatic films (which replace action on stage, especially for large-scale sequences like battles and demonstrations that would be difficult to portray with actors) and commentary films (which function like a chorus).[57] Sometimes these films also served to intensify the tempo and rhythm of scenes or as a design element that expanded the perspectival depth of the stage.[58]

Films and projections were only one part of the massive multilevel sets that Piscator and his longtime set designer Traugott Müller developed. *Rasputin* (1927) featured a half globe that was divided into multiple rooms. The outer walls of the globe lifted to expose different playing areas, and the whole globe rotated on a spinning stage. The set design for *Hoppla, Wir leben!* (Hoppla, We're Alive!, 1927), seen in Figure 3.1, resembled an enormous dollhouse with multiple levels of stacked rooms. Sometimes action would take place in multiple rooms simultaneously, at other times live action would take place in one room while films were projected onto the back walls of other rooms.

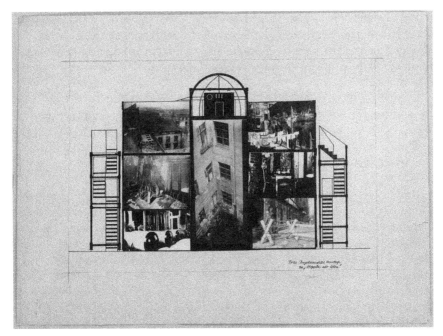

FIGURE 3.1 *Sketch for the set of* Hoppla, Wir Leben!, *designed by Traugott Müller (Orphan. Source: Institut für Theaterwissenschaft der Freien Universität Berlin, Theaterhistorische Sammlungen, Nachlass Traugott Müller).*

Much of the technology was cutting edge, and Piscator's theatre consistently faced technical difficulties and often lacked the time and manpower to fully render the visions of Piscator and his collaborators.[59] For example, the machinery used in *Die Abenteuer des braven Soldaten Schwejk* was so loud that it was impossible to hear some of the lines of text over the noise it made.[60] The dress rehearsal for Piscator's first productions at the Volksbühne, Alfons Paquet's *Fahnen* (*Flags*, 1924), was such a technical disaster that Piscator demanded the entire cast and all of the stage workers stay in the theatre and rehearse straight through from 1.00 am until the curtain went up the next evening.[61] Piscator's productions were chronically under-rehearsed; the final scene of the *Des Kaisers Kulis* (The King's Coolies, 1930) was written during the intermission on the night of the premiere![62]

Piscator's use of stage technology reflected a deep concern with social and technological changes that extended beyond one political party or ideology. Some of Piscator's theatre celebrated the new possibilities of technology, but this technology also had a sinister side, expressing the smallness and vulnerability of individuals confronted with new technologies of war. The philosopher Walter Benjamin (a close friend of Brecht's) wrote about how the experience of the First World War changed not only soldiers themselves but also their capacity to talk about their experiences with others. In an essay called 'Der Erzähler' (The Storyteller), Benjamin writes that the First World War, and the social, economic and political turmoil that followed it, fundamentally changed people's understanding of their own place in the world:

> A generation that had gone to school on a horse-drawn streetcar now stood under the open sky in which nothing remained unchanged but the clouds, and beneath these clouds, in a field of force of destructive torrents and explosions, was the tiny, fragile human body.[63]

In this new world, the 'tiny, fragile human body' is rendered powerless against the forces around it and incapable of communicating with others. By using documentary footage from the First World War in *Trotz Alledem!*, Piscator indicates that this magnitude of violence cannot be conveyed through conventional acting. The scale of war, Piscator's production suggests, goes so far beyond the human individual that it simply cannot be represented on stage, no matter how many extras are employed. During the war, the human body was rendered mere refuse. In the highly controversial ending of his 1929 production *The Merchant of Berlin*, three street sweepers walk across the stage, sweeping away the garbage of Berlin's streets. Among the piles of garbage they first sweep away paper money that was rendered worthless by the inflation, then a soldier's helmet and finally a human corpse, which is tossed out with the other garbage as the street sweepers exclaim, 'Filth! Get rid of it.'[64]

Piscator saw in new technology the possibility for reflecting the tempo and sensory overstimulation that came with life in a modern metropolis. In 1903, the German-Jewish sociologist Georg Simmel wrote about the urbanization of Berlin in a classic essay, titled 'The Metropolis and Mental Life.' In his essay, Simmel argues that the experience of living in a modern metropolis changes people. He describes how the experience of the city and 'the rapid crowding of changing images, the sharp discontinuity in the grasp of a single glance, and the unexpectedness of onrushing impressions' alters the 'sensory foundation of psychic life'.[65] Piscator and his collaborators, such as Brecht, also believed that modern life had changed people's sensory perception and even their very understanding of reality. If life itself is experienced as fragmented, contradictory and disorienting, art would have to reflect this shift. For art to reflect this new reality, Piscator believed that it had to develop new, experimental forms using the latest technologies. Playing on Lenin's famous line that 'Communism is Soviets plus electrification,' Brecht wrote that Piscator, 'electrified the theatre, and rendered it capable of tackling major themes'.[66]

In Piscator's production of *Die Abenteuer des braven Soldaten Schwejk*, we can see Benjamin's arguments about the human body in war and Simmel's arguments about modern society come together. Simmel writes that the modern individual's greatest struggle is to preserve their own individuality and autonomy in the face of overwhelming social, cultural, economic and political pressures.[67] Piscator used new stage technologies to represent how individuals could become mere cogs in the machine, struggling to maintain agency in the face of almost irresistible social pressures and institutions. Here, Piscator's use of stage technology reveals a dark underbelly to the Soviet dreams of industrialization and collectivization that he celebrates in other works.

Die Abenteuer des braven Soldaten Schwejk, based on a satirical novel by Jaroslaw Hašek, shows the adventures of a naïve soldier marching from Prague to join his regiment in Budweis. In the stage adaptation, Schweik moves through many individual episodes without a strong overarching plot; in fact, Schweik is the only character to appear in more than a single episode. To show Schweik's journey, Piscator built two large conveyer belts into the stage and throughout his journey, Schweik walked along one of them, against the motion of the belt (staying in the same place as he marched forward). On the second belt, various props and scenery like trees and milestones moved past Schweik, while a film with both actual scenery and cartoon illustrations by Grosz were projected behind him.[68] This technology revealed that despite his best efforts to move forward, Schweik wass caught in the machine, believing that he was making progress while in reality he was on a conveyer belt heading toward his own death. Although framed in a comic light, this stage portrayed the very smallness and impotence of humans that Benjamin describes in 'The Storyteller.' Today, the technical possibilities of stage machinery have certainly developed beyond Piscator's innovations. But Piscator's use of technology both to show the promise of innovation and to reveal its dangers is still relevant today. This ambivalent relationship to technology resonates with how many of us see technology in our world, as a tool with great potential for bettering our quality of life but also as a potential threat to meaningful human interaction.

The contemporary political reception and legacy of Piscator's Weimar work

At the height of his fame, Piscator was a controversial figure creating art in an era of aesthetic and political controversies. Even though Piscator believed that his productions furthered the communist cause, important critics in the Communist Party of Germany were skeptical. In response to the opening of the Proletarian Theatre, the Communist Party's newspaper, *Die Rote Fahne* (The Red Flag), published an article criticizing Piscator's ambition to dissolve the boundaries between art and politics, instead insisting that workers needed art that was separate from politics for relaxation and edification.[69] This was only the first example of tension between Piscator's political theatre and the cultural polities of the Communist Party of

Germany and the Communist International. Although *Trotz Alledem!* was a huge success with its audiences, it only played two nights: the Communist Party, still suspicious of Piscator's political theatre, decided not to support any additional performances.[70]

In the 1920s and 1930s, artists, activists and critics with similar political beliefs had very different ideas about the role that art could or should play in politics. Piscator's tensions with the Communist Party reveal the difference between two approaches to portraying reality. Piscator reflected reality in a way that was photographic and documentary, seeking to objectively reflect current events. Influential critics within the Communist Party of Germany, however, rejected this approach as superficial, and instead claimed that artists must filter reality through ideology in order to reflect its essential truth.[71] Following *Trotz Alledem!*, *Die Rote Fahne* criticized Piscator for being too documentary and sticking too close to the facts, 'Don't all stick so slavishly to "that's the way it happened",' the critic wrote.[72] This unease between Piscator's mode of production and critics in Communist Party papers such as *Die Rote Fahne* mark the beginnings of bitter arguments about art and politics that took place in international German-language publications in the 1930s.[73]

Piscator's use of massive technology, and particularly the huge expense of his productions, also drew criticism from leftists on other grounds. Not everyone was convinced by Piscator's claims that he was creating a revolutionary theatre. The scope of Piscator's projects in the 1920s required both capitalist philanthropists and a wealthy bourgeois audience willing to pay high prices for theatrical novelty.[74] When Piscator left the Volksbühne in 1927 to start his own, more stridently proletarian-revolutionary theatre, he began with 400,000 Marks donated by a wealthy businessman, Ludwig Katzenellenbogen, introduced to him by Tilla Durieux, an actress and *grand dame* of Berlin. To build the *Totaltheater* that he designed with Gropius, he asked Katzenellenbogen for 1.8 million Marks. After a series of spectacular financial failures, and unable to repay his capitalist investors, Piscator asked his proletarian subscribers to help him rebuild the theatre.[75]

Piscator's reliance on capitalist finance and bourgeois audiences drew criticism from contemporaries, such as Brecht, who were also critical of Piscator's lifestyle. Gropius designed a fashionable apartment for Piscator and his first wife, which was featured in a women's magazine, leading to more friction with communist comrades.[76] Brecht's poem 'The Theater-Communist' is a thinly veiled attack on Piscator from this period:

For 3000 Marks a month
He is prepared
To stage the misery of the masses
For 100 Marks a day
He shows
The injustice of the world.[77]

Piscator's comfortable life as Berlin's 'Theater-Communist' did not last long and neither did his image of what political theatre was. Piscator left Germany in 1931, and headed first to the Soviet Union and then, as Stalin's purges began to decimate Piscator's circle of friends and collaborators, to Paris. On the first day of 1939, Piscator and his wife, Maria Ley Piscator, sailed into New York's harbour. The former star was now a political exile in search of both a new home and a new form of political theatre. The communist revolution never arrived in Germany, and Piscator watched as the great promise of early Soviet theatrical innovations was brutally dashed in the 1930s.

The spectacles of Fascism and Stalinism unsettled Piscator's faith in the transformative power of theatre and the creation of mass audiences. He also began to reconsider his earlier ambitions to collapse the distinction between art and politics. The mass spectacles of the Nazis offered a nightmarish example of what it might look like to fully collapse art and politics. In the essay 'The Work of Art in the Age of Mechanical Reproducibility,' Benjamin argues that Fascism 'render[s] politics aesthetic', turning war and human destruction into the objects of aesthetic contemplation. He quotes the manifesto of the Italian Futurists, an artistic movement aligned with fascist politics, celebrating the beauty of war:

> War is beautiful because it initiates the dreamt-of metallization of the human body. War is beautiful because it enriches a flowering meadow with the fiery orchids of machine guns. War is beautiful because it combines the gunfire, the cannonades, the cease-fire, the scents, and the stench of putrefaction into a symphony [...] ... Poets and artists of Futurism! ... remember these principles of an aesthetics of war so that your struggle for a new literature and a new graphic art ... may be illuminated by them.[78]

People are turned into mere 'human material', and mankind reaches such a degree of 'self-alienation' that 'it can experience its own destruction as an aesthetic pleasure of the first order'. In response to this aestheticization of politics, Benjamin calls on communism to respond by 'politicizing art'.[79]

Piscator's work in interwar Berlin demonstrates just how hard it can be to differentiate between work that 'aestheticizes politics' and work that 'politicizes art'. Unlike the Futurists, Piscator never sought to render war beautiful, his films and depictions of mutilated bodies on stage were designed to show war's horrors. But at the same time, the sort of collective energy as well as the large-scale spectacle that Piscator prized in an event like *Trotz Alledem!* bears an uncomfortable resemblance to the mass spectacle of the Nazi Party Congress in Nuremberg in how it used spectacle to forge solidarity and commitment. Starting in the 1940s, Piscator turned away from these large scale rallies and instead looked back to the German tradition of aesthetic philosophy, as well as to canonical German plays in order to develop a new form of political theatre, one that did not seek to dissolve the boundaries between stage and audience or between theatre and politics. Instead, Piscator emphasized the public importance of theatre as an institution uniquely suited to teaching people how to respect and share space with others who are unlike them and to respect difference rather than to demand homogeneity.

4

Moving Theatre Back to the Spotlight: Erwin Piscator's Later Stage Work

Klaus Wannemacher

Erwin Piscator left Germany shortly after the phase of his greatest achievements on the stage. During two decades of exile and after his final return to Germany, he remained true to the general conception of a theatre engaged with pressing political questions. Still, his theatre would never be the same again with regard to a desired unity between a topical, activist approach and its prodigious scenic and technical realization. For almost a decade he was occupied with film projects and coordination tasks in theatre associations in the Soviet Union and France. For another, he became a theatre educator in the United States with occasional directing practice at drama schools that facilitated a continuation of Weimar Republic theatre. His return to Germany in 1951 finally ushered in a return to continuous stage work. But only after another decade was he given a chance to manage a theatre again and, as he wrote in 1955, to 'move the theatre back to the spotlight'[1] with premieres of political plays, as he had done during the 1920s.

In his later productions, Piscator would revive and refine many of the theatrical approaches and techniques that he had developed during the interwar period: adapting plays in close cooperation with the author before and during rehearsals, updating older plays, having actors interact with spectators, making use of projections of stills, statistics or quotations, applying multifunctional scaffolding constructions, experimenting with alternative stage forms, producing topical plays at political party conventions, etc. His later stage work retained the maxim that had informed his earlier work: theatre had to contribute to the critical scrutiny of political, social and economic realities and was supposed to contribute to a more humane society. Nevertheless, the political context and his troublesome personal situation as an emigrant during Nazi rule, the Second World War, German partition and the onset of the Cold War, caused Piscator to change his agenda and to tone done the political impulses of his productions.

The aggressive representation of issues, such as antimilitarism, social revolution, unemployment, inflation or back-street abortion, in Piscator's activist and political theatre of the early interwar period turned into the still determined but less provocative representation of issues, such as the contingencies of war, the daunting machinery of dictatorships, the human susceptibility to manipulation or discrimination against black women, in the following decades. However, it required a sweeping change of social framework and a readiness for questioning established patterns of thought in post-war Germany, to allow for a broader public acceptance and wider impact of Piscator's new approach to a politically engaged theatre in the 1960s.

This chapter will set out the adaptations Piscator made to his model of political theatre in relation to changes in the general political context and his personal circumstances. It will roughly follow the stages of Piscator's later biography with a focus on the 1940s and 1960s. Distinctive features of his directing conception will be exemplified by some of his more prominent later productions and his theoretical considerations, while also shedding light on Piscator's educational approach as a teacher of directing. Two of Piscator's late productions (Rolf Hochhuth's *The Deputy* and Peter Weiss's *The Investigation*) will particularly help us understand the circumstances under which theatre could become a forceful medium of social discourse and self-reflection again.

The chapter will reveal the main paths, byways, detours and dead ends of Piscator's interpretation of a political theatre. It will particularly examine the question of why Piscator could not fully recover the unified realization of a political theatre that had characterized his stage work of the 1920s. Why did the director limit himself to largely relying on topical content in some of his most significant later productions at the expense of innovative scenic and technical solutions?

Deliverance from political persecution and a decade devoid of stage work

One of Erwin Piscator's final productions in the Weimar Republic, a stage adaption of Theodor Plivier's novel *Des Kaisers Kulis* (The Kaiser's Coolies,

Lessing Theatre, Berlin, 30 August 1930), had driven critics to the view that this haunting narrative about the dire conditions on German Navy warships during the First World War would have been a perfect subject for a film. The theatre director, known for his ground-breaking incorporation of cinematic content into his stage productions, had immediately entered into negotiations with Soviet film companies. Since his Berlin-based troupe of actors had faced growing economic pressures, Piscator hoped for a chance to acquire new funding through a motion picture project. He left Germany in April 1931 for the Soviet Union. In the years he spent there, Piscator produced an anti-Fascist motion picture (*Revolt of the Fishermen*), made plans for an 'International Theatre' performing in the Soviet Union and in Germany, headed a leftist theatre association, worked out plans to reorganize the institutional structures of Soviet cinematography, devised a French–Russian film company and conceived an emigrants' theatre in the German Volga Republic.

After he had finished his first motion picture, Piscator's situation as an emigrant in the Soviet Union slowly but steadily worsened. He considered himself deliberately sidelined. As for his role as a film director, his former client, the Mezhrabpomfilm company, postponed follow-up projects. Piscator's plans for the comprehensive reorganization of an international theatre association that he headed as president were declined by Soviet authorities.

In this precarious situation, a news item immediately seemed to open up new perspectives for him. It came from the East Coast of the United States: an imaginative Piscator-style theatre production in rural Pennsylvania had been well-received by US critics. With limited resources, the small non-commercial Hedgerow Theatre had arranged a stunning production of Piscator's stage adaptation of *An American Tragedy* in the borough of Rose Valley, Pennsylvania, in April 1935. The play was based on Theodore Dreiser's bestselling 1925 novel of the same name. It focused on the ambitious Clyde Griffith, a young man from a humble background, and his attempt to 'free himself from a relationship with the working-class Roberta in pursuit of the wealthy Sondra, and Griffith's subsequent execution for murdering Roberta by overturning their rowboat'.[2]

In keeping with Piscator's practice, Hedgerow's director, Jasper Deeter worked with a two-tiered stage symbolizing the economic status of the characters. A lot of action was mimed to accompanying offstage sound effects, and he employed a speaker freely roaming over the stage and audience space commenting on the action and drawing attention to the economic disparity between the classes.[3] In one of the key sequences, Deeter showed the protagonist's transformation from poor to rich in a barber shop.

Newspapers in Philadelphia and New York acknowledged an intriguing adaptation and production.[4] As Hedgerow chronicler Barry Witham reports, the success of the production 'created a storm of interest among agents and producers vying to bring *An American Tragedy* to New York'.[5]

Impresario Milton Shubert, who had seen the production, was among those who expressed a strong interest in bringing the script to a Broadway stage.[6] As statements by Piscator in Soviet periodicals from 1935 show, contact had been established and an invitation for him to stage a play in New York City seemed feasible.[7]

It was not long before Piscator, whose ambitious artistic and cultural-political plans had resulted in discrepancies with the authorities for quite some time, began to cause Soviet officials growing dismay. In the autumn of 1935 he gave cues to his intention to accept work offers by American theatre managers. He considered asking permission to exchange roubles for hard currency for the passage to New York.[8] Piscator's impolitic behaviour probably contributed much to his timely (and life-saving) departure from the Soviet Union a few months later, with Stalin's Great Purge imminent.[9]

However, due to a long process of reorientation after having left his manifold projects in the Soviet Union behind, it took another two and a half years before he finally arrived in North America.[10] The *Anschluss* (annexation) of his second wife's native country, Austria, into Nazi Germany in March 1938 and the infamous Munich Agreement between Germany, Italy, France and Britain permitting the German annexation of portions of Czechoslovakia in September 1938 had confirmed Piscator's resolution to finally take refuge in the United States.[11] Since Hitler had already voiced further demands regarding ethnic Germans in Poland and Hungary, expectations of an imminent war steadily increased.

When Piscator entered the United States in January 1939, he had not been working on the stage for almost a decade. Since he had left Germany in 1931, he had neither managed a theatre nor had a chance to direct plays. He lacked adequate backers who would allow him to realize his sumptuous projects. The avant-garde stage director who was renowned for his extensive use of cinematic projections, scaffold and simultaneous stages, treadmills and lift-bridges in the Berlin of the 1920s and who had established the concept of a 'political theatre' through his practice and his writings, was determined to resume stage work. He was ready to see how his theatre model could be adapted to new cultural and political circumstances. The world stood on the verge of another world war in the late 1930s. Piscator felt that it was precisely the theatre that had to assume a new role in this decisive moment.

Shortly after his emigration to New York City in 1938, Austrian actor Alexander Granach believed that conditions were perfect for his friend Piscator to work in the United States: 'his prospects are huge here. The local theatres experiment a lot and many imitate him. He is very well-known here'.[12] Given the turbulent American politics of the 1930s, left-wing activists had been increasingly vocal in the American theatre and had prompted directors such as Hallie Flanagan to experiment with epic theatre set-pieces such as graphs, projections or lighting effects. What sympathetic Granach had not taken into account was that meritorious approaches to renewing US theatre on the part of the Neighborhood Playhouse (1915–27), the Civic Repertory Theatre (1926–32) or the Theatre Union (1933–7) were already in serious decline. A whole era of American theatre initiatives and companies such as the Federal Theatre Project and the Group Theatre, devoted to experimentation in theatrical form and technique, and partly to social issues, had come to an end. Moreover, a general swing to 'bourgeois realism' that had taken place in American leftist theatres by the mid-1930s clearly contravened Piscator's earlier understanding of theatre as a tool of radical political and social intervention.[13]

Arriving in New York City, Piscator was aware that he had to reinvent himself after years of deadlock in exile. He revived old acquaintances and established contact with theatre authors, producers and experts. In New York, he was introduced to Alvin Saunders Johnson. Johnson, an American economist and literary scholar, was co-founder and president of The New School for Social Research, a private, non-profit institution focused on adult education that had been founded by former Columbia University professors. Johnson had established a 'University in Exile' as a graduate division of the New School serving as an academic haven for scholars who had to flee Europe after the Nazis' rise to power in Germany. Piscator and Johnson immediately entered into negotiations about founding a theatre department at the New School. For some time, Johnson had intended to concentrate the scattered theatre activities of the New School in a separate 'Department for Dramatic Art'. The president of the New School asked his guest: 'Why not teach your theatre here?'[14] He also wanted to have the existing acting courses systematically complemented through seminars on dramatic composition, directing, repertory and role studies, elocution and other subjects.

Immediately, Piscator started to draft a plan and work schedule for the new department that would put a special emphasis on closely connecting theatre education with practical experience in the professional theatre, as he conveyed to Alvin Johnson:

> perhaps closer contact could be established with the Playwright Association, [Robert Emmet] Sherwood, [Maxwell] Anderson, Elmer Rice, and others, and connections made with the theatres where their plays are staged. Also, through my practical work on the stages of New York, I hope to be able to make a good practical connection between the School and the real artistic world.[15]

This intention, as well as Piscator's declared purpose of offering courses that would impart knowledge of all the different interconnected processes of a theatre production, appealed to the president of the New School. That Piscator's affluent second wife, Maria Ley, would pay her husband's salary for the proposed department's initial two years of operation seems to have added further to a prompt agreement.[16] Maria had inherited the estate of her former husband Frank Deutsch, a member of a German industrialist dynasty.

En passant: Establishing a National Repertory Theatre in Washington, DC

As one of his American students put it later, 'Piscator was never without grandiose ambitions.'[17] While the preparations for establishing a Department for Dramatic Art were underway, Piscator explored another auspicious option for securing his livelihood. Louis Nizer, a lawyer in New York, part-time author and dedicated supporter of emigrant concerns, asked Piscator to produce George Bernard Shaw's play *Saint Joan* in February 1940. Piscator was supposed to cooperate with the Washington Civic Theatre on this project. As Piscator's former assistant, Leon Askin, remembered, the 'Civic Theatre was a group of amateurs, many of them government workers, who rehearsed after the day's labors and on weekends, and who had the opportunity to work with professional directors and guest stars.'[18] The *Saint Joan* performances were to take place as Red Cross fund-raisers at the Shubert-Belasco Theater in Washington, DC, a theatre that had long been disused.

Piscator agreed to direct the Shaw play. He was able to engage famed German actress Luise Rainer in the lead role. In previous years, Rainer had won two Oscars for best leading actress. As the first actor to win multiple Academy Awards, she had written cinematographic history. *Saint Joan* opened under the joint direction of Erwin Piscator and the local director of the Washington Civic Theatre, Day Tuttle, on 10 March 1940. Working with a cast of Civic Theatre actors, Piscator made occasional use of techniques of his epic theatre, as a critic reported:

> He goes about it by building the stage out into the middle of the orchestra, by leaving the curtain up throughout, by using a minimum of three-dimensional props, by projecting backgrounds onto a screen covering the entire rear of the stage, by announcing successive locales with placards, and by shifting scenery, when need be, before the audience's eyes [...] frequently a single shaft of light or a simple shadow generated more colorful illusion than a stageful of intricately designed settings could have done.[19]

While the critic realized that all of Piscator's directorial decisions were meant to be a means to an end, neither he nor other critics actually commented on a specific topical end that the director had envisaged. Through the projection of images – for eample, masses in concentration camps or the burning of synagogues – superimposed upon the burning of Joan at the stake, Piscator had established a link between the France of 1431 and the Germany of 1940.[20] Whether this attempt at drawing an arc from the past to the present was perceived as a minor aspect of the production or whether it was difficult to relate to (with many Nazi crimes not yet widely known at this early stage of the Second World War) remains unclear.

An honourary committee had accompanied the benefit production. Washington society acknowledged sympathetically that Piscator and Rainer had worked without reward and that the proceeds were intended for the American Red Cross's European war relief. Local theatre critics celebrated an outstanding success. *The Washington Post* concluded: 'the Washington Civic Theatre stands on the brink of its most distinguished achievement and the fulfilment of its most cherished ambition'.[21] After almost ten years of having refrained from active theatre work, Piscator felt relieved that he had not forfeited his creative abilities, as he disclosed to his mother: 'despite the prolonged inactivity, I have neither lost my power nor my imagination, that much is proved by this production'.[22]

Piscator knew how to seize a favourable moment. After the warm welcome in Washington, he began to advocate no less than an American National Theatre in Washington. Among the open-minded actors of the Civic Theatre as well as the dignitaries of Washington's society, such as US Secretary of Labor, Frances Perkins, or the British Ambassador in Washington, Philip Kerr, Marquis of Lothian, Piscator referred to the proud and renowned national theatres of other nations in February and March 1940. He pointed to the bitter absence of such a building in the cityscape of the US capital.[23] Civic Theatre representatives supported Piscator's arguments and tried to appeal to potential financial backers with the notion that America, similar to European nations, had reached a point where it had the beginnings of a classical tradition of its own. They argued: 'it is at the same time the repository of that European culture which in whole or in part has been destroyed or lies under the threat of destruction. In the cultural history of the world after 1940 America will occupy first place'.[24]

Piscator's proposals fell on fertile soil. In view of his ambitious suggestions, during a general meeting of the Civic Theatre on 9 May 1940, it was decided to dissolve Tuttle's contract. Piscator was designated his successor.[25] A preliminary programme for the Civic Theatre as a National Repertory Theatre was drafted. The theatre was supposed to produce five plays per season. At a meeting on 19 June 1940, the Board of Governors adopted the plan to convert the Washington Civic Theatre into a National Repertory Theatre.

While Piscator faced increasing demands on his time through the newly founded 'Dramatic Workshop', as the Department for Dramatic Art at the New School had been named, the Washington newspapers heralded him as the future 'Director of the Washington Theatre, formerly the Washington Civic Theatre'.[26] Piscator's twofold strategy for establishing a National Repertory Theatre in Washington and a theatre school in New York soon turned out to be overstretching his capacities. He had to leave the responsibility for the ambitious theatre project in the US capital mostly to his wife, Maria Ley.

Lee D. Butler from the Board of Governors of the Civic Theater informed the press in September 1940 that Piscator had been contracted for five further productions and that nine lectures on theatre art with American playwrights and scriptwriters such as Robert Emmet Sherwood should additionally take place during a timeframe of eighteen weeks in Washington.[27]

As a first production, a revue was planned at the Civic Theatre, which was supposed to capture the 'rhythm of Washington', called *D.C. Melody (A Satirical Revue)*. However, due to Piscator's lack of time, the revue became no more than a flawed experiment, as Maria Ley conceded in her memoirs: 'there was no book, no music, no texts. There was nothing apart from the white pages and the pretty faces of the students, amateur actors and talented singers. I wondered how we could possibly hire professional staff for the Civic Theatre without any financial means'.[28] They asked Leon Askin, who had been Piscator's secretary in Paris, to assist. Askin had acquired some experience of his own in directing. While Maria took over the choreography, Piscator, commuting between New York and Washington, supervised Askin's directing.

The Advisory Committee for the Repertory Club of the Washington Theatre was presided over by the First Lady, Human Rights activist and diplomat Anna Eleanor Roosevelt. In preparation for the premiere, Eleanor Roosevelt commented: 'I am delighted to know that your club is really moving to establish a National Repertory Theater. Such an enterprise is valuable because it can be an educational factor, as well as providing a constant and changing entertainment for any community.'[29] She attended the opening night on 8 December 1940 in the Wardman Park Theater.

However, Piscator and his wife had spent too little time and care on the decisive production. The revue on emigration and resistance with texts by Maria Ley, Harold L. Anderson, Jay Williams and John Arbor failed with the critics and the audience. The directing team had underestimated the demands of Washington's theatre connoisseurs and moreover told them too clearly what they wanted to hear. The critic of *The Washington Post* commented disappointedly: 'D.C. Melody is a surprisingly amateurish effort to have sprung from the ashes of the Washington Civic Theatre.'[30] Considering the shattering reviews, Piscator took responsibility and resigned from the artistic direction of the Civic Theatre.

A Dramatic Workshop in New York City

While the American National Theatre project led to outright failure, the plans to establish a Department for Dramatic Art at the New School for Social Research had made good progress. After successful negotiations with Alvin Johnson, Piscator opened his Dramatic Workshop with some twenty students enrolled for evening classes in January 1940. When the second semester approached in the autumn, the Dramatic Workshop received more than two hundred applications. The first course catalogues already contained a broad range of classes such as Directing, General Preparatory

Training, Acting, Dramaturgy, Motion Picture Writing, Criticism, American Drama in Our Times, The Musical Stage, Design and Production.

In accordance with the maxim of 'learning by doing' that the New School for Social Research had adopted from its co-founder, the American philosopher and educational reformer John Dewey, Piscator announced in the bulletin for the autumn term 1940/1 that the Dramatic Workshop offered an interdisciplinary theatre education that would militate against narrow specialization. The learning objectives of the Dramatic Workshop were detailed in the catalogue:

> To educate students to make a living in the theatre of today. To lift the student's vision of the full possibilities of the living theatre, with its social and cultural potentialities. To stimulate the development of the repertory theatre as a non-commercial institution of artistic expression with the same position in our society that the symphony or the art museum enjoys.[31]

In the first semesters, the educational approach that would shape the Dramatic Workshop in the long term already became visible. Through his educational programme, Piscator tried to ensure that specialists in one theatrical area would also acquaint themselves with other areas of theatre art (e.g. playwriting, directing, acting, stage technique, incidental music). Piscator was convinced that having future playwrights, directors, actors and technicians switch roles would 'replace many years of the slow and uncoordinated work that face the newcomer in the theatre'.[32] Piscator wanted to make the students familiar with the history of dramatic literature and production styles in the broadest sense as well. Essential for this aim was the 'March of Drama Repertory.' In this lecture series, John Gassner and Paolo Milano covered masterpieces in the history of dramatic literature. In later years, Piscator augmented the lectures through staged readings by advanced students and invited guests.

True to his earlier theatre practice, Piscator sought technical means of presentation which would be adequate for the immediate present. In this regard Piscator wanted to make the Dramatic Workshop a 'laboratory in which new ideas could be inexpensively tested for value prior to their application in the commercial theatre'.[33] Most important to implementing the vision of interdisciplinary theatre education was the creation of a Studio Theatre that could bridge the gap between academic training and a professional career in the theatre. To Piscator's mind, only such a facility would make the school an effective institution in the teaching of theatre.

Piscator had already maintained a Studio Theatre, at his Piscator-Bühne in Berlin during the 1920s. Its supposed function had been similar: being a 'laboratory in which the members of the theater [...] can put their ideas to the test in practice, can learn to see the whole field of theater from every angle, helping and complementing each other's work in the process'.[34]

Junior directors had been given a chance to develop components of a 'perfect theater'[35] there. Even though Studio directors had occasionally experimented with scaffolds, projections of self-produced film scenes, or workers' choruses, the Studio productions of the 1920s had not revealed the innovatory character that Piscator had envisioned. For the Studio Theatre at the Dramatic Workshop of the 1940s (see Figure 4.1), however, the educational objective of enabling students to acquaint themselves practically with a number of different areas of theatre art clearly dominated the aspect of testing new theatrical ground. Although the theatre productions at the Dramatic Workshop exhibited a strong semblance of Piscator's approach to epic theatre (actors walking on a turntable that revolves against them, single spot-lit faces as the theatrical equivalent of a close-up, use of simultaneous stages, etc.), clearly the Studio Theatre at the New School did not serve the purpose of developing new components of a political theatre as its predecessor.

To produce versatile graduates who were familiar with all relevant areas of theatre art, a wide-ranging team of educators was necessary. The Dramatic Workshop's faculty of up to sixty instructors comprised some of Piscator's old Weimar acquaintances such as Herbert Berghof, Hanns Eisler and Carl Zuckmayer, but also many American theatre specialists such as Stella Adler, Brooks Atkinson, John Gassner and Lee Strasberg.[36] Piscator himself taught the directing seminar, which served as the curriculum's core.

Among the students of the Dramatic Workshop were Bea Arthur, Marlon Brando, Tony Curtis, Walter Matthau, Rod Steiger, Elaine Stritch and – at an early point of the Workshop's existence – Tennessee Williams (1940) and Shelley Winters (1941).[37] Most of the students mentioned here attended the Dramatic Workshop in the second half of the 1940s after the passing of the G.I. Bill (see below). Actor, singer and social activist Harry Belafonte remembered Piscator as a great, but remote, instructor who was noticeable to students primarily when he held his lectures at the Dramatic Workshop:

> Yet the workshop bristled with his energy and sense of mission, and all of us were inspired by it. Drama was serious; it was a tool to speak truth to power, to change society and, especially, to show the folly of war. [...] Inspired, I read these [i.e. *The Flies* and *All the King's Men*] and every other play that Piscator mentioned, and all the classics I could get my hands on. In those first months at the Dramatic Workshop, I felt my whole world opening up.[38]

Fellow student Judith Malina, the co-founder of the New York based theatre company Living Theatre, likewise remembered that Piscator had a 'great gift for transmitting ideas, and taught his classes and seminars with evident passion', notwithstanding 'teaching was always for him, what he later called "an interim achievement"'.[39]

FIGURE 4.1A *Dramatic Workshop public relations material with reference to the Studio Theatre, New York, 1942/3 (Photo: Klaus Wannemacher; PR material: New School University).*

FIGURE 4.1B *Dramatic Workshop public relations material with reference to the Studio Theatre, New York, 1942/3 (Photo: Klaus Wannemacher; PR material: New School University).*

Perhaps in the context of the directing seminar, Piscator began to reconsider acting from a more theoretical perspective. Towards the end of this phase of his life in the United States, he summarized central guidelines of his acting approach in an essay on 'Objective Acting'[40] which was driven by the general conception of an actor as someone who conveys ideas more than emotions. In this text he argued for understanding the actor as an original creator, not merely a craftsman or an 'object in the hands of the playwright'.[41] He advocated putting the auditorium at the core of the actor's attention and specified that the audience had to become an integral part of the actor's performance. In Piscator's view, the actors and the audience build one entity with two poles. The action and the actor's attention has to be 'directed constantly toward the center of the theater',[42] i.e. towards the audience (rather than to fellow actors). Focused eye contact with audiences was supposed to increase the vibrancy and immediacy of the stage action. The actor aspires to entertain the audience. At the same time he or she has to comment on the action and on emotions through the specific form of playing and perhaps convince the audience of his or her case. In contrast to Brecht's *Verfremdung*, Piscator advocates a moderate form of role distance. The modern actor is not supposed to improvise 'his emotions behind the "fourth wall", but we want him to give us commentaries on these emotions – playing not only a result but the thought which created the result'.[43] The actor has to make the roots visible, not the fruit alone. This requires superior control so that the actor will not be overcome by his or her emotions.

Since Piscator aspired to a mode of teaching that allowed for plenty of theatrical practice, he required a stage. With the start of the Dramatic Workshop's second semester in September 1940, he could establish a 'Studio Theatre' in the central auditorium of the New School building on 66 West 12th Street. Joseph Urban had designed the auditorium in the style of the Viennese Secession with a great semi-circular arch above the stage. It had never been conceived as a theatre stage, though,[44] and it was ill-equipped to accommodate Piscator's technically ambitious productions.

On this makeshift stage, Piscator wanted to produce theatrical material not presented on established stages, offering subscribers 'plays which cannot be done on Broadway, because of their uncertain appeal, or sophisticated level of intelligence, or overlarge cast'.[45] Piscator's casting director and assistant was James Light, the former director of the influential New York non-profit theatre group Provincetown Players. In subsequent years, Piscator began to establish a large repertory of classical and contemporary plays on his small experimental stage, making the Dramatic Workshop 'the most important source of contemporary European drama in the United States'[46] for a whole decade.

Initially, selected plays were staged with students with the occasional involvement of professional actors. Among the early productions were Shakespeare's *King Lear* with Sam Jaffe playing the lead (14 December 1940), Gotthold Ephraim Lessing's 'dramatic poem' *Nathan the Wise* with

Herbert Berghof (11 March 1942), a stage adaptation of Leo Tolstoy's novel *War and Peace* (20 May 1942) and Dan James's partisan drama *Winter Soldiers* (28 November 1942) on the attempts of resistance groups to halt the advance of Hitler's Wehrmacht on Soviet territory. Many of Piscator's and his collaborators' early productions in New York can be interpreted as statements targeted at that larger part of the American public that (had) opposed any direct military intervention into the Second World War. In the wake of the failure of the appeasement policy towards Nazi Germany and the German conquest of its neighbouring countries, Piscator had come to the belief that 'peaceful thinking and living are not enough to maintain peace'.[47]

Piscator and his students tried to make the best possible use of the restricted spatial and technical possibilities of the Studio Theatre with its maximum capacity of 500 seats. The first production, *King Lear*, may illustrate this intention. Piscator's approach to this Renaissance play was one of creating connections between the past and present. He saw 'Lear in the company of the dictators who are remaking the map of the world. What he did in dividing his kingdom is in line with the ideology of a tyrant'.[48] Piscator recognized in Shakespeare's tragedy the social forces and political tactics of more contemporary dictatorships. In terms of the staging, the director had rows of seats removed from the auditorium to enlarge the playing space and make room for architectural constructions such as a pyramidal stage structure located on a makeshift revolving stage. This structure had a symbolic function: depending on their social status and relative success, the figures moved on the higher or lower pyramidal steps. After a highly symbolic pantomime relating to the biblical narrative of Cain and Abel (one man slaying another), actors entered the stage from the rear of the audience. The members of Lear's court conversed on their way down the aisles, directly addressing the audience. When the disempowered and expelled King Lear later wandered through the storm on the heath, he was accompanied by a multiplicity of effects: Piscator used the revolving stage and a sophisticated system of sound and light. A whirling rainstorm was projected on mist. Here, the humiliated king was merely heard as a voice for most of the time. A sound system with thirty-two loudspeakers placed around the ceiling rim made Lear's mournful wails heard wandering through space, overlapping each other.

Piscator's unconventional interpretation of Shakespeare and his technical embellishments made many New York critics feel uneasy with the production. The unconventional aesthetic approach of a former avant-garde director who worked on a (makeshift) experimental stage associated with a theatre school in New York seemed to pose a dilemma to professional reviewers. Their set of critical standards were informed by the practices of commercial Broadway stages and hardly corresponded to a theatrical venture such as the Studio Theatre. Critic Burns Mantle found an elegant response to this challenge, emphasizing the great pedagogical potential inherent in such productions. He acknowledged 'carefully studied new readings and new posturings which probably mean more to the student body than to the layman. And it is the student body which will profit most from this enterprise'.[49]

In his production of Tolstoy's *War and Peace* in 1942, Piscator employed a stage consisting of no less than five different segments allowing for a complex practice of simultaneous play, interlacing several monologue sequences. Documentary picture and film projections on gauze (e.g. of speeches by Hitler and Mussolini and of battle scenes in the Soviet Union) partly visualized contemporary parallels between the Napoleonic Wars of the early nineteenth century and Nazi Germany's attack on the Soviet Union of 1941. Critic Arthur Pollock commented: 'It is only occasionally that one sees a production so fluid. Scenes are changed with something a little like magic, spotlights pick out actors here and there, characters walk through great hunks of time and space in a few steps.'[50] The Studio Theatre production of Dan James's war melodrama *Winter Soldiers* (under the direction of Broadway's Shepard Traube) returned to a more traditional stage conception and directing practice, but came up with vivid auditory collages on a darkened stage under Piscator's supervision. The hissing of steam, trampling of numerous feet, commands and grinding steel noises represented troop movement, thus indicating changes of setting.

Since Piscator hoped for a chance to gradually enter the larger commercial stages, he mostly restricted himself to advocating a theatrical programme of pluralistic Modernism and general humanist commitment instead of openly vouching for a more specific political agenda. Furthermore, he soon decided to remain in the background of the small Studio Theatre productions. While guest directors (such as James Light of the Provincetown Players or Sanford Meisner of the Group Theatre) as well as workshop students took over the directing, Piscator mostly restricted himself to the role of a supervisor. However, only the production of Lessing's *Nathan the Wise* was given the privilege of a transfer to Belasco Theatre on Broadway in April 1942. When this happened, professional New York critic Burns Mantle felt that relocating the piece from a studio setting to a professional environment would necessarily bereave the undertaking of some of its original congeniality: 'it is still effective drama, staged with skill and acted with frequent touches of moving eloquence. But now it becomes just another theatre attraction for the crowd and loses something of its appeal as a pilgrimage for the few'.[51] Further attempts with Broadway productions by Piscator were ill-fated.[52]

As several theatre productions attracted the attention of professional critics, conflicts arose with theatrical labour unions such as Actors' Equity Association. The unions positioned themselves against the uncontrolled, increasingly 'commercialized' productions of amateur theatres in New York. Due to a failure to raise the subsidy necessary to continue productions at union scale, the Studio Theatre had to be closed in March 1943. However, a few weeks later, Piscator encouraged former Studio Theatre subscribers to attend the popular 'March of Drama' lectures. This lecture series, originally initiated by John Gassner of the Theatre Guild, had been subsequently complemented through illustrative performances. Gassner's lecture series began to attract a growing audience to the New School's auditorium, i.e. the previous Studio Theatre location.

After Piscator had been permitted to organize a successful revival of *Nathan the Wise* with professional actors in the wake of anti-Semitic riots in New York in February 1944, the New School treasurer pushed through the final closing of the Studio Theatre with support from the influential dean of the Graduate Faculty of Political and Social Science because it contravened the New School's fire regulations.[53] Despite all the publicity the Dramatic Workshop created for the New School, many actually believed that it had no place in an institution devoted to adult education and that it 'drained resources needed for other activities'.[54]

Piscator had to seek out new approaches and locations for student productions. In this context, he began to establish a series of annual summer theatres that were held at summer resort towns such as Sayville, Great Neck, Lake Placid or Falmouth. Piscator adopted a tradition that had begun some twenty-five years earlier in New England where summer stock theatres had presented different plays in weekly or biweekly repertory, typically between June and September. During the 1930s, the New York-based Group Theatre had repeatedly rehearsed new productions in the summer. In July 1944, Piscator withdrew with a group of some twenty-five Dramatic Workshop students and a small staff of colleagues for the first time to Sayville on Long Island, New York.

He had encouraged his students to earn $100 each in part-time jobs in order to be able to jointly rent the Sayville Playhouse. During the first summer season, he used a tight weekly budget of $375 to present plays such as *Dr. Sganarelle* (a student adaptation of Molière's farce *The Doctor in Spite of Himself*), Shakespeare's *Twelfth Night* with a young Marlon Brando and Elaine Stritch, and Carl Sternheim's salon piece *Die Marquise von Arcis* (Mask of Virtue). Until his departure from the United States, the annual summer retreat remained a stable component of Piscator's educational and theatrical practice. The summer productions gave students a chance to gain practical theatre experience once again.

For some time, the Dramatic Workshop had participated in the New School's 'Bachelor of Arts Program', entitling students to attain a 'Bachelor of Drama' after finishing a two years' undergraduate study. Since the Servicemen's Readjustment Act, the so-called 'G.I. Bill', had been enacted in January 1944, the New School for Social Research and, in turn, the Dramatic Workshop experienced a rapid growth from 1945 on. The G.I. Bill provided a range of benefits for returning Second World War veterans such as payments of tuition and living expenses to attend university or vocational education. As a result, the Dramatic Workshop temporarily became 'one of the largest dramatic schools in the country'.[55] Piscator was taken aback by the strong demand for theatre education. He even felt that he had to warn applicants of a potentially insecure future in the theatre business: 'I am astonished and slightly bewildered at this desire of so many young people to go into the theatre. I ask them to what theatre, where, but I can't hold them back.'[56]

Furthermore, many of the new veteran students appeared 'intimidated, had lost their friends and always had their war experience in mind. [...] They hoped to raise new energy in themselves and to gain new skills through stage acting'.[57] A focus of the training was therefore laid on the perceptiveness of veterans in order to contribute to the dissolution of traumatic war experiences. While the Dramatic Workshop had had 40 to 60 full-time students and about 250 part-time students in the previous year,[58] the number of students suddenly rose to 160 regular students and 300 part-time students in the spring semester, 1946. Yet further changes were emerging. Due to a continued budget deficit in the Dramatic Workshop, the New School's Board and Piscator reached an agreement to relocate the Dramatic Workshop in 1946. Piscator rented the small, but fully equipped, President Theatre with 299 seats at 247 West 48th Street, 'a small midtown enclave of serious work in the midst of Broadway'[59] that served as the Dramatic Workshop's new home. As a positive side effect, Piscator could now continuously work on authentic theatre premises.

The Dramatic Workshop's relocation and release into independence

In spite of the rising challenges Piscator had to face as the director of the Dramatic Workshop, his general situation as an emigrant, if compared to those of some of his colleagues, was one of the better ones. Quite a number of seminal figures of 1920s German-speaking theatre had been driven to emigration and experienced difficulties in securing a living in their respective host countries. Leopold Jessner, former director of Preußisches Staatstheater Berlin, had failed to establish a theatre company in Los Angeles in 1939, and thereafter worked anonymously as a reader for MGM. Austrian-born directing legend Max Reinhardt had established a 'Workshop for Stage, Screen and Radio' on Hollywood's Sunset Boulevard in 1937/8. With his ingenious art of directing hardly having regained its powers for years, he died in New York in the autumn of 1943. Bertolt Brecht (who had been received as an upcoming and increasingly influential author rather than a stage director in the Weimar Republic) had spent years in Denmark, Sweden and Finland, before emigrating to the United States in 1941. While he became a prominent writer of 'Exilliteratur', he rarely had a chance to direct his plays on American stages.

More or less successfully, Piscator had adjusted his agenda to the cultural and political climate of 1940s America. He admired the United States for its long tradition of democracy, for its achievements as the economically and technologically most advanced country, and he cherished the openness and frankness of many Americans.[60] In a first contribution to *The New York Times*, he expressed his admiration for the American theatre and acknowledged the outstanding quality of contemporary drama.[61] Historical events of national (and international) resonance, such as President Franklin D. Roosevelt's death, moved the stateless immigrant deeply. With recourse to Greek mythology, Piscator gave an emotional, almost patriotic obituary in front of his Theatre Research class in April 1945, acknowledging the far-sighted founder of the New Deal as a 'true Agamemnon of the present time'.[62] After the end of the Second World War, Maria Ley acquired a house in New York's Upper East Side close to Central Park. Even at a point where a return to Germany would have been possible in 1946, the Piscators were determined to become US citizens and to stay in the United States permanently.

The Dramatic Workshop was facing further transition. As a consequence of resource conflicts within the New School, a first step to the Dramatic Workshop's future independence had to be taken. Piscator consolidated the Dramatic Workshop in the President Theatre as its new home and began to experiment with the professional theatre equipment available at West 48th Street. In his memoirs, Dramatic Workshop student Ben Gazzara recalled the imaginative character of the occasional production that Piscator staged at President Theatre:

> These twice yearly shows were lessons unto themselves. He took a little stage, the President Theatre on West Forty-eight, which was the size of a small living room, and turned it into Radio City Music Hall. I don't know how he did it. He required a week just to light a show. He called this Epic Theater and it *was* epic. It was fantastic. It was the first time I saw a director work creatively with light and space. Piscator tricked the audience into seeing what was not there. Suddenly, theater for me was not only what you see onstage but also what you don't see [emphasis in original].[63]

Nevertheless, a stage of 299 seats did not fully correspond to Piscator's demands. He additionally rented the larger Rooftop Theatre with 800 seats at 111 East Houston Street. It was situated atop the Yiddish National Theatre in what had formerly been Minsky's Burlesque House. Reactivating the successful lecture series 'March of Drama Repertory' as a live course in theatre history, now with purely student theatre performances, the Dramatic Workshop once again began to attract a large subscription audience that could see six plays for four dollars. At the President and the Rooftop Theatre, Piscator was now able to offer his audience an 'array of postwar drama unparalleled in New York'.[64]

Even though the President Theatre had to operate under the same constraints that the labour unions had imposed earlier on the Studio Theatre, a range of topical productions such as Jean-Paul Sartre's *Résistance* drama *Les Mouches* (The Flies) with a young Walter Matthau (President Theatre, 17 April 1947), a stage adaptation of Robert Penn Warren's Pulitzer Prize winning novel *All the King's Men* (President Theatre, 17 January 1948), Wolfgang Borchert's *Draußen vor der Tür* (The Man Outside) (President Theatre, 1 March 1949), Géza Herczeg and Heinz Herald's trial drama *The Burning Bush* (Rooftop Theatre, 16 September 1949) and John F. Matthew's stage adaptation of Franz Kafka's novel *Der Prozess* (The Trial) (President Theatre, 19 April 1950) could be produced at the new locations. Some of these productions, that had to do without professional actors, still attracted the attention of professional critics, such as *The Flies* with a 'newsreel curtain-raiser depicting the Nazi heyday'[65] appealing to Lester Bernstein of *The New York Times*, or *All the King's Men* whose stage design, a spiral staircase graphically illustrating the upward striving power, attracted coverage from *Life Magazine* (see Figure 4.2).

FIGURE 4.2 *Robert Penn Warren's* All the King's Men, *President Theatre, New York, 17 January 1948 (Herbert Gehr/The LIFE Picture Collection/Getty Images).*

After years when the Graduate Faculty had gained ever more importance within the New School while the adult education sector had to deal with considerable financial challenges, the New School's Board of Trustees finally took a decision on 9 February 1948 to sever the Dramatic Workshop with its steadily rising budget entirely from the New School. Piscator negotiated with Bryn Hovde, Johnson's successor as president, to defer the separation for one year. In February 1949, Alvin Johnson and Erwin Piscator announced a 'complete change in the future operating policy' of the Dramatic Workshop during a press conference: 'Dr. Johnson said the Workshop had outgrown its original function, which was to provide courses in dramatic appreciation as part of the school's adult education program. Now employing a faculty of fifty to teach 540 students, it offers professional training for careers in acting, directing, playwriting and other phases of theatre.'[66]

Since 1940, the Dramatic Workshop had become one of the most important hubs for the continuation of the German theatre practice of the Weimar Republic under the conditions of exile. Piscator had not only presented central elements of his own political theatre model to New York audiences, but had also inspired many American students to believe that the theatre could contribute to a shift in public awareness on social and political issues. Dramatic Workshop students had learned from some key figures of the Weimar Republic's literature, theatre and music scenes, and Piscator had brought some of the more important contemporary European plays to the attention of American audiences. As agreed, the Dramatic Workshop was finally separated from the New School in June 1949. Even though Piscator and his wife continued its operation in the rooms of the Rooftop Theatre on a reduced scale, the general conditions for running the school were unfavourable.

In February 1947, the US Immigration and Naturalization Service had refused Piscator's application to become a US citizen with the perhaps surprising rationale that 'through his actions he had not contributed to the fortune and welfare of the American people'.[67] Another factor was that the financial consolidation of the Dramatic Workshop suffered a severe setback when it was denied the eligibility for support from the G.I. Bill due to its dissociation from the New School in September 1949. This resulted in an immediate loss of students. Not least, a shift in the nation's political climate with the onset of the Cold War had made many artists the subject of anti-communist inquiries. In the wake of early Cold War events such as the Soviet Union testing an atomic bomb in 1949, Mao Zedong's communist army gaining control of mainland China and the beginning of the Korean War in 1950, fear of communist influence on American institutions was on the rise. Assertions by Republican Senator Joseph McCarthy of Wisconsin that he held a list of known communists working for the State Department, resulted in a campaign spreading fear of communist influence in American institutions. Many American government employees, entertainment-industry staff, educators and union activists became the subject of investigations and questioning before government panels, committees and agencies.

As an artist, theatre educator and leftist intellectual, Piscator was part of various circles most affected by the repression. In the summer of 1951 it came for him. The Catholic weekly *The Tablet* accused him of unchanged affinities to communism and postulated that his educational institution was actually a communist front.[68] The article claimed that at least nine part-time employees of the Dramatic Workshop had been communist sympathisers. The material provided by the right-wing newsletter 'Counterattack' seemed to be drawing on detailed information gathered by the FBI and the House Committee on Un-American Activities (HUAC).

In September 1951, the contract for the President Theatre was cancelled. On 4 October 1951, Piscator found the request of an investigating officer in his letterbox to call him back. The officer invited him to a hearing in Washington and asked for a preparatory meeting.[69] It was clear to Piscator that a hearing before HUAC would lead to a call to initiate a deportation process against him. A refusal to comply with the summons would have led to the cancellation of his US residence permit. Hastily, Piscator decided to return to (West) Germany.

After his devastating experience in the Soviet Union and the large-scale political purges and prosecutions of so-called enemies of the people that had taken place after his departure, leaving for West Germany seemed a more calculable option to him. It had also been suggested to Piscator in the late 1940s that Communist Party leaders in East Berlin did not speak well of him.[70] Piscator knew he would run a great risk of being sidelined if he went to East Germany without an official invitation. He boarded a flight to Hamburg on 6 October 1951.[71]

A hurried new beginning in post-war Germany

When Piscator abruptly returned to Germany, he had only few contacts in the theatre after almost twenty years of absence. Unlike other theatre directors, he had received no official invitation to return. The Director of the National Press Office in Hamburg, Erich Lüth, had invited him to stage a guest production in Hamburg at a ceremony hosted by American philosopher Horace Kallen in New York in 1950. This tentative offer was the most concrete starting point Piscator had in West Germany. His return to Hamburg initially went unnoticed. While the director gathered first impressions of post-war Germany, news was circulating about one of his old collaborators who had taken up residence in East Germany. Bertolt Brecht had established himself as an internationally famed author and theatre director in the capital of the German Democratic Republic (GDR), East Berlin. GDR President Wilhelm Pieck awarded Brecht the First Class National Award in the Deutsche Staatsoper, Berlin, on the very same day that Piscator returned to West Germany from emigration.[72] Brecht, who had tried to attract Piscator to return to Germany repeatedly in the late 1940s, had been well received since he had finally (re-)turned to directing in 1949.

The Socialist Unity Party of Germany (SED), the GDR's governing Marxist-Leninist party, had adopted a resolution on the 'Struggle against Formalism in Art and Literature for a Progressive German Culture' in March 1951. This resolution imposed binding guidelines of Socialist Realism on GDR artists. In the wake of this disturbing policy, Brecht was compelled to make changes to his opera *The Trial of Lucullus* in October 1951. Piscator observed these incidents with great concern[73] and felt confirmed in his decision against returning to East Berlin.[74] He was determined to contribute to Germany's democratic renewal through the rather limited means of theatre. Preferably without state intervention.

He had received several warnings in New York with regard to the situation of the German theatre. Gerhard Jacoby, one of his former lawyers in the 1920s, pointed to a general lack of plays, money and audiences:

It is completely different from the period after World War I when everything that had been experienced had been translated into a tremendous productiveness. This time, an outright lethargy has resulted. People have nothing to say, perhaps mainly because they have been content with having been allowed to express nothing or merely what was desired. Thus, the plays that I saw were mostly old or foreign. [...] The audience has been weaned off decent theatre. It desires a good deal more 'to escape' like the audience in the States. They don't want problems, and if they relax in the evening they want to see something simple and enrapturing.[75]

Just like other returning emigrants, Piscator painfully recorded that the political transformation in the Federal Republic of Germany was making slow progress. The hesitant avoidance of authoritarian and anti-democratic habits, the ostentatious anti-communism and the increasing importance of security and prosperity as guiding ideas in West Germany disturbed him. He perceived the lacking, at best selective debate on the Germans' Nazi past as a disconcerting shortcoming. The exile who had escaped Nazi prosecution, had found no home in the Soviet Union under Stalin and had to leave the United States of the McCarthy era was given a cool reception at home. In the autumn of 1951 he delivered a rushed, flawed premiere of a love story adapted from Thomas Middleton's and William Rowley's *The Changeling* at Schauspielhaus, Hamburg, Fritz Hochwälder's *Virginia* (4 December 1951). After the failure, attractive follow-up jobs failed to appear.

Apart from rare exceptions such as P. Walter Jacob, the General Director of Städtische Bühnen Dortmund, or Carl Ebert, the General Manager of Deutsche Oper Berlin, who were both former emigrants, West German theatre and opera of the early 1950s was being directed by theatre or opera makers who had remained in Germany. Piscator felt that returning emigrants had the status of near-pariahs in the theatre: 'emigrants were cumbersome admonishers. No one wanted to take in their moral positions, their claims were not really understood'.[76] Much like others in his situation, Piscator was at odds with the coping strategies practised in the Federal Republic of Germany. The returned emigrant was convinced of a social renewal which had yet to materialize after the end of the Nazi regime.

Limitations of an interventionist theatre aesthetics during the East–West confrontation

After the underwhelming production in Hamburg, Piscator worked as a guest director at various West German state and municipal theatres throughout the 1950s. Invitations from theatres in Switzerland, the Netherlands and Sweden occasionally provided a change of scene. As a guest director, Piscator staged plays declined by in-house directors. Otherwise, he mostly pursued the emphases of the broad theatre repertory that he had cultivated in New York City. He had to switch between staging classical, existentialist, bourgeois and psychologically realist plays. Only once in a while was he assigned productions that allowed him to formulate a commentary on contemporary events. In a production of Lessing's *Nathan the Wise* (Schauspielhaus Marburg, 14 May 1952), Piscator prominently tried to confront former Nazi fellow travellers with their involvement in the Shoah (in a key scene Nathan's lament for his seven sons was illustrated by the projection '7 – 70 – 700 – 7,000 – 70,000 – 700,000 – 7,000,000 promising sons burnt!'). Thus he aimed at promoting a democratic consciousness and spirit of tolerance free from resentment.

   Piscator's programmatic terminology had entirely changed during his years of emigration. The decidedly leftist political rhetoric of the 1920s had gone. In reaction to new political frameworks, social realities and his personal experiences as an emigrant, his functional aesthetics had acquired a less fundamental and a much more pragmatic character. An entry from Piscator's diaries, reflecting on his own development in the early 1950s reads: 'What has he learned? To work with caution, to avoid *shock*. Not to stand still.'[77] Thus, Piscator began to propagate a 'theatre of commitment' or 'confessional theatre' (*Bekenntnistheater*) that should facilitate a deep inward reflection. He wanted to convert theatre into a laboratory in the search for truth and 'ideas to live for'. Critics tended to reproach Piscator for the diffuseness of the key term 'confessional theatre'. As Barbara Elling pointed out, the strangely inexplicit term ultimately embodied a quite specific substance: 'of course, [...] "confession" took on a special meaning in post-war Germany, pointing directly to the national guilt and Germans' unwillingness to confront it'.[78]

Two years after *Nathan*, Piscator staged Arthur Miller's modern didactic play *The Crucible* on the seventeenth century's witch trials (Nationaltheater Mannheim, 20 September 1954). The play that Miller had written as an allegory of the era when the US government blacklisted accused communists had moved Piscator deeply. After all, Piscator had been compelled to leave the United States during McCarthy's heightened repression of supposed communists. The director arranged *The Crucible* on a thrust stage to create a closeness to the audience. A narrator entered the stage from within the audience. He presented extracts of Miller's commentary on the historical background and individual characters of the play along with his contemporary references, for example, to the challenges of political opposition in times of the Cold War. Selected scenes of the final act, when court representatives try to extort false confessions, were played partly from the auditorium; actors were placed within the front rows of the audience.[79] Central events were accompanied by illumination from below, creating a distressing atmosphere. Location and time were displayed through projections. The stage design of the acclaimed production at National Theatre Mannheim contained an illustrated chronicle of persecution and resistance, encompassing Socrates, Joan of Arc, the German officers executed in Berlin on the night of 20 July 1944, etc.[80] Thus, the production took on the character of a universal warning against the dangers of a doctrinaire exercise of power and the persecution of dissenters.

In view of the peripheral position Piscator held as a former emigrant in the German theatre, it took him several years until a first production in West Berlin materialized. Here he presented a revised version of his stage adaptation of Leo Tolstoy's novel *War and Peace* (Schiller-Theater, Berlin, 20 March 1955).[81] He had originally conceived his stage adaptation as a play against war. To entwine the historical events with individual strands of action, the director employed a complex, segmented stage. The 'stage of destiny', a heightened, sloped area on the main stage, was reserved for representing central historical events (e.g. battles during the French invasion of Russia). Here, the director staged a pivotal battle scene depicted by an actor moving ranks of foot-high toy soldiers. Projections of sketch maps and bottom-up lighting served to make the action more transparent. A lectern for a narrator commenting on events stood on the leading edge of the stage of destiny. Interpersonal scenes took place on a red 'stage of action' in the front. Three rostra on the forestage ('stages of reflection') were reserved for personal reflections of the central characters. Piscator conceived his staging as a model production[82] to be reproduced (though, without the in-depth photographic documentation associated with Brecht's later 'model' productions).

In the light of the intensifying conflict between the nuclear superpowers, the United States and the USSR, the premiere of *War and Peace* was designed as a deliberately untimely appeal to peace and understanding among nations during the early East–West conflict. The Warsaw Pact was about to be founded and 'two days prior to the premiere, the Bonn–Paris conventions were agreed in Bonn. The accession of the Federal Republic of Germany to NATO was settled, the defence alliance agreed upon. The premiere took place on 20 March 1955'.[83]

Piscator had wanted to show the 'timeliness of the material in view of new preparations for war'.[84] In fact, the production, staged by a director who was still remembered as the incommodious theatre innovator of the Weimar Republic, was perceived as a deliberate provocation by some critics. In the face of enthusiastic audience reactions, Friedrich Luft spoke of a 'theatrical Pyrrhic victory' and a 'seemingly victorious defeat'. Luft deplored the 'marvellous, strong fabric of Tolstoy's novel being meticulously unravelled' and the 'false pleasure in simplifying the complex'.[85] Piscator, as an experienced adaptor of novels for the stage, was irritated by Luft's remark in that it was generally impossible to bail an 'ocean out with a bucket',[86] i.e. that the adaptation had not fully exhausted the novel. In a letter to a literary scholar, he commented on the feedback to his first post-war production in Berlin: 'at very least we wanted to scoop out some crucial thoughts from Tolstoy against the war, and on any account use the bucket for collecting water, instead of letting it become a steel helmet once again'.[87]

Despite various scathing reviews, *War and Peace* frequently sold out and became the most successful production of the Schiller-Theater that season. The audience in West Berlin regularly celebrated it with standing ovations. East Berlin's press encouraged a guest performance in Brecht's Theater am Schiffbauerdamm. In June 1956, *War and Peace* was invited to the 'Festival Théâtre des Nations' in Paris. Piscator's stage adaptation was subsequently produced in many countries and received several TV and radio broadcasts internationally.[88] Nevertheless, Piscator's aspirations to permanently return to his former theatrical domain, Berlin, suffered a setback because of the mixed reviews.

The director believed it was important that 'none of what we have suffered must be lost'.[89] He sensed that the Nazi past would eventually become relevant to German theatres. And he wanted to set standards again, to 'unleash discussions! In order to move the theatre back to the spotlight!'.[90] In the period between 1954 and 1958, he staged his disturbing production of *The Crucible* and his adaptation of *War and Peace* at five different theatres in West Germany and Sweden. By focusing on theatrical topoi such as mass hysteria, persecution of dissenters and the contingency and imponderability of war, Piscator wanted to send out clear signals against the vagueness and cumbersomeness of the average repertoire in post-war West German theatres.

When the conditions at larger stages permitted, Piscator's later productions reflected directing conceptions and techniques from his work of the 1920s.[91] Thus, his earlier attempts at making audience members active participants in his productions were sporadically reflected in his later stagings. For example, Piscator wanted to back the party executives' intention to initiate a non-binding referendum on a nuclear build-up in the West German army in the single performance of Günther Weisenborn's anti-nuclear piece *Göttinger Kantate* (Göttingen Cantata) on the occasion of the Social Democratic Party's Convention in 1958 (Liederhalle Stuttgart, 18 May 1958). Weisenborn's piece consisted of the recital of a manifesto that leading German scientists had put forward against the government's armament policy, debates on the risks of nuclear armament and musical parts by composer Aleida Montijn (e.g. songs by fishermen on nuclear-weapons tests at Bikini Atoll). The piece was supposed to encourage the roughly four hundred party delegates to support a nationwide referendum. Then, in his production of Max Frisch's dark comedy *Biedermann und die Brandstifter* (The Fire Raisers) (Nationaltheater Mannheim, 22 May 1959), Piscator had Frisch's chorus of firemen rise from within the audience. The firemen interacted with spectators, for example, through demanding matches from them. The provocative actions aimed at stimulating self-reflection on the ordinary citizens' inclination to ignore the potential 'fire hazards' involved in the arms race of the Cold War of the 1950s.

The 'proto-postdramatic' quality of his earlier work, in the sense of rejecting literary theatre and practicing a theatre focused on performance, was also in evidence. Even the first production after his return from the US, Fritz Hochwälder's *Virginia* in Hamburg in 1951, was characterized by long and heated debates between director and author. Hochwälder's tragedy was set in Mexico in the early twentieth century. Piscator considered adaptations to the play necessary in order to capture the economic and social conditions of Mexican society prior to the Mexican Revolution. In August 1959 he gave a speech at a performing arts conference in Bayreuth on 'Performing Arts and Playwriting' in which he emphasized the paramount importance of acting (as opposed to the written text). Piscator underlined the original creativity of the actor and demanded: 'The actor and acting have to be delivered from the literary work, from the wrong claim of literature to lead.'[92] He proposed considering acting as an art form in its own right which did not lag behind the author's work, but could instead advance drama through giving vital impulses to authors. During the 1960s, a close collaboration with authors such as Rolf Hochhuth and Peter Weiss would loosely tie in with Piscator's earlier practice of developing plays and performances before and during rehearsals with his 'dramaturgical collective' of the 1920s.

Piscator maintained his practice of producing stage adaptions of epic texts such as the adaptation of Tolstoy's *War and Peace* or Bertolt Brecht's posthumous text, *Flüchtlingsgespräche* (Refugee Conversations).[93] He also applied strategies in order to make older plays more topical. In a staging of Georg Kaiser's expressionist antiwar plays *Gas I and II* (Schauspielhaus Bochum, 28 September 1958), Piscator paralleled the poison gas of the First World War with modern nuclear weapons. In this production Kaiser's proposal of a new kind of human being culminated in an apocalyptic vision of nuclear mass extinction. In the dystopian final scene, absolute silence contrasted with nuclear thunderbolt, darkness with tremendous light, revealing a skeleton tower (see below). His first production as the manager of the Freie Volksbühne Berlin was a condensed version of Gerhart Hauptmann's *Atreus Tetralogy* (Theater am Kurfürstendamm, 7 October 1962), written in Nazi Germany. Piscator wanted to make Hauptmann's encoded 'protest' against Nazi rule visible. He mostly played down archaic elements. On an abstract stage with skeletal metal scaffolds and a gigantic solar disc, he underpinned the story taken from Greek mythology with documentary material from the Second World War such as pictures of destroyed cities and cacophonous airplane, bomb and tank noise.

He occasionally made use of projections of stills, statistics, captions or quotations. In the production of the *Atreus Tetralogy* projections played an important role. Two black panels framing the stage displayed the time of origin of the different plays (1940–4) and major events of the respective period of the Second World War. The curtain and background screens presented decorative elements (e.g. abstract patterns and shadow silhouettes) and information adding a second temporal reference point to the tetralogy (e.g. Hauptmann's death mask, his lament on the destruction of Dresden in 1945 and images of a destroyed city). In his production of Shakespeare's comedy *The Merchant of Venice* (Freie Volksbühne Berlin, 1 December 1963), Piscator linked scenes with projections that reflected on the economic, social and political situation of sixteenth-century Venice (e.g. trade statistics or general information such as 'The Jewish inhabitants of Venice were excluded from Merchant Shipping'). The projections were supposed to facilitate an understanding of the social situation of Jews in a prosperous Christian Renaissance society. In addition, the projections served to reinforce emotional responses. When Shylock's malicious daughter Jessica received the information that she would inherit her father's estate (though she had stolen from him), the scene darkened and Shylock's magnified face was projected on the cyclorama. And when staging Heinar Kipphardt's documentary play *In the Matter of J. Robert Oppenheimer* (Freie Volksbühne, 11 October 1964), a dramatization of the controversial Oppenheimer security hearing on the American theoretical physicist and 'father of the atomic bomb' Oppenheimer, Piscator returned to the use of film projections. A large projection screen above the stage visualized central locations and subjects of the play: there were aerial views of Washington, earlier security hearings, countdowns, atomic explosions and nuclear bomb victims (see Figure 4.3).

Most prominently, Piscator experimented with alternative stage forms (e.g. traverse stage, thrust stage or theatre in the round)[94] and with alternative spatial arrangements (segment and simultaneous stage). He employed dualist stage constructions that casually referred to different spheres of action[95] or to social disparities.[96] Through his frequent use of non-standard stage forms in the 1950s, Piscator wanted to reduce the

FIGURE 4.3 *Heinar Kipphardt's* In the Matter of J. Robert Oppenheimer, *Freie Volksbühne Berlin, 11 October 1964 (Harry Croner/ullstein bild via Getty Images).*

distance between actors and audience inherent in the classical proscenium stage, and to increase the immediacy of stage action while, nonetheless, providing the audience with a rich thematic texture, expressed though the treatment of space. In the newly erected National Theatre, Mannheim, for example, Piscator staged Friedrich Schiller's *Die Räuber* (The Robbers) (Nationaltheater, Mannheim, 13 January 1957) on a traverse stage. The audience was divided up in two blocks. On the outer edges of the barren central stage lay the two poles of the action, the von Moor castle and the Bohemian forests (realized as a huge red staircase and a tall green wood construction, respectively). No proscenium arch was to be seen. The actors on the central stage played to two sides. The unconventional traverse stage allowed for a greater proximity between actors and audience, and brought out the dramatic conflicts more clearly. Yet, while Piscator used thrust and traverse stage repeatedly, he was reluctant to apply the (even) less familiar theatre in the round. In his production of Frisch's satirical play *The Fire Raisers,* four seating blocks encircled a slightly expanded square main stage. The house of the simple-minded hair-tonic manufacturer Biedermann, who lets arsonists settle in his attic, was realized as a multilevel construction. Above the main stage, an iron grid and a lighting bridge accessible through pull-down stairs provided for further playing space. The theatre in the round was supposed to facilitate self-recognition with the protagonist's astounding, self-destructive action.

Occasionally Piscator began to revive his earlier practice of applying multi-functional scaffolding constructions on stage. The revolving, hinged half-dome he had used in his milestone production of *Rasputin* in 1927 (Alexei Tolstoy/Pavel Shchegolev, *Rasputin, die Romanows, der Krieg und das Volk, das gegen sie aufstand* [Rasputin, the Romanovs, the War and the People that Rose Against Them], Piscator-Bühne, Berlin, 10 November 1927) was echoed by a metallic half-globe representing a gas factory in his staging of Kaiser's *Gas I and II*. In his final production, Hans Hellmut Kirst's *Aufstand der Offiziere* (The Officers' Uprising – Freie Volksbühne, 2 March 1966), he used a revolving half-globe as an accessible, hinged scaffolding construction again. On the exterior of the half-globe, documentary and other film was projected. During phone calls, real actors spoke with their cinematic interlocutors who were projected in close-up on the outer half-globe.

During the 1950s, Piscator offered new approaches in stage lighting and developed a light-focused dramaturgy designed to 'suspend' conventional space. He was convinced that light 'organises every corner wherever it shines and integrates every corner into the entire (aesthetic) conception'.[97] He used light as a descriptive dramaturgical element. Apart from strong light/dark contrasts or back-illumination, Piscator experimented in many productions of the 1950s with bottom-up lighting based on a light grid on which the actors could play.[98] The light grid originally consisted of metal bars with spotlights installed beneath, but was later constructed with a glass plate. Piscator applied this bottom-up lighting technique in and after his production of Jean-Paul Sartre's *Im Räderwerk* (L'engrénage; In the Mesh) (Städtische Bühnen Frankfurt am Main, 27 September 1953): 'The grid: its exclusive significance is in the lighting. […] That space as well as the floor will be reversed.'[99] Piscator used the light grid regularly to emphasize monologue sequences or key statements of main characters. Thus, in his production of *The Robbers*, he had the moving, self-reflecting scenes in which Karl von Moor, who had left his promising aristocratic life behind to become the leader of a gang of robbers, played out on such a grid. The grid allowed for powerful atmospheric lighting effects in Piscator's later opera productions as well.[100]

During his years of emigration in the United States, Piscator had begun to outline his approaches to acting more theoretically. His activity as a theatre educator and his tentative approach at a theory of acting were reflected in a stronger focus on acting and a more refined elaboration of roles in various of his later productions. Often, he analysed words and sentences in much detail with actors and, in doing so, took an ever-greater interest in the 'inner affairs in man and in the actor'.[101] When Piscator presented Eugene O'Neill's larger dramatic trilogy *Mourning Becomes Electra* (Bühnen der Stadt Essen, 12 January 1958) on the inexorable self-extinction of a puritan industrialist family after the end of the American Civil War, the director received much critical acclaim for the quality of how the actors were directed and how they made full use of the stage space: 'Piscator aims at the dialogues time and again, the handling of conflicts in one-to-one encounters. The space is bustling continuously since the director composes and dissolves the tensions of these resolving and clarifying, developing and devastating dialogues over the whole stage.'[102] Another critic highlighted the positioning of the actors: 'Piscator's directing, [which is] tremendously symbolic, dynamic and mathematically accurate in terms of the positions of the actors, reproduces the demonic interlinking of events with captivating magic.'[103]

Returning to a repertoire of topical plays and premieres

The impact of Piscator's early theatre had been closely connected to potential fields of resonance in society and possibilities of addressing controversial political and social topics. In the first years after his return to Germany, he had hardly found opportunities to resume this practice. Several controversial political developments in the late 1950s would finally enable Piscator to reflect on political issues in the theatre in a more profound way again. Among these events were the onset of the nuclear arms race between the United States and the Soviet Union, the re-founding of a (West) German army in May 1955, and subsequent reports by West German newspapers that the nuclear armament of the German army was scheduled sooner or later.

In the light of this possibility, dissent emerged in the general public. In April 1957, a group of eighteen leading West German nuclear scientists presented a declaration against the government's aspiration, the so-called Göttingen Manifesto. During ongoing parliamentary debates in the Bundestag on the issue of nuclear armament in early 1958, an extra-parliamentary committee 'Combating Nuclear Death' was formed to urge the population to resistance. The political protest was driven by a broad alliance of Social Democrats, trade unions, Liberals, churches, scientists and authors.

In the context of the peace movement emerging in West Germany, several theatre managers assigned productions to Piscator that were more or less closely linked to the topic of nuclear armament. These early productions on the new arms race and the threat of a nuclear war received mixed receptions. Kaiser's *Gas I and II* caused a stir due to Piscator's decision to parallel the poison gas of the First World War with modern nuclear weapons. The dystopian production culminated in a universal vision of death with a tower of luminous skeletons, a nightmarish theatrical apocalypse pointing to a potential third world war. Other topical productions were less successful: Piscator's choice of an experimental, three-storey 'theatre in the round' stage for Max Frisch's *The Fire Raisers* was rejected by critics as overwhelming the play and its satirical nature.

Yet another timely subject led to the writing of compelling, topical plays. In 1958, many cities in West Germany had seen swastikas daubed on the walls of private homes and public buildings. The general public across the political parties were outraged by these scandalous, anti-constitutional acts. During the late 1950s, intellectuals such as the German philosopher and returned emigrant Theodor W. Adorno initiated a discourse on the *Aufarbeitung der Vergangenheit* (working through the past).[104] This debate corresponded to Piscator's long-held conviction that the theatre had to take up this issue. In 1960, he produced Jean-Paul Sartre's *Les séquestrés d'Altona* (The Condemned of Altona), a play about the suicide of a German officer, instigated by insights into his involvement in Nazi crimes (Bühnen der Stadt Essen, 2 May 1960). On a stage with a characteristic prison atmosphere, Piscator showed the demanding process of introspection endured by former officer Franz von Gerlach who had been known as the 'oppressor of Smolensk'. Apparitional projections on a vitreous ceiling signified an imaginary 'court of crabs' extorting speeches of self-justification from the former lieutenant. Two years later, Piscator premiered a stage adaptation of Bertolt Brecht's series of dialogues *Flüchtlingsgespräche* (Refugee Conversations, Munich Kammerspiele, 15 February 1962), a humorous examination of the situation of German emigrants. Piscator framed the *Refugee Conversations* as a revue with a narrator reading the introductory texts to Brecht's amusing dialogues and two uniformed revue girls moving Brechtian half-curtains across the stage. Two popular solo cabaret artists, Willy Reichert and Werner Finck, embodied the main characters, Kalle and Ziffel, conversing in a railway pub in front of a selection of huge mobile caricatures, for example, of an SS officer marching over a street paved with human skulls or of a guard staring over the recently built Berlin Wall at the Victory Column.

Plays and adaptations such as these allowed Piscator to contribute to a discussion that interested and affected him vitally as a returned German struggling for his place in post-war society. The successful production of the Sartre play resulted in several restagings by Piscator in other cities. The Brecht text drew much spontaneous applause from Munich audiences. Both productions proved that it was possible to theatrically address the Nazi past to the approval of audiences and critics alike. Not by coincidence, from this point on, premieres of new writing became the backbone of Piscator's repertoire once again as they had been in the Weimar Republic.[105] Soon, Piscator was able to produce an, albeit small, range of contemporary plays on the Nazi period, the Holocaust and the policies of dealing with the past. A new approach to a politically engaged theatre beyond the fundamental social opposition Piscator had championed during the 1920s seemed within reach. Two of the corresponding productions bringing back Piscator's work to the attention of an international public, the premieres of Rolf Hochhuth's 'Christian tragedy' *Der Stellvertreter* (The Deputy) and Peter Weiss'

Auschwitz oratorio *Die Ermittlung* (The Investigation), will be examined more closely.

Revealing the blind spot: A new play raises international controversy

A highly successful try-out production of Arthur Miller's *Death of a Salesman* with Leonard Steckel as Willy Loman in West Berlin (Theater am Kurfürstendamm, 6 October 1961) finally put an end to what long-time freelance director Piscator called his own activities as a 'travelling salesman in theatre matters'.[106] During rehearsals for the premiere of Brecht's *Refugee Conversations* in Munich, Piscator received a message changing everything. He was appointed General Director of the Theater der Freien Volksbühne in West Berlin in February 1962. The theatre was operated by the Freie Volksbühne Berlin, a theatre organization with a long tradition and a membership of more than 100,000. Back in the 1920s, Piscator had experienced his breakthrough as a theatre director at the predecessor institution, the Volksbühne Berlin, a theatregoers' organization with close ties to the labour movement and a theatre of its own. It had been established to bring 'art to the people'.[107] In the selection interview in 1962, Piscator had successfully brought into focus decisive conceptual qualities that could make the Freie Volksbühne stand out from other Berlin stages again (such as a programmatic scheduling policy instead of improvising a repertoire from play to play; developing a consistent production style).

Two weeks after the Executive Board's decision had been made public, Piscator received what would prove to be a momentous message by publisher Heinrich Maria Ledig-Rowohlt from Hamburg. Ledig-Rowohlt drew Piscator's attention confidentially to an unpublished play by an upcoming author. The dramaturges of renowned theatre directors such as Heinz Hilpert (Deutsches Theater Göttingen) and Hans Schweikart (Munich Kammerspiele) had dismissed the piece as unplayable.[108] Ledig-Rowohlt on the contrary affirmed: 'The play packs a punch provided it is launched and got up and running.'[109]

The drama *The Deputy* was a 'well-founded and sensitive study of the Vatican's policy towards the Nazi extermination camps'.[110] It was based on the author's perception that Pope Pius XII had failed in the face of the expulsion and murder of millions of European Jews during Nazi rule in Germany. In his debut piece, a then editor for the Bertelsmann book club, Rolf Hochhuth, developed the thesis that the Pope's function as a religious authority and as the leader of the Catholic Church had implied the moral obligation to express a public protest against the Holocaust during the Second World War. In the playwright's judgement, a note of protest against the Nazi's policy of exclusion could have potentially forced Hitler to back down and saved countless lives. At the same time, Hochhuth's play raised the uncomfortable question of individual responsibility under the dictatorship. During a working visit to Rome, well-versed Vatican diplomat Bruno Wüstenberg had confided to the book club editor in 1959 that Pope Pius XII had effectively never protested against the extermination of the European Jews or asked Hitler for mitigation.[111]

Central characters of the play are the fictitious Roman Jesuit priest Riccardo Fontana and the historical character of SS-Obersturmbannführer Kurt Gerstein, member of the 'Bekennende Kirche' (Confessing Church) and of the Hygiene Institute of the Waffen-SS. As Gerstein enters the Berlin Nunciature in order to disclose strictly confidential information on the extermination camps in the East to Vatican representatives, only the young Jesuit priest Fontana is willing to listen. Fontana is convinced that Pius XII must use his moral authority and political weight for a protest against the Nazis' extermination policy. The following acts in Rome depict Fontana's 'neutralization' and relocation through a cardinal, and the deportation of the Roman Jews. Fontana's involvement culminates in a confrontation with the pontifex who is not prepared to enunciate more than a general public appeal in which the Jews are not explicitly mentioned. As a result of realizing his failure, Fontana decides to share the Roman Jews' fate and travels with them to Auschwitz.

Piscator's deliberate, calm style of directing was supposed to confirm the discovery of a major new playwright. Apart from accompanying sacral music, and text and image projections between scenes indicating locations, Piscator renounced the dramaturgical effects and elements of a director's theatre. Exactly this directorial caution and the factual, text-oriented presentation were recognized by leading critics such as Willy H. Thiem as a strength, considering the play's controversial contemporary theme: 'Thus, in renouncing the means of cheap ruckus and bold trivial intonation [... Piscator] achieved through rigour and modesty his most effective, most artistic and most concentrated accomplishment in years.'[112]

The reduction of the play to half of its original length meant that all scenes which presented an insider's view of the Nazi regime were eliminated. The arrest of the Jewish Luccani family in Rome or the round-up of the prisoners in the Roman Gestapo headquarters were not shown in order not to distract the audience from Fontana's self-imposed mission to 'retain' Catholicism's ethos and dignity and to avoid any touch of sensationalism. The final act, in which Fontana has accompanied the Roman Jews' on their deportation to Auschwitz and is confronted with a fiendish Nazi physician in Auschwitz, was cut heavily. Piscator focused his staging on Fontana's intra-church opposition and his martyrdom. Though concentrating on Riccardo's struggle to convince Vatican officials of the necessity of an official protest against the mass murder, the director toned down the Jesuit priest's claims that a deputy of Christ had knowledge of those crimes and remained silent for political reasons in the second act. Piscator eliminated many references to the exploitation and abuse of concentration camp prisoners and forced labourers through large industrial companies as well since these could have impaired the thematic focus on the failure of a religious authority in view of unprecedented historical challenges.

The premiere (Theater am Kurfürstendamm, 20 February 1963) instantly turned *The Deputy* into the most discussed theatrical event not only of the year, but in the previous history of the Federal Republic of Germany. Even before the premiere, in January 1963, a nationwide dispute on the play had erupted. The Catholic Berlin weekly *Petrus-Blatt* voiced a vigorous protest against the premiere of a play that accused the Pope of faint-heartedness in the face of the Holocaust. The church saw its self-image as an institution driven to martyrdom by fascism imperilled. The Catholic news agency subsequently printed highly selective quotations from the stage script on 12 February 1963, without permission. Hochhuth defended his 'Christian Trauerspiel' on 22 February 1963, against manifold hostilities in turn as a 'pronouncedly catholic piece' that 'openly expressed a long overdue criticism of the conduct of the pontifex in the years from 1942 to 1944'.[113]

During the 1962/3 season, Piscator's production was performed 117 times. In the following season, the play received another 141 performances in the Freie Volksbühne's new theatre building in Schaperstraße and a successful nationwide tour through twenty-one West German cities. After a delay of a whole year, the play was subsequently staged at other West German theatres and internationally. Productions of *The Deputy* in other countries frequently sparked unrest and even riots.[114] The play and production turned into a political issue. The Vatican's diplomatic representative in the West German capital Bonn, nuncio Corrado Bafile, examined opportunities for a legal challenge, based on paragraph 189 of the criminal code penalizing the defamation of those deceased. The governments of Italy and Belgium expressed grave concerns with the West German government's refusal to clearly dissociate itself from Hochhuth's accusations.[115]

Challenging response strategies to the question of guilt: The Auschwitz trial on stage

In conversations with young intellectuals after the Second World War, Bertolt Brecht had pointed to the limitations that dogged a potential literary treatment of Nazi crimes: 'the events in Auschwitz, in the Warsaw Ghetto, in Buchenwald would doubtless not bear any literary description. Literature was not prepared for such events, nor has it developed any means of describing them'.[116] The perception of the impossibility of a direct literary description of the Holocaust resulted in the development of a 'Holocaust literature' that used indirect forms of representing the Nazis' extermination policy. A central driver of the literary treatment of Nazi crimes were the

Frankfurt Auschwitz trials, a series of hearings running from 1963 to 1965 that charged twenty-two defendants for their involvement in the Auschwitz-Birkenau death and concentration camp complex. Fritz Bauer, the Hessian Attorney General in charge of the arraignment, noted in October 1965: 'we lawyers in Frankfurt, deeply horrified, have called for the poet who could articulate what the process is not able to articulate', and whose texts could contribute to 'prevent Auschwitz both now and in the future'.[117]

The literary initiative had been taken by Swedish-German author Peter Weiss. Weiss had attended some of the court hearings in the 'Criminal proceedings against Mulka and others' (*Strafsache gegen Mulka und andere*) – the actual term for the Frankfurt Auschwitz trials – since March 1964. When Piscator received the manuscript of Weiss's play *The Investigation*, he immediately agreed to premiere it. Through factually and soberly presenting statements of (anonymized) witnesses against the former SS concentration camp staff and guards, the play, set in a courtroom, depicts the Holocaust victims' path from the ramp upon arrival at Auschwitz to the gas chambers and ovens. Considering the exceptional importance of the play, Piscator and the Suhrkamp Theatre Publishing House, in a most unusual arrangement, decided on a multiple, simultaneous premiere. In a circular from May 1965, Suhrkamp Theatre Publishing invited stages throughout Germany to participate in a massed premiere. In addition to the Freie Volksbühne Berlin, another three theatres from West Germany, eleven stages from East Germany as well as the Royal Shakespeare Company in London accepted the invitation. All productions opened on 19 October 1965.

Piscator was convinced that Weiss' text was predestined to stimulate the underdeveloped public debate on the crimes of Nazi Germany and to 'impede the general desire to forget in matters of our recent history'.[118] He perceived the production as an 'attempt to reinstall the theatre's position as a moral institution' in Friedrich Schiller's sense.[119] The director was anxious to give a rather factual representation of the play and to replicate the formal rigour of the text scenographically. The stage design of the West Berlin production (Freie Volksbühne, 19 October 1965) showed a condensation of the Frankfurt jury court room without giving a true-to-life imitation. The titles of the different scenes ('cantos') were projected in white on the black, triangular stage. On the stage sat the eighteen defendants, all visible to the audience, to the right the judge and prosecutor, between them the defender. The witness box located on the proscenium was intended to allow for an identification between audience and witnesses (see Figure 4.4).

Only the ten witnesses moved across the stage. If individual defendants were addressed, they were illuminated from above. Piscator wanted to avoid any touch of pathos and had much of the text presented in a conversational tone. Many of the accusations were presented in 'blazing' sobriety. In order to structure the long statements, Piscator used optical and acoustic breaks. The defendants collectively turned to the right or left on their chairs once in a while. They partly supported their evasive answers, excuses and

FIGURE 4.4 *Peter Weiss'* The Investigation, *Freie Volksbühne Berlin, 19 October 1965 (Heinz Köster/ullstein bild/Kontributor via Getty Images).*

downplaying of their responsibilities with a gesture of washing hands. At the end of each trial phase, the last sentence was spoken like a 'punch line'. An atonal electronic musical intermission, described by critics as a blaring, yelling, whistling soundscape, was contributed by Italian composer Luigi Nono.

After excerpts of Peter Weiss's preliminary work on *The Investigation* had been printed in the first edition of the influential cultural journal *Kursbuch*, edited by author Hans Magnus Enzensberger in June 1965, and a complete preprint had been published in the almanac of the *Theater heute* magazine in August 1965, a public dispute commenced several weeks before the premiere. Diverse objections were raised against presenting 'Auschwitz on stage' by critics. In light of these reservations, Walter Jens, Professor of General Rhetoric at Tübingen University, subsequently acknowledged Piscator's production as fully appropriate and conclusive: 'it was a *theatrical* evening, indeed: thanks to Erwin Piscator; he devised the visual emphases, jumping up and sitting down, Pilate gesticulation of the accused, witness dances in front of the tribunal, with consistency, determination and gravity [emphasis in original]'.[120]

The programmatic character of *The Investigation*'s premiere was reinforced through linking it to the ceremonies on the seventy-fifth anniversary of the founding of the Volksbühne Berlin. The ceremonies, running from 17 to 21 October 1965, comprised lectures, theatrical performances, an exhibition and the bestowal of the Gerhart Hauptmann Literary Award. During the ceremonies, Karl Hans Bergmann, Vice-Chairman of the Freie Volksbühne's Board, announced that the premiere of *The Investigation* had provoked some 2 percent of the 120,000 members of the Freie Volksbühne to cancel their membership.[121]

Once more: Theatre as an institution of political and social discourse

Piscator's readiness to take a risk as the General Director of the Freie Volksbühne Berlin had proved momentous. While in the early 1960s he had been the only director willing to premiere *The Deputy* (after his earlier politically charged theatre productions had failed), topical plays increasingly met with the interest of other directors in its wake. Piscator had to share the world premiere of Heinar Kipphardt's play *In the Matter of J. Robert Oppenheimer* in 1964 and of Peter Weiss's *The Investigation* in 1965 with one or more of his colleagues. While Paul Verhoeven co-premiered the Kipphardt play at Munich Kammerspiele, multiple stages participated in the open premiere of Weiss's disturbing play. The plurality and poignancy of the reactions to Piscator's late productions[122] shows that the director had actually achieved what he had pursued once again. Theatre had taken on a function that had scarcely been present after the Second World War. Piscator's provocative productions of the 1960s particularly urged theatregoers to reflect on the crimes that had been committed in their country some two decades beforehand and to express their opinion. Through provoking broad national debates, theatre became a driving force in the shift in consciousness in those years.[123]

Nevertheless, Piscator had not been able to fully recover the unity between an activist topical approach and the intensive and extensive scenic and technical realization that had characterized his stage work of the 1920s. At that time, he had frequently emphasized the functional character of his epic staging techniques and their inseparability from a specific political content.[124] In spite of multiple attempts to reapply his earlier directing and scenic techniques during the 1950s, his most successful productions of the 1960s such as *The Deputy* or *The Investigation* were successful due to Piscator's hesitation in using sophisticated stage technique and due to restricting himself to a topical approach in its own right. Many factors have contributed to this process of separating what should have originally been inseparable in Piscator's theatre (i.e. content and specific epic technique):

- the limited production conditions Piscator faced as a freelance director at West German theatres (and even as the director of the Theatre of the Freie Volksbühne)
- a cultural climate favouring strict faithfulness to the original text over theatrical experimentation
- conflicting expectations of a director who was supposed to have overcome the 'aberrations' of his earlier technology-focused theatre but, nevertheless, was still expected to deliver a permanent directorial imprint.

Additionally, the weighty topics of some of his late productions would not have allowed for all too dominant directorial solutions. Some plays had to rely on their own powerful subject matter.

Thus, characteristic of Piscator's late productions was less the concerted use of stage technology linked to dramaturgical concepts as in earlier years, but his extensive use of documentary material such as reports, photos and statistics. Piscator had thereby become the inspiration to a generation of young dramatists such as Hochhuth, Kipphardt and Weiss. This group of authors would rely on documents, a critical dramaturgical feature of Piscator's earlier work, as pieces of evidence that were supposed to make it more difficult for audiences to dispute the exposed historical facts.

Not all of Piscator's productions relating to a theatre of the immediate German past achieved the clarity and forcefulness of the premieres discussed above. With the intent to provide no space for anti-Semitic interpretations, Piscator rendered the Venetian money lender Shylock as a noble Jew in a 1963 production of Shakespeare's *Merchant of Venice*, contrasting with the author's representation of Shylock (Freie Volksbühne, 1 December 1963). Much to the displeasure of the critics, he reduced Shakespeare's text to Shylock's political tragedy.[125] Likewise, Piscator's final production, the premiere of Hans Hellmut Kirst's *The Officers' Uprising* (Freie Volksbühne, 2 March 1966) on the 20 July plot to assassinate Adolf Hitler and to overthrow the Nazi German government led to disappointment and severe criticism. Piscator had invited Kirst to produce a stage adaptation of his recently published novel *Aufstand der Soldaten* (The Soldiers' Revolt), but the collaboration with an author who had no experience as a dramatist progressed slowly. All attempts to mitigate the poor text with additional directorial efforts (e.g. the use of a revolving half-globe stage and film projections) failed. Several first-rate actors had returned their contracts during the rehearsals. Relatives of the executed resistance fighters protested against historical inaccuracies. The critics felt that the important historical material had been trivialized. During the rehearsals, Piscator had been very ill. A few weeks after the premiere, he died after an emergency gall bladder operation.

Notwithstanding, the uneven end of Piscator's career, productions such as *The Deputy* and *The Investigation* constituted an effective monument to his work on the post-war stage. They had contributed to a palpable change in West German memory culture. To some degree, the success of documentary theatre rested on Piscator's thoughtful dramaturgical and scenographic preparation of the texts (it had taken almost a year of intense collaboration between Piscator and Hochhuth to finalize the premiere of *The Deputy*). In a letter to his wife, Piscator took pride in the fact that the premiere of *The Deputy* had been spared the distraction of becoming a theatrical scandal. While he had used all theatrical means available to achieve a greater effect in his stage work of the 1920s, he now argued that the hostilities in the run-up to the premiere of *The Deputy* had necessitated a very cautious directing approach: 'In my production the play became covertly an intimate play, and this was good in view of the difficult and fastidious material. In fact, Catholics had fiercely demonstrated beforehand [...] in a nutshell, there was great excitement beforehand, more than afterwards. The anticipated "boisterous Piscator" was not to be seen. The sensation was reversed. Earnestness and calm dominated.'[126]

This ability to deliberately exercise directorial restraint in favour of a strong dramaturgical effect where necessary was perhaps the one of the most substantial features of Piscator's later stage work. It allowed him to temporarily move theatre back to the spotlight of political debate under the challenging conditions of post-war German society.

Bertolt Brecht

5

Brecht as Corrector: Directing Away From Conventional Theatre

David Barnett

Bertolt Brecht (1898–1956) was a towering figure of twentieth-century culture. He made significant contributions to playwriting, poetry, the theory of theatre-making, and directing, among other things. Yet while many volumes have been written on his plays, poems and theories, relatively little work has been done on his work as a director and theatre practitioner. This is both understandable and surprising. On the one hand, published texts can endure far longer than theatre productions that may achieve great success in performance but be surpassed or forgotten as time moves on. On the other, the Berliner Ensemble (BE), the company Brecht co-founded with his wife, Helene Weigel, in 1949 was internationally celebrated from the mid-1950s, and Brecht insisted that its work, in rehearsal and on stage, be documented to serve as a model for other theatres.

This chapter examines how Brecht approached directing three different genres of play, a comedy, a propaganda piece and a tragedy. In each case, Brecht took over direction from another director, twice without credit. An examination of these three productions allows insights into the conditions under which Brecht felt compelled to intervene and reveals how he responded to the more conventional fare the original directors were offering the actors and potentially the audience. This contrast will shed light not only on Brecht's aims for the theatre but the means by which he sought to realize them. First, however, I will outline Brecht's development as a director in the decades preceding the BE's foundation in order to show how he later modified and challenged certain ideas that emerged early in his practice.

Early seeds of directing practice

Brecht's engagement with theatre practice started when he was in his teenage years. A school friend considered him the 'director and artistic director' of a second-hand puppet theatre bought from one of their teachers.[1] One of his school friends recalled how Brecht had directed puppet shows in various rooms around his home town of Augsburg, Germany, from 1914. His first experience of directing in the professional theatre came some years later in 1922. By this time, he had made something of a name for himself as a playwright and decided to direct *Vatermord* (Parricide), a play written by his friend, Arnolt Bronnen. The rehearsals were a disaster: Brecht made himself unpopular with the actors and withdrew from the production.[2] The curtain finally went up on 14 May, over a month after the advertised premiere, and was directed by Berthold Viertel, who would stage Maxim Gorky's *Vassa Zheleznova* at the BE in 1950. This was hardly an auspicious start to a directing career that would be marked in part by its productive and enabling dialogue with actors.

Before Brecht fled the Nazis in 1933, he was involved in a great number of projects that he either directed or co-directed. However, only a few of them offer concrete material that allows for focused analysis. One of the most important productions Brecht directed in the Weimar Republic (1918–33) was an adaptation of Marlowe's *Edward II* as *Das Leben Eduards des Zweiten von England* (The Life of Edward the Second of England) that he wrote together with Lion Feuchtwanger. It premiered in Munich on 19 March 1924 and reveals some important features associated with his theatre. First, and most importantly, Brecht directed with great clarity: there was no room for movement or deliveries that did not contribute to the overall meaning of any given scene. He was also concerned with the relationship between character and the architecture of the play as a whole. As actor Asja Lacis observed: 'he wanted the whole character to be expressed in every movement. [...] He wanted to break [the actors'] habit of fuzzy nebulous, general expression'.[3] Brecht was thus not concerned with presenting characters as naturalistic slices of life but as figures in a fictional drama, looking backwards and forwards to what they had done and what they were yet to do. Edward Braun observes that after this experience, 'nothing in the theatre was more important for Brecht than the story (*Die Fabel*)'.[4] I will return to this term below, but I will note at present that here, the *Fabel* refers to prioritizing the dynamics of the plot over those of the characters. That is, Brecht looked beyond the characters to the stage world and the demands it made on them; he was interested in the relationship between character and wider contexts, not in character as an autonomous dramatic agent.

Another key idea emerged during rehearsals, one that Brecht would only name later in the 1930s. As Bruce Gaston writes, Brecht's 'concern over just how Baldock should pass the king a handkerchief, or how a noose is tied, contains the embryo of his concept of the "Gestus"'.[5] This term, which connects gesture to ideas beyond the gesture itself, also undermines the individual character's claims to sovereignty over his or her actions. Instead, characters are aligned with ways of behaving that exist beyond them. In the above example, Baldock was to betray his king, and so the gesture had to include the element of treachery; it had to exist in a gestural language that was not limited to the activity itself. Brecht was serving the *Fabel* rather than the character as a way of clearly setting out the action to the audience. As is evident, he felt no compunction about using consciously theatrical methods that did not seek to reflect everyday life. Elsewhere, for example, he famously had soldiers wear white make-up to represent fear. Already it is evident that Brecht was developing a theatre of signification, where the clear communication of ideas, actions or feelings formed the basis of actorly virtue.

An aesthetic of interruption also emerged. An announcer declaimed the scenes' titles and a singer delivered the songs specially written for the adaptation.[6] Interruption is a central idea in both Brecht's playwriting and his theatre practice in that it can dislocate the reader and the spectator, respectively. Dislocation requires activity on the part of the recipient in order to make sense of the disparate elements, such as when drama is interrupted by song. This drive to activate spectators by making demands on them from the stage would be developed with greater focus in the years to come.

The last significant motif in Brecht's direction was his pragmatic approach to the text that, in this case, he partially wrote himself. Bernhard Reich, who attended rehearsals, noted that Brecht the director would continually revise the text, taking issue with Brecht the playwright, in order to develop ideas and address perceived shortcomings in the lines that emerged in rehearsal.[7] This 'disrespect' for the playwright represented the primacy of theatrical efficacy for Brecht the director over whatever lines he found on the page. In future years, he would have no qualms about re-writing, adapting, cutting or adding material to the existing text, be it his or another's.

Brecht was to refine many of these features over time. He directed, for example, a new version of his first major play, *Baal*, in Berlin (premiere 14 February 1926) in which he introduced a 'compère or announcer in a dinner jacket who announced directly to the audience what would happen in the following scene'.[8] This development of the narrator figure in *Edward* disrupted a staple of conventional theatre: tension. Brecht preferred to concentrate the audience's attention on *how* an action unfolded by suspending the audience's speculation about the outcome of a particular scene. Brecht showed here that he valued the process of a dramatic event over its outcome. Spectators were invited to engage with the course of events and not simply to be sucked into them because they wanted to know what would happen in the end. The production of *Edward* already registers features that would reappear later in Brecht's directorial career. Yet it is important to avoid the trap of believing, as John Fuegi does, that 'from first to last, essentially Brecht had remained the same'.[9] It is true that Brecht laid certain foundations and principles early in his directing career, but these were to evolve in the light of his study of Marxism that took place in the mid-1920s, after the two productions discussed above. The influence of this encounter can be felt in particular in two productions from the early 1930s.

Brecht directed his own *Mann ist Mann* (Man Equals Man) in Berlin, and it premiered on 6 February 1931. The play is about the conversion of a simple porter, Galy Gay, into a fully-fledged soldier, Jeriah Jip. The central character's journey constitutes an attack on the notion that the individual has an inviolable identity, and production amply traded on the discontinuous nature of his transformation. One of Brecht's close allies, the theatre reviewer Herbert Ihering, criticized the characterization of Galy Gay as being 'spoiled by an overly nuanced approach'.[10] Brecht observed that 'the speeches' content was made up of contradictions, and the actor had not to make the spectator identify himself with individual sentences and so get caught up in contradictions, but to keep him out of them'.[11] The crucial word 'contradictions' is worth dwelling on here, as it reflects Brecht's debt to his new political philosophy. Karl Marx, following the philosopher Hegel, believed that reality was not in some way stable or innately self-regulating, but profoundly unsteady and potentially volatile. This was because he considered society and its economic structures to be defined by contradictions. Capitalism, for example, is a boon to those who profit from it and a bane to those who suffer to produce that profit. The single idea has contradictory qualities. Contradictions can be ignored, but can never be eliminated without action, and this idea is a source of revolutionary hope. Contradictions do not only exist on a societal level; they are also to be found in individuals. For example, people might appreciate that cheap clothing comes from exploiting sweatshop labour from overseas, but they may continue to buy that clothing because they cannot afford to spend more. What Brecht's plays and theatre increasingly began to demonstrate was that analysis of individuals could prove a useful means of exposing grander contradictions that originate in society itself. Addressing Ihering's criticism, Brecht countered that the actor 'has to be able to show his character's coherence despite, or rather by means of, interruptions and jumps'.[12] The means Brecht the director employed to dramatize contradiction in Galy Gay upset the theatre reviewer but represented reality more closely, according to Brecht. Rather than passing over contradictions, Brecht sought to bring them out as clearly as possible. Thus, the devices identified in the earlier productions were re-focused for Brecht's new political experiments to achieve new ends: the exposure and articulation of contradiction.

Brecht co-directed his play *Die Mutter* (The Mother) which had its world premiere in Berlin on 17 January 1932. Laura Bradley notes how the blocking clearly demonstrated the relationships between the characters in every scene.[13] The predilection for clarity, that appeared in the *Edward* production, is again refocused and put to the service of a different kind of meaning. Formerly, Brecht was concerned with shining the light of clarity onto the complexities of the text for the benefit of the spectator. Here, the impulse is not dissimilar but it is serving a different purpose. Bradley suggests the clarity of Brecht's direction was not an end in itself but a means of setting out the play's *Fabel*.[14] One of Brecht's assistants at the BE, Carl Weber, offers a useful definition of the term: '"Fable" was, of course, Brecht's preferred term designating a play's plot as it is retold on stage from a specific point of view [...] A fable was always to reveal the contradictions of a plot.'[15] (I will retain the German *Fabel* to avoid confusion with the English 'fable'.) The centrality of a play's *Fabel* is again connected to Brecht's interest in Marxism. Marx, in his sixth thesis on Feuerbach, understood the individual to be 'the ensemble of social relations'.[16] As such, the individual is formed and informed by the contradictions of its given society at a given time. In order to understand more about a society, the theatre can start thinking about the social forces that exert an influence on the individual, and it does this by developing a scene's *Fabel*. Thus, the figures on stage can illuminate wider social contradictions through the way the actors are arranged on stage and how they behave towards each other. Friendly words can be spoken in antagonistic onstage formations; social interests, such as the protection of private property, can be identified while the lines themselves may contradict their social meaning. In short, the dramatization of contradiction can take place on both an individual level and the broader social one by playing out the scenes' *Fabel*.

Brecht's early career as a director was then drastically interrupted by the rise of the Nazis. His access to theatres was severely curtailed as he lived the uncertain life of an exile in various European countries and the United States until his return to Germany in 1948. However, he used his exile to write plays and poems, and to develop a range of theoretical positions that would further inform his directing.

Brief excursus: Theory and practice – a not-so-fraught relationship

Brecht is often arraigned for producing elaborate theories that had no place in the rehearsal room. As Margaret Eddershaw notes: 'Brecht's lack of interest in promoting or referring to his own theoretical ideas in rehearsal and the company's concern with the telling of the story are recurring themes in the comments on Brecht's work from Ensemble actors.'[17] This observation, however, requires qualification. As Meg Mumford notes:

Archive documentation testifies that under Brecht's leadership rehearsals at the Berliner Ensemble were heavily indebted to the concept of *Gestus*. Contrary to statements that Brecht rarely mentioned his theories and related terminology during rehearsal, 67 quotations in rehearsal notes amply demonstrate that he often used the term *Gestus* [...] Moreover, his co-workers' frequent recourse to the term suggests that, within the Berliner Ensemble, gestic acting was a familiar and popular approach to performance.[18]

Similarly, my own readings of rehearsal documentation at the Berliner Ensemble have shown occasional use of the term *Verfremdung* (discussed below) both in rehearsal and by the note-taking assistants. Thus, while Brecht avoided theoretical discussion in rehearsal, the tenets of his ideas were not alien to either the actors or the creative team. Over time, practical approaches to Brecht's theoretical positions clearly emerged and developed.

In his book on Brecht the director, Fuegi notes in a bracketed introductory comment – for which he provides no supporting argument – that for Brecht, theory 'had a valuable place outside the theatre but almost none in the actual day-by-day staging practice'.[19] However, Fuegi's claim that theory did not play a role in Brecht's work as a director is based on a misunderstanding of the meaning of taking theoretical positions in rehearsals. Mumford points out the category error implicit in the separation of theory and practice: '"practice" is defined as the action of doing something, so theorizing – i.e. thinking or writing about ideas and principles of practice – is *a part of*, inseparable from, practice, and not *apart from*, in opposition to, it [emphasis in the original]'.[20] One can appreciate that theory and practice are two distinct entities, but acknowledge that they are also connected as related activities. Brecht's close collaborator and sometime mistress Ruth Berlau lists the words she most frequently heard Brecht use in rehearsal: 'show, try out, contradiction, dry, speak, *Fabel*, why?, why?, and again: why?'.[21] This short list combines imperatives to cool down delivery ('dry', 'speak') and questions of the actors' activation and interrogation of the text and events. Berlau's inclusion of the terms 'contradiction' and '*Fabel*' show that Brecht set down parameters linked to his Marxist worldview but sought input in terms of practice to answer the recurring question 'why?'. As a result, it is clear that Brecht was working from a theoretical position that saw the world and its inhabitants in terms of contradictions. His direction itself did not engage in theoretical debate with the actors but instilled sophisticated ideas as tenable and applicable practice. The philosophical underpinnings of Brecht's Marxist theatre are complex, and I have deliberately avoided terms like 'dialectics', 'antitheses' and 'sublation' in this chapter because they may well serve the analyst but can perhaps confuse the actors in the rehearsal room.[22] Brecht himself focused on the notion of contradiction with his actors, and this concept served his direction throughout his tenure at the BE.

A classic example of his sparing use of theoretical terminology in rehearsal, coupled with staged implementation of theoretical principles, is the treatment and embodiment of the term 'Verfremdung'. *Verfremdung* was once widely translated as 'alienation', but is nowadays left in the German original.[23] The process of 'making the familiar strange' sounds complex, yet consider this example from Brecht's play *Mutter Courage und ihre Kinder* (Mother Courage and her Children). At the end of Scene 6, Courage curses the war that has destroyed her family; at the beginning of Scene 7, she praises the same war that is generating wealth for her. The character has been made strange by delivering two contradictory lines: there is nothing mysterious at work here, and the director does not have to explain difficult theoretical positions. Complexity does arise but in the minds of the spectators: they are the ones who have to account for the contradictory positions in the female lead. However, direction was often required to bring out contradictions to engender *Verfremdung*. Brecht directed his play *Der kaukasische Kreidekreis* (The Caucasian Chalk Circle) at the BE in 1954. One scene includes a sequence when an abandoned baby is discovered on the doorstep of a poor peasant couple. There is nothing explicit in the script to describe their response, yet Brecht wanted to establish the contradiction that would characterize their condition. As a result, a photograph from the production shows the two facing away from each other, the man with his head trained on his soup, the woman cradling the baby. There is no illusion of harmony and the stakes of taking on an extra mouth to feed are made clear: self-interest is in conflict with selfless concern. Neither option solves the problem: the baby will either die without support or it will drain the couple's ability to survive. Yet this image did not make itself: it was the result of directorial intervention. According to the documentation of the production, however, there was no mention of *Verfremdung* even though the effect of such an image is to make the familiar strange. That is, the articulation of a contradiction gives the audience a pause for thought. The couple do not simply pick up and nurture the child; the husband draws attention to his own needs and shows that charity always carries a cost.

Going beyond a comedy of character: *The Broken Jug*

Brecht co-founded his own theatre company, the Berliner Ensemble, in September 1949. He had chosen to remain in the eastern sector of a Berlin that would soon be formally divided. He sided with the Soviet Union, the socialist republic which best represented his political views and set about developing actors and directors as a way of making the company viable. In October 1949, the German Democratic Republic was declared by the ruling party, the Sozialistische Einheitspartei Deutschlands (Socialist Unity

Party – SED). Initially, Brecht had planned to instil a fairly eclectic approach to direction: while he shared directorial honours on two of the first season's three productions, he was happy to allow his old friend Berthold Viertel to direct Gorky's realist play, *Vassa Zheleznova* in 1950. By 1951, the potential plurality of directing approaches had effectively become the continual refinement and development of the Brechtian method. Brecht's assistants, usually under his watchful eye, were delegated directing duties, and the work itself found popular acclaim. However, in 1951, things had started to turn nasty. The SED had imposed artistic dogmatism on its theatres, supporting Stanislavsky's System [see **Volume 1**] as a way of portraying reality with photographic accuracy. Brecht's theatre, that used the theatre's own artificiality to investigate the processes behind human behaviour, was under attack and faced an uncertain future. As a result, Brecht invited guest directors to stage productions as a way of deflecting attention away from himself and his approaches to making theatre. Two actors, with no previous directing experience, but with reputations that were supposed to insulate them from official criticism, were contracted to direct two potentially safe plays: a classic German comedy and a propaganda play from the Soviet Union. Later, a director with apparently impeccable communist credentials began directing a tragedy set in the Second World War. However, as rehearsals progressed on each production, Brecht could not resist the temptation to observe and respond. What he saw did not please him and he proceeded to direct the shows himself, and so he undid his own cultural-political aims of distracting the SED by moulding the productions with his own methodologies. In the following sections, I will consider these projects, what Brecht considered to be their shortcomings and his strategies to combat them and make improvements.

Heinrich von Kleist (1777–1811) completed his play *Der zerbrochene Krug* (*The Broken Jug*) in 1806, and it stands today as one of the great German-language comedies. The play is set in a rural Dutch village and, as the title suggests, has at its centre a jug, owned by Marthe. The judge, Adam, is charged with discovering the identity of the person who broke it. With a nod to Sophocles' *Oedipus*, Kleist makes the judge the perpetrator, yet Adam, unlike Oedipus, is fully aware of this fact. It was his dalliance with Eve, Martha's daughter, that led to the accident, and when the truth is exposed, Adam makes good his escape. Like all comedies, *The Broken Jug* has a potentially dark side, such as when Adam seeks to send the innocent Rupprecht, with whom Eve is in love, to prison to hide his own crime, and this is the point at which the truth is finally revealed. In addition, the court is being inspected by Walter, and Adam is continually looking over his shoulder at his scribe, Licht, who covets Adam's position.

The play is multilayered. It is potentially a wonderful comedy of character, with a duplicitous judge, his scheming assistant, an officious inspector, an innocent girl and her mother who is a righteous plantiff, all of whom struggle to establish or conceal the truth. Kleist's use of language and the comedy of some of the arguments may suggest that the comedy is character-driven. In addition, the play has a more universal aspect: the names are often symbolic. There is the tempted fall of Adam and Eve; Walter is literally one who presides over matters in German ('walten' is the verb to rule), a small-scale God-like figure; and Licht is German for 'light'. Yet the comedy is also a gentle satire on the workings of the law. By its conclusion, the criminal has been discovered, yet he effectively evades justice and is implicitly pardoned for his initial weakness regarding Eve and his more serious attempts to frame and sentence a rival. Suffice it to say, the play offers several interpretations and consequently several approaches to direction.

As already noted, the director was drafted in for political reasons, to deflect attention from Brecht's staging ideas and to offer a different kind of theatre at the BE. Therese Giehse was a renowned actor who had gone into exile in Switzerland to escape the Nazis and played Mother Courage in the world premiere in Zurich. Her presence as a guest in the GDR was thus quite a coup for the socialist nation, and she had previously taken the title role in the BE's production of *Vassa Zheleznova*. However, she had never directed in her career, although she had recently appeared as Marthe in Salzburg, Austria, and thus knew the play well. Although she had initially intended to direct exclusively, she later decided to reprise the role of Marthe, and the plan was to have her alternate the part with another BE actor, Angelika Hurwicz. The director was thus under an amount of pressure not only to manage the comedy but also to play one of the major parts.

Not surprisingly, Giehse's direction was fairly conventional in that she was interested in understanding the characters as independent agents who served the overall aim of making the audience laugh. After three weeks' rehearsal in December 1951, Brecht started to take an interest and was making suggestions towards the end of that month before taking over direction early in January 1952 (see Figure 5.1). The story of the production process is fairly well preserved in the notes taken by Brecht's assistants. It should be acknowledged, however, that the record is not one of faithful description of what took place. Brecht insisted that his assistants took notes, or *Notate* as they were known, that not only described the most salient elements of a rehearsal but also reflected on them explicitly and sometimes made suggestions of their own. As such, the *Notate* were not merely a record but a more active contribution to the rehearsal process as a whole.

In an undated *Notat*, the anonymous assistant summarized the problems of Giehse's approach. I will deal with the criticisms in turn and consider how Brecht chose to address them. A central issue was that 'the figures were constructed psychologically, not socially'.[24] Before addressing this distinction, I would like to dwell on the term 'figures'. In German, it is customary to call a character a 'Figur', although the word 'Charakter' is also used. The contrast between 'figure' and 'character' in English is more illuminating because it helps to differentiate between two ways of considering the actors' conception of what they are doing on stage. A 'character' has characteristics,

FIGURE 5.1 *Brecht discusses* The Broken Jug *with Therese Giehse (Hainer Hill, Akademie der Künste, BBA-FA 13/004.17).*

and these may be used to define the way it behaves. A 'figure' is more elusive and unfixed, and it was this quality that appealed to Brecht. Marx's assertion that the individual was the 'ensemble of social relations' suggests that there is no necessary 'core' to human identity but that it is constructed out of potentially contradictory forces in perpetuity. In addition, we are children of our time, because society is always located at a particular point in history and, thus, adopts attitudes and behaviours typical of that time, although it should be noted that any time allows for a wide variety of positions and these change as time goes on. Thus, it is unlikely that most people consider slavery a good and justified idea in contemporary Britain, yet it was acceptable to those in power in earlier centuries and, indeed, slavers still exist in Britain, although their numbers are small.

The idea of a 'figure' rests on the mutability of human identity, that people change as their situation changes. This would seem self-evident: we tend to speak and behave differently towards our parents than towards our friends. Yet this simple example reveals something important about interpersonal relationships, too. If they are, at least in part, shaped and limited by the social situation, then by changing the social situation, people might change their behaviour. This dynamic interaction lies at the heart of Marxist thought; if people are flexible figures and not fixed characters, then attempts to alter social conditions will affect the ways people behave towards each other. If spectators note, for example, both that figures on stage treat each other badly *and* that this behaviour is related to prevailing social conditions, then they can start to imagine different conditions that may bring about different, more felicitous behaviours.

Consequently, Brecht was opposed to a psychological approach to building a figure. Psychology restricts the opportunities afforded to a figure because it allies them with qualities that are somehow intractable, as it were, given as biology or inheritance. Many of the great figures of world drama simply do not support the psychological position. Lady Macbeth, for example, is often considered a model of ruthless ambition and strength. Yet once she achieves her aims, she falls apart. Where have these qualities gone? The same could be said of Richard III, who, on finally becoming king, finds that the new situation makes him doubt his abilities, make poor decisions and eventually lose his realm. The shrewd tactician becomes a blunderer, unable to read the political situation. In both cases, it is impossible to ascribe characteristics to the figures; they become functions of their changing environments. Brecht thus proposed that it was not psychology that should inform the actors' work but, instead, an appreciation of the figures' social position *and* their social relationships.

The *Notat* mentioned above continues to note that Giehse had constructed her characters through 'backstories that aren't known [from the text] and were constructed individually'.[25] The individual character is the antithesis of the social figure because individuality, in this sense, treats the character as if it were cut off from society and social relations. An example given is the figure of Walter, the official sent to observe and examine the workings of Adam's court. While Walter is often interpreted as innately honourable, Brecht offered a different analysis: 'Walter knows full well where his class interests lie – we no longer have any need of traditional nobility in him.'[26] That is, Walter is not an inspector because he is a decent person and has an instinctive desire to see justice served. On the contrary, Walter is a member of a privileged middle class, a bourgeois in this interpretation, and wants to ensure that the law works because it supports his own property-owning privileges. Such an inversion, from a character-based decency to a class-based self-interest, informed the subsequent performance.

Brecht thus directed Walter to act with restraint: 'the figure of Walter gets more powerful the more privately and gentlemanly he speaks his lines; above all: not in verse'.[27] The instruction is predicated on a contradiction: Walter does not need to assert himself to attain a powerful position. The audience is thus provoked to ask why a soft-spoken and upright man can have such an effect. The answer is to be found in the social situation. Walter has power due to his middle-class birth and the office he has attained. His class confers benefits that do not need to be established through bluster or haughtiness. The *relationship* between Walter and the rest of the figures becomes an object of interest. It is also an example of *Verfremdung* insofar as the audience has to ask itself questions that, in a more psychologically constructed production, would have been superfluous because Walter would have a 'natural' superiority.

To remain with Walter just a little longer, it is worth noting the way in which his manner affects his relationships. Early in the play, before the trial has begun, he tells Adam of the suicide of a neighbouring village's corrupt judge. For Walter, this is 'routine', yet for Adam this is 'a tragedy, something terrible'.[28] The contrast Brecht sought to bring out between the two responses may tell the audience something about Adam's psychology, but it also says something about the rule of law and what happens when it is violated. Adam realizes early that Walter is a powerful figure because of the authority vested in him. As a result, he loses his autonomy, as can be seen in the following direction:

> Adam finds the tale of the judge terrifying. The inspector [Walter] finds it funny, so Adam can find it funny as well [...] From now on, Adam no longer has a life of his own, he is dependent on Walter. He finds nothing tragic or comic. He is at his mercy.[29]

Adam, understanding the power relation that is based on class, finds himself a shadow of his former self. The authority that he wielded in the local context of his courtroom is completely usurped, and he surrenders what appeared to be his personality as a result. Again, the audience is presented with a contradiction between two performances of Judge Adam and is asked to reconcile the erstwhile confidence and swagger of the judge with his craven behaviour.

The criticism of Giehse's psychological approach draws the conclusion that 'it was wrong to proceed from a settled conception of Kleist's figures, on the contrary we should explore the possibilities our actors have for portraying Kleist's figures realistically'.[30] There are two important ideas to be considered here: how Brecht related to his actors as director and the meaning of realism in his theatre.

When the *Notate* mention 'the possibilities our actors have', they make implicit reference to Brecht's rehearsal methods. Actor Regine Lutz, who played Eve in the production, was relatively inexperienced and was still cutting her teeth when working with Giehse. In a letter, she initially felt that she was working with a 'proper' director because Giehse was busy telling the cast what to do.[31] Lutz was used to a very different way of working, one based on granting the actors a greater say in how they represented their figures. As Manfred Wekwerth, at that time one of Brecht's directing assistants, stated: 'the actors are to make "offers". The director develops [the offers]

through correction. To repeat: the *Fabel* [the interpreted events of the play]
decides everything. The final understanding of a figure only comes about
through this interplay'.³² The actors were thus entrusted with constructing
their figures not through preparation the night before a rehearsal but in the
rehearsal room itself. They could only understand their figures by playing
them off the other figures. Actor Käthe Reichel, who was not involved in
The Broken Jug, but was a member of the BE, said that actors had to 'learn
to think "dramaturgically"' under Brecht.³³ That is, they were encouraged to
think through their roles, their social contexts and their relationships with
the other figures. They were to be activated by such rehearsal practice,³⁴ but
this was not just a democratic gesture on Brecht's part.

Brecht was also concerned with 'realism', itself a slippery term, especially
in the theatre. Realism tends to signify a performance style in which the
action on stage mirrors behaviours we encounter in our everyday lives.
This was not, however, the way Brecht understood the term. He drew on a
Marxist interpretation formulated by Friedrich Engels and reprinted in the
book that documents the first six productions at the BE: 'the representation
of typical people under typical circumstances'.³⁵ The emphasis on typicality
shifts realism away from the particularity and individuality of the more
conventional understanding of realism in the theatre to something more
general. Thus, realism is not derived from reproducing reality but from
asking questions of it. In a piece written in 1938, Brecht understood the
term as a complex of elements, which I have enumerated for clarity:

> *Realistic* means: [1] revealing the causal complex of society/[2] unmasking
> the ruling viewpoints of the rulers/[3] writing from the standpoint of
> the class that has in readiness the broadest solutions for the most
> urgent difficulties besetting human society/[4] emphasizing the factor of
> development/[5] concretely and making it possible to abstract.³⁶

In the first instance, realism is active (1–4): it is no longer a reflection of a
situation but an interrogation of it. The aim is to reveal the processes that lie
beneath the surface (1, 2 and 4) and to take up a perspective solely based on
class (3). Realism, because it is predicated on the collective rather than the
individual, also strives to take the particular and to make it general (5). In
Brecht's definition, realism is a philosophical rather than an aesthetic category,
and it was the actors' job, in concert with the director, to determine just what
was realistic by pooling their resources and making offers to each other in
rehearsal. Thus, Brecht's means, the activation of collective input, and his end,
to achieve realistic performances, were in harmony with each other.

Another criticism of Giehse's approach was that

> the play's *Fabel* was not discernible [...] In terms of the play's language,
> the director had done great work, but it did not make its presence felt
> because it wasn't an organic part of the story. A sequence of many often

excellent set pieces lacked a 'guiding thread' that linked them to each other and only then made them comprehensible.[37]

Again, this comment needs to be unpacked in order to understand the original director's perceived failings. The key term is *Fabel*, the interpretation of the play's plot based on its contradictions. Another *Notat* makes clear what kinds of work the *Fabel* in this production was supposed to be doing: 'written by Kleist as entertainment, as parable (Adam, Eve, the Fall of Man), not as critique [...] Amazing that there's still something to bring out today from our critical perspective'.[38] The *Fabel* understood the text not on Kleist's terms but on that of contemporary GDR society, as a critique of bourgeois justice and its mechanisms. Without such interpretive 'glue', this meaning of the play was submerged beneath the comic vignettes Giehse had worked on. By taking an approach like this, the new director, Brecht, was able to clarify many aspects of the action. Thus, Brecht noted with respect to Marthe that: 'her property is more important (bourgeois!) than her daughter's honour. She's not concerned with justice, but compensation'.[39] By clarifying objectives in social terms, Brecht was able to provide the 'guiding thread' and maintain interpretive coherence throughout the production. Such an approach differentiates itself from Giehse's, which was allied far more closely to Kleist's 'entertainment': she was more concerned with perfecting the comic moments, even if they did not make sense when taken together.

Making sense was a concern for Brecht because he believed that it was the theatre's job to demystify the workings of society. The clarity noted in his production of *Edward II* in 1924 was thus later applied to social relationships in a bid to set out the interplay between individual and society. In his quest, all aspects of the text were open to critique. The play's status as a comedy was called into question in the name of displaying 'realistic behaviour': 'yes, the play is a comedy and so it's justified to play short sequences comically. The lines are not decisive, but the behaviour'.[40] The acknowledgement of comic moments in the play is qualified by the imperative of the *Fabel*: to expose the contradictions of bourgeois justice and the behaviours they engender in the courtroom. As it happened, comedy *was* established but reconfigured because it rested on the contradictions of the class society portrayed on stage. Elsewhere, a somewhat cavalier attitude to the text itself was also evident: 'fundamental position established by Brecht: we should show no undue reverence to Kleist's language [...] Whatever appears to weigh things down or isn't understood can go. We're not making theatre for professors'.[41] Again, the comedy that originally resided in Kleist's turns of phrase deferred to the comic social relations that arose from the new interpretation.

Giehse was most offended that Brecht had taken over 'her' direction,[42] yet she retained the directing credit and was perhaps pleased with the reviews for the production, which premiered on 23 January 1952. The overwhelming critical response in the GDR was that it had radically reinterpreted a classic text without doing damage to the classic text.[43] The response registered how

Brecht's approach could take dramatic material, consider it from a different standpoint from which it was originally conceived, and stage it in such a way that a new socially contextualized reading could emerge. Brecht had developed a methodology that started with the *Fabel* and allowed its contradictions to pervade the performed relationships and behaviours on stage.

Tidying up the propaganda: *The Kremlin Chimes*

The decision to stage what was essentially a propaganda play in the same season as *The Broken Jug* was, to all appearances, an attempt to placate the GDR's increasingly hostile ruling party, the SED. *The Kremlin Chimes* by Nikolai Pogodin gives a fictionalized account of how Lenin electrified the Soviet Union and thus dragged it into the twentieth century. The landmark achievement is represented by the electrification of the Kremlin's chimes as they play the anthem of socialism, the Internationale, at the play's climax. The choice of guest director also seems to have been designed to win approval. Ernst Busch was a committed communist who had fought in an International Brigade in the Spanish Civil War and was imprisoned by the Nazis in the Second World War. He was both an actor and a singer, whose renditions of political songs were immensely popular at the time (and remain popular with the German left today). In short, his political credentials were beyond reproach.[44] It would seem, then, that the production could effectively 'direct itself' and achieve the desired aim of presenting the party with a celebratory show.

The rather thin documentation of this production tells a different story, and I discuss it to cast light on Brecht's techniques. Just like Therese Giehse, Ernst Busch had no directorial experience and consequently fell into similar traps of conventional theatre-making, that is, to ignore social context and to present characters rather than figures. It is clear from the few extant papers that Brecht could not tolerate work that did not conform to his artistic and political standards. The problem for Busch was that the action appeared to do his work for him, and he was concerned far more with providing atmosphere than engaging with content.

The first scene, for example, is set in a black market. Busch had filled it with extras and a flurry of activity. A critical comment registered: 'the black market feels like a legitimate market'.[45] Brecht intervened by reducing the actors on stage by two thirds and having two events at most taking place at any one time. The scene came alive 'through clarity and not quantity'.[46] Here, one notes the difference between Brechtian realism, discussed above, and theatre's more usual understanding of the term as a reproduction of everyday life: a black market may well be alive with activity, yet in order to show that Brecht focused on typical details that set out the workings of the market without overwhelming the audience with naturalistic reproduction (see Figure 5.2).

FIGURE 5.2 *The black market in* The Kremlin Chimes *(Photographer not known. Akademie der Künste, BBA BE-FA 044 Bogen 005/017).*

As may be expected, the revision of the production proceeded from the establishment of the *Fabel*, which was not to glorify Lenin and the Soviet Union as an end in itself, but to show the processes that led to the successes and then to imply glory. The interpretation of the play's story ran along the following lines: the first act established the energy of the Bolsheviks in the behaviour of its soldiers, peasants and workers. Lenin was thus inspired to electrify the new republic. The second act showed how Lenin tried to realize his plans and how he found himself in conflict with the remnants of Russian bourgeois society. The third act offered a vista onto the future through the construction of a socialist society.[47] Contradictions, with which a director could work, are visible in the first two acts. There is a tension between the nascent energy of the new republic and the ability to harness that energy. By the second, this energy is in conflict with the old order and seeks to win it over to the revolutionary cause.

With the grand scheme in place, Brecht proceeded to home in on the details of the relationships on stage. The idea of a 'detail' is connected to Brecht's understanding of semiotic synecdoche in the theatre: 'the *distinguishing features* [*Merkmale*] stand as realistic parts to the realistic whole [emphasis in the original]'.[48] The German word 'Merkmal' contains a particle from the verb 'merken', 'to notice' – and so the details were not in some way minor or accidental, but significant and designed to catch the spectator's eye. An example from the third scene of the first act shows how a peasant's son responds when he bumps into Lenin. In Busch's version the man 'greeted Lenin with obsequious theatrical delight'.[49] This was the kind of congratulatory kitsch Brecht could not suffer. Instead, he directed the encounter in a manner steeped in his understanding of the play's realism. The man was taken by surprise by the chance meeting with the great man and responded with military stiffness because he had just been demobilized from the army. The attention to social and historical context was a way of anchoring the action and relationships in the reality of the situation. Thus, Brecht sought to construct the production from a chain of realistic details that could carry the propaganda piece and lend it social depth and interest.

Brecht's theatre was also driven by contradictions, and by the need to bring them out and display them. Erasing these meant that political content was lost or passed over. For example, when two young people were chatting, it was noted that the scene was 'too much lovey-dovey talk between equals' whereas they were actually of a different class and that that had to be shown in performance.[50] The two examples may appear trivial, but Brecht considered them vital tools for pointing to the ways that a specific society pervades human interaction. This is an example of picking out the politics immanent in the most mundane of events on stage. Brecht insisted that political details should emerge and not be ignored in order to demonstrate a relationship between individual and society.

As this brief discussion suggests, Brecht was 'polishing a turd', in common parlance. The play was weak, its meaning clear and its function obvious. Yet he attempted to lend it depth by bringing out contradictions, founded in the *Fabel* and the realistic details present in the text's situations. One reviewer of the production, which premiered on 28 March 1952, noted how carefully the tempo and the dialogues were treated, something 'that makes [...] Ernst Busch one of our most important directors'.[51] Little did he know that he was actually praising Brecht.

Resisting humanist tragedy: *Battle in Winter*

The final example of Brecht's remedial direction came in 1954, once the BE had become an internationally renowned theatre company after triumph at the Théâtre des Nations festival in Paris that summer. That is, the BE was now out of the political crisis that had led to the appointment of Giehse and Busch to directorial positions to which they were unsuited. Brecht's decision to invite the Czech director Emil František Burian to stage a play with the company, thus, had very different motives. Brecht had seen a production of Johannes R. Becher's *Winterschlacht* (Battle in Winter) in Leipzig in early 1954 and believed that his company could offer a far better production.[52] The choice of Burian was based on his pedigree and experience: he was a convinced communist and had successfully staged Becher's play in Prague in 1952. Indeed Brecht wrote to the director prior to his arrival at the BE noting that he believed his actors could learn a great deal from Burian.[53]

However, Burian's methods differed greatly from Brecht's, and it is this contrast that will form the basis of the final case study.

The play is set during the Battle of Moscow (1941–2) and follows the young German soldier Johannes Hörder who opens the play with an heroic deed for which he is awarded the Knight's Cross, only to discover the horror of the Nazi *Wehrmacht* when he is ordered to kill Soviet partisans and instead shoots himself. The play is set in two locations: the Eastern Front and Germany, where Hörder's father is a Nazi judge and where his brother is executed for his anti-Nazi resistance. Becher described the play in a preface 'as a modern-day "Hamlet tragedy"'.[54] Becher's description was problematic for a director like Brecht for two reasons. The genre of tragedy sat awkwardly with Brecht as a Marxist, for reasons set out in a dialogue from *Buying Brass*:

> Philosopher The causes of a great many tragedies are outside the control of those suffer them, or so it seems.
> Dramaturge So it seems?
> Philosopher Of course it only seems so. That which is human cannot be outside of humanity's control and the causes of these tragedies are human ones.[55]

Brecht registers a profound suspicion of tragedy as something to which a play's characters are subject. His scepticism is founded in the view he expressed in the political meditations of his unpublished book, *Me-ti*: 'the fate of man is man'.[56] The comment locates human activity in the material world, not in anything supernatural, metaphysical or mystical. Thus, it effectively criticizes tragedy as an entity that is assumed to exist beyond human beings and invites them to deal with problems that only appear insurmountable.

In a note on *Battle in Winter*, Brecht wrote that 'the tragedy is a bourgeois tragedy'.[57] That is, what appears to be tragic is brought about by a class-based politics and its attendant opinions and behaviours. What is really at stake is the struggle between the classes, as represented by the working-class characters who persuade a middle-class German, Hörder, to change sides. Becher's reference to Hamlet adds a further dimension to the problem in that Hamlet was often seen as a reactive figure, unable to deal with and overwhelmed by the circumstances he found himself in. Brecht rejected this interpretation in favour of a more materialist one. He considered both Hamlet and Claudius representatives of a new, modern approach to the world, as opposed to the feudal view taken by Hamlet's father. Hamlet's failure to pursue a more reasoned approach to the problems of the day lead to a 'relapse'[58] into the old ways of revenge and murder; he is unable to emancipate himself from an older mindset that is still present.

Brecht's critique of a 'Hamlet tragedy' is rooted in two Marxist principles: materialism and historicization. Materialism states that there is no reality beyond matter. That is, there are no supernatural forces that act on people. It does not discount supernatural beliefs, such as religion, but traces them back to material need, in this case, the need to explain apparent mysteries or provide solace to human suffering. Materialism seeks to trace causes for human action in what is present in terms of human society and activity. Historicization asserts that human problems are specific to humans' place in history. Thus, the problems of a Renaissance prince of Denmark are not the same as those of a soldier in the Nazi *Wehrmacht* because the historical conditions are profoundly different. Historicization seeks to identify the historical factors that influence human thought, action and behaviour in order to contrast them with the audience's experience of the present. The cleavage between the two should make the audience aware that differences in social context can produce differences in human beings and their actions.

One might assume that Burian, himself a committed communist, would have acknowledged these Marxist principles when approaching *Battle in Winter*, but this was not the case. The notes taken record an altogether more conventional approach to staging the play. He recommended that the actors delve deep into their characters in order to understand them, and he directed one actor not to follow his directions regarding her position on stage but to 'submit herself to the text because that alone will tell her where she should go'.[59] In short, he was prepared to understand human behaviour on stage as something that did not need to be historically contextualized or made clear to an audience. Brecht's predilection for clear stage positions that set out relationships between figures and their contradictions was replaced by movements based on the actors' interpretations of their characters. In addition, Burian was happy to impute qualities to the characters. A Russian prince, who works with the Nazis on their assault on Moscow, was described as having the 'Dostoevskian sentimentality of an émigré' when remembering his time working as a chauffeur in France.[60] In Brecht's production, one finds this note: 'the Prince has a stronger class consciousness than the German officers [...] Even if he's been a chauffeur in Paris, then precisely because of this. He's seen these revolutionaries up close, who won't be told anything and who are thus dangerous'.[61] In Brecht's production, the prince's characteristics were located concretely in his bitter experiences, and so his attitude was rooted in material reality.

Suffice it to say, Brecht was not pleased with what he found when he visited rehearsals. One of the actors reported that Brecht was incandescent with rage at the quality of the work, but then proceeded calmly to make adjustments scene by scene.[62] At a rehearsal on 1 December 1954, Brecht told Burian: 'What I didn't understand was changed. The audience can't understand what the actors don't understand [...] That wasn't the fault of the actors.'[63] Here it is clear that Brecht found the production offered no insights for the audience; it lacked clarity when it was needed most. Dramaturge Käthe Rülicke noted that the production was one of the most difficult for the BE because it confronted its German audience with their own failure to resist the Nazis.[64] Brecht thus believed that he had a moral and political duty to direct the play in such a way that set out the contradictions of the historical piece with clarity and precision. He set about re-directing the play, together with Manfred Wekwerth, and the production premiered on 12 January 1955. Burian's response has not been recorded in the documentation.

The starting point for the new interpretation of the play centred on Hörder. Brecht, alluding to Goethe's *Wilhelm Meisters Lehrjahre* (Wilhelm Meister's Apprenticeship), considered the play to be 'Johannes Hörders Lehrjahr',[65] in that the production was to set out the processes that bring him to understand his place in the *Wehrmacht* and his final act of resistance that ends in his death. Brecht understood the *Fabel* of the play as a whole as: 'at the beginning of the play, Hörder is blind; as he starts to see, his eyes are violently closed'.[66] In both descriptions, Hörder has limited agency and finds himself in a series of situations that constrict his appreciation of what is really happening. In order to show that Hörder was subject to forces beyond his control, the actor had to shift from playing a character to playing a figure. A rehearsal note explicates the distinction by contrasting two different approaches. First, Ekkehard Schall played Hörder as an unsympathetic character because he was a Nazi soldier. In the second attempt, 'Schall played a likeable young man who, however, talks and acts like a Nazi. It is clear that a young man has been turned into a Nazi [...] The social insight is greater.'[67] The comment shows how a Brechtian actor can show two contradictory facets in order to problematize a sense that a figure is acting autonomously.

Brecht offered advice to Schall, who was developing his craft as an actor in this production. In a letter Schall noted that he had struggled to 'hit the right tone' in his characterization. Brecht countered:

> You should really not try to fix a particular tone, but rather the behaviour of the figure to be played, independent from (if also occasionally connected to) the tone of a given scene. And the most important thing is your behaviour towards this figure, which determines your figure's behaviour.[68]

It is worth dwelling on these words because they sketch some important Brechtian directing principles. First, the idea of seeking to find the 'right tone' is a mistake because tone changes as situations change. Yet Brecht also objects to the word 'tone', preferring more precise instances of 'behaviour'. Tone is perhaps a little too concerned with character as a generalized entity, whereas behaviour encompasses different specific deliveries and physical bearing. Behaviour is set against the tone of a scene, so that contradiction can emerge: thus a celebratory scene might in fact evince anger or frustration in a figure. Second, Brecht wants the actor to think carefully about his relationship to Hörder, not, as in Stanislavskian practice, to transform himself to become a character. The actor has to develop a fluid relationship in order to show aspects of a figure that he might find strange, questionable or with which he might agree. The actor thus has to negotiate both the scene and the figure in order to 'show the join' between actor and figure, and allow the audience to see that join between the actor's and the figure's behaviours.

Of course, the context in which Hörder found himself also needed to be presented, as Brecht noted:

> this colossal chain of command with its particular customs, military ranks and traditions has to be right not only because the majority of our audience are familiar with it, but all the more so because our hero is stuck in its mechanisms.[69]

Great efforts were thus expended to offer a picture of the *Wehrmacht* as a machine that was regulated along class lines. In one scene, for example, the officers were asked to behave differently from the soldiers when drunk. Their sense of Prussian discipline meant that they got stiffer the more they drank and fell over stiffly, too.[70] The edifice of the army became a metaphor for the class society of which Hörder and the rest of the cast were members. Brecht's aim, as always, was to suggest that if that edifice was changed, the barbaric behaviour would change as well.

Brecht applied the same principle of opening up a character so that it could become a figure to the working-class actor, who played a *Wehrmacht* major's wife. She complained that she had been miscast, but Brecht told her that she was all the better suited to playing such a role. He concluded: 'the manners and customs of high society have to be shown when they're being exposed'.[71] By this he meant that by showing and not hiding her roots, she was able to shed light on the ways in which a particular class operated by pointing to its peculiarities and, through this, making them strange. Performing the rituals of any particular social group was important in Brecht's theatre because it linked individuals to a specific set of behaviours that exist beyond them. Again, Brecht was keen to emphasize the connection between human behaviour and social context. By doing this, he could point to the values of each specific class and invite the audience to ask why different classes behaved in different ways.

An example of this emphasis can be seen in the scene when Maria Hörder, Johannes's mother, shoots her husband dead for having their other son executed for opposing the Nazis. Brecht observed that Becher's style employed 'great bourgeois pathos and the iambic verse of Lessing and Schiller', and believed that his own stagecraft could effect a critique of 'bourgeois heroism that can only appear in the form of kitsch this epoch'.[72] The task of the direction was to ironize the activity of the middle-class figure in order to show that her apparently noble decisions to resist the Nazis were too little and too late. This action was implicitly contrasted with her son's transformation from war hero to enemy of the state, a process that was galvanized by the agitation of proletarian soldiers.

However, the performances were not universally directed to show the join between actor and role. In some cases, the social foundation of the scenes was laid with more detailed mimetic representations of life at the time. The actors playing Nazi soldiers had originally delivered their lines ironically, so as to expose the distance between themselves and their roles. This method was, however, rejected: 'their critical relationship to the events of the play prevented them from portraying Fascist soldiers'.[73] By happy accident, a rehearsal that took place with real vehicles on stage meant that the actors had to bellow their lines and thus attained the desired tone for delivery. Here, then, it was necessary to give a concrete sense of how things were in order for Hörder to respond appropriately. This attention to social and historical detail was also present in the costume choices. Brecht insisted that the uniforms age over the course of the production in order to show the effects of time on the figures.[74]

The production of *Battle in Winter* is difficult to assess in the light of newspaper reviews. The play's praise of Soviet forces split critics, with those from the East praising the work and identifying the lack of pathos,[75] while those in the West predominantly attacked the play while acknowledging the BE's artistic rigour.[76] It is clear from the rehearsal documentation that Brecht actively disrupted the play's aspirations in order to focus on the individuals' actions and to frame them socially. In doing this, he offered the audience a view into the complex interactions between the classes on stage, making society and its dynamics the focus. This historicization of the play demonstrates how stagecraft can draw out material that is latent in the text and present it as a fresh interpretation to an audience.

Conclusion: The tasks of Brechtian direction

The three productions discussed above deal with very different genres of plays, but two principles can be detected that run through Brecht's directorial practice: the critique of the apparently natural and the articulation of contradiction. I will deal with them both in turn.

In character-based theatre, individuals can appear to be behaving 'naturally' or 'as people do'. Such interpretations ignore the fact that people think and behave in different ways at different times in different places. It would be absurd, for example, to consider that men held the same views on their relationships with women today as they did a century ago or that views on human rights are universal across the world. Opinions and behaviours are closely linked to one's social and historical position. What can appear outrageous today may have been completely acceptable in the past. Brecht was concerned with highlighting the connections between individual and society in order to account for actions and ideas that may strike a contemporary audience as odd or unusual by contextualizing the figures' deeds and speeches in their time and place. However, this did not only apply to plays set in the past. By historicizing the present, Brecht could achieve similar results, as was the case when he directed his own play *Herr Puntila und sein Mann Matti* (Mr Puntila and his Man Matti) in 1949. The production was praised for the clarity it brought to the class relations between a wealthy bourgeois landowner and his proletarian chauffeur even though the play was set in the present. (Meg Mumford considers the revival of the production in the following chapter.)

The problem with the 'natural' is that it suggests that human beings are prisoners of their own personalities and that change is not possible. This position is sometimes located in observations about human emotional response, that love or hate, say, are in some way universal, trans-historical and independent of the social. Much has been made of the role of emotion in Brecht's theatre with a repeated assumption that he tried to frustrate an emotional bond between the stage and auditorium for fear that spectators would not view the figures critically. Yet Brecht asserted that his theatre both produced and investigated emotions.[77] Furthermore, he insisted that emotion always had 'a quite particular class-based foundation [...] Emotions are never universally human and timeless'.[78] Emotions such as shame would appear to be most noticeably social (why would one be ashamed of introducing a partner of another colour to one's parents if their society were founded on equality?). Yet others also start to reveal social qualities on closer inspection. Might an emotion like jealousy be something found more frequently in those who earn or possess more because they define themselves through what they own? Or are there different types of compassion, such as the type that assuages the conscience and the type that brings about change? It is not that Brecht is saying that all emotions are in some way false, but that they are often falsely understood: emotions are not 'things in themselves' and thus need to be understood just as much as more rationally made decisions. The natural thus becomes a site of enquiry and not acceptance. And if the natural is produced by society, then changing society might change apparently 'natural' responses, too. Emotion, properly understood, is thus of great importance to Brecht as director.

The means through which a critique of society, emotion and nature is effected is the articulation of contradiction on the Brechtian stage. In Marxist thought, contradiction is the motor of change because, by definition, contradictions persist until they force change. However, before a contradiction is articulated, it has to be identified, and this is one of the main responsibilities of the Brechtian director. But, as noted above, the director does not work in isolation, and the actors in concert with the director need to uncover contradictions and work together to make them clear to an audience. It is worth emphasizing that making contradictions clear does not answer the question of how they are to be resolved. That is the audience's job and, in Brecht's theatre, that cannot be taken away from them.

As should be evident, Brecht's approaches to direction may be painstaking and involve great efforts from the director and the cast, but the focus is unwaveringly on the audience. The stage presents the results of an analysis that seeks out contradiction and clear ways of presenting it, yet contradictions are themselves a kind of question for the audience: how can these two opposing qualities exist at the same time and what can be done to eliminate them? If the stage were to offer answers, the audience would have to do less work and run the risk of becoming more passive. Conversely, by soliciting the question 'why?' from the audience, Brechtian theatre is able to transfer the dynamics of the stage world into the auditorium in the hope, at least, that the spectators might start to see their own lives outside the theatre in clearer terms and perhaps change them as well.

The emphasis on analysis and precision in rehearsal might, however, give a false impression of Brecht's theatre as overly serious or weighty, and devoid of enjoyment. This is a false opposition. Brecht criticized 'we Germans' as understanding learning as 'not a cheerful process of finding out, but having something shoved under our nose'.[79] In order to make learning pleasurable, performance had to have a lightness to it. He wrote in a published documentation of the BE's first six productions: '[the actor] has to organize his [sic] movements [...] in such a way that through rhythm and shaping [Plastik] they are fun for him. These are all sensuous [and not exclusively intellectual] tasks and training is physical. If an actor doesn't make things easy for himself, he doesn't make it easy for the audience either'.[80] It is also worth noting that Brecht considered understanding the ways contradictions riddled human relations and society as something that required a good sense of humour.[81] Rehearsal documentation often records Brecht's raucous laughter when a problem was creatively addressed, and so it would be wrong to consider Brecht the director and facilitator of rehearsals and productions as a grave, forbidding taskmaster. His aim was to offer audiences both enjoyable and insightful work with which they would willingly engage. The BE filled 71 per cent of its seating capacity in 1954 and 74 per cent in 1955; by 1960, the figures had risen to an enviable 98 per cent.[82] It would appear that the audience voted with its feet and very much accepted the theatre's invitation.

Brecht's great achievement as a theatre theorist and practitioner was to look afresh at dramatic material and to ask questions of it. His critical approach opened up often latent aspects that were passed over by conventionally realist directors and actors, whose conventions stressed 'coherence' and 'unity' of character and plot. His aim was to reveal connections between actions, opinions and social contexts. The method that he developed had wide-ranging manifestations in rehearsal, as discussed above, and aimed to provoke curiosity in the audience. Even today, Brecht's impetus is radical. In a society that still reverberates with Margaret Thatcher's dictum that 'there is no alternative', Brecht invites theatre-makers and spectators alike to look further and resist such rhetoric, safe in the knowledge that politics and reality itself are always capable of change.

6

Brecht's Perspectives, Then and Now: Class, Gender and the Social Stakes of Performance

Meg Mumford

Bertolt Brecht fully established himself as one of the world's most significant directors during his artistic leadership of the Berliner Ensemble (BE) in the German Democratic Republic (GDR). Co-founded by Brecht and his actor-wife Helene Weigel in September 1949, this company offered him a rare opportunity to work as a theatre-maker with a high level of resources at his disposal. Under Brecht and his general manager, a role ably carried out by Weigel, the company quickly began to deliver quality productions that were fêted both at home in Berlin and at international theatre festivals. Due to factors such as the company's rigorous attention to production documentation, as well as the training of numerous talented artists and the opening out of the rehearsal room to an array of keen observers, Brecht's staging practices from this period have been disseminated across the world.

As this chapter demonstrates, factors that profoundly shaped these practices include Brecht's responses to the development of a communist state in East Germany and his Marxist-inspired desire to forge an activist theatre that interrogated the dynamics and impacts of social systems. In order to illuminate some of the ways Brecht's most famous directorial work was shaped by his perspectives on social reality and theatre's relation to it, this chapter explores his approach to portraying class and sex–gender regimes during rehearsals at the BE when staging two of his own playtexts. To this end it discusses aspects of the stagings of the company's well-received opening production, the 1949 version of the comedy *Herr Puntila und sein Knecht Matti* (Mr Puntila and his Man Matti) that was co-directed by Brecht and Erich Engel, as well as the 1952 revision of the same production involving a collaboration between Brecht and the young director Egon Monk. Additional aspects of Brecht's interpretive and experimental approach, particularly his attention to the oppressive and interlinked nature of ruling-class and patriarchal ideology, are then addressed in a brief discussion of rehearsals for the historical drama *Leben des Galilei* (Life of Galileo). Premiered in 1957 under the baton of Erich Engel, this would be the final show that Brecht worked on in a directorial capacity before his death in 1956. The features of Brecht's directing that come to the fore in these three stagings include his approach to choreography, gesture and bearing, and contradiction. All of these elements draw attention to the changeable and interrelated nature of social structures that forcefully shape human behaviour. Many of these directorial approaches have ongoing relevance today. Some require a form of revision in keeping with Brecht's own practice of modifying the theatre so that it is better equipped to address current social reality.

The BE's opening production: A comedy about class conflict

Through its satirical treatment of Puntila – a Finnish owner of land, a sawmill and flourmill – as well as its depiction of the legal, religious and diplomatic figures Puntila invites to his rural estate, Brecht's comedy offers a firm indictment of capitalist societies and their ruling-class elite. In the case of the production that premiered on 12 November 1949, the play's political relevance was highlighted through a slight alteration to the Prologue so that parallels could be drawn between Puntila and those landowners – wealthy and/or Nazi – whose estates were divided and redistributed as part of the land reform movement in the Soviet-controlled area of Germany immediately after the Second World War. For the 1952 restaging, the play's topicality was further underscored through the inclusion in the programme of information about GDR land reform.[1] According to a 1951 commentary, later published in the company-authored documentation of the BE's first six productions called *Theaterarbeit* (Theatre Work, 1952), Brecht argued in the wake of the land reform and in a world that had witnessed more active proletarian fighters than the eponymous servant Matti, *Puntila* remained relevant. This was because: there was much to be learned not only from struggle but the history of struggle; the residue of vanquished epochs lived on for a long time in people's souls; victory on one battle field during the class struggle had to be exploited in order to ensure victory on another; and because life for the people freed from their oppressors could initially be as difficult as it was for pioneers because the emancipated have to exchange the system of the oppressor for a new system.[2]

Brecht's comedy was also likely to appeal to its patrons, the Socialist Unity Party of Germany (SED), on ideological grounds because it clearly demonstrated the exploitative nature of class-based society and finishes with an act of rebellion on the part of Puntila's chauffeur, Matti, an event that gently points forward to revolutionary change. Over a revue-style series of scenes, Puntila is depicted as repeatedly succumbing to his weakness for alcohol. When drunk he is a more humane figure who seeks to overcome his isolation through companionship with Matti, expresses compassion for his workers and shows insight into the shortcomings of his would-be son-in-law, the Attaché. He attempts to befriend Matti, engages himself to four women from Kurgela village and invites them to his daughter Eva's engagement party, and promises jobs to a number of farm labourers at a hiring fair. When sober, however, he is a calculating and mean preserver of his own interests, vowing to sack Matti without a reference, turning away the Kurgela women when they arrive at his estate and dismissing the men he wooed to his home with false promises of work. Throughout, Matti shows himself to be a hard-working, agile and clever employee who, despite the fatigue and frustration of dealing with the whims of both Puntila and Eva, nevertheless, remains servile. This is the case at least until the finale where Matti, angered by Puntila's treatment of a group of farm workers, turns subordination into its opposite. Upon drunk Puntila's command that Matti build Mount Hatelma in the library so that they can both enjoy the famous view, Matti rather too energetically obliges, destroying much furniture in the process. Shortly thereafter Matti leaves the estate, proclaiming that it is time for the servants to turn their backs on Puntila: 'They'll find a decent master pretty fast / Once they've become the masters here at last.'[3]

Both the conflict between the classes depicted in the play and the change it precipitates – in this case a marked development in Matti's class consciousness – embodies a Marxist materialist dialectical vision. That is, a dialectical belief in the transformative power of opposition within realms such as thinking, human history and nature, as well as a commitment to the view that contradiction is at the heart of (progressive) social development. Because one of the distinguishing features of Brecht's approach to directing at the BE was the way it embodied a Marxist-inspired way of interpreting behaviour, society and social change – particularly through a specific approach to staging contradiction – it is important to understand his materialist dialectical philosophy. According to this interpretive framework, key social contradictions include tensions between new *forces* of production (e.g. industrial machinery) and old *relations* of production (e.g. under the feudalist mode of production the lords owned the land, the means of production, and serfs were subordinate to the landowners and unable to become the wage earners industry requires). These tensions usher in struggles for power between old and emergent owners of production (e.g. the landowning aristocracy and the bourgeois owners of merchant, industrial and money capital). The ensuing revolutions increase a society's capacity to provide for all humans and sets the conditions for liberation from subsistence and class rule. Under capitalism, however, such liberation is hindered by the private ownership of the means of production by the bourgeoisie. It is the collision between that ruling class and the industrial proletariat that Marx believed would precipitate a further significant revolution and ultimately a shift to a classless and egalitarian communist society. However, unlike Marx, Brecht would have to come to grips with historical developments that did not fit easily with a narrative about the rise of the revolutionary proletariat, particularly the formation of communist East Germany. In 1948, Brecht described this political event as an 'imposed socialism', one that forced an unprepared proletariat, many of whom had supported the Nazis, to take power.[4]

The play's relation to the kind of dialectical thinking that inspired both Marx and Brecht is indicated in its German title which refers to Puntila as *Herr* ('master' and/or 'Mr') and to Matti as *Knecht* ('servant' or 'slave'). Here the title evokes a passage from philosopher G.W.F. Hegel's *Phenomenology of Spirit* (1807) that contains a famous discussion of lordship and bondage, often known as the master–slave (or, more accurately, master–servant) relation. One of Hegel's observations that seems to have had considerable impact both on the *Puntila* playtext and the BE productions is the idea that the master–servant relation is contradictory: the almighty lord is actually dependent on the subservience and work of the bondsman, and the latter's servile work is a source of his freedom. This idea resonates through Brecht's playwright-director depiction of the ruling elite as vulnerably dependent on the constant efforts of the servants, and by Matti's creative destruction of the library furniture.

Clarifying a class-conflict scenario through *Arrangement, Gestus* and realist stylization

The rehearsal notes for the 1949 production testify that from the very first scene onwards Brecht strove to create imagery that communicated the socially significant or typical nature of individual and group behaviour. During his time at the BE, Brecht used the terms 'significant' and 'typical' quite specifically to denote that which is decisive for the developmental processes of society and the progress of humankind.[5] In order to communicate the significant in a vivid manner Brecht worked with what was referred to by his directorial team and during rehearsal as *Arrangement* and *Gestus* (pl. *Gests*). This team encompassed co-directors, designers, and a crew of directorial and dramaturgical assistants. Their tasks included compiling the rehearsal notes that recorded and accounted for decisions, as well as the instructive Modelbook for each production which combined selected photographs and textual commentary. Both as a playwright and director Brecht sought collective working practices, actively inviting creative input and solutions from an array of collaborators. Together the notes and Modelbooks provide extensive records of how *Arrangement* and *Gests* were used to represent the *Fabel*. The latter refers to the interpretation of plot incidents according to a dialectical point of view. The *Fabel* was embodied through *Arrangement*, a dynamic form of blocking or choreography that includes groupings, gestures and movements.[6] *Gestus* refers to the artistic presentation of a thinking body's socially conditioned relation to time, space, materials and people.[7] When creating a *Gestus* the director and actor consider how gesture, movement, vocal delivery and body-shape can draw attention to both the individual's social position and to how his or her behaviour is moulded by particular social and historical forces rather than being a purely natural expression of a given 'innate' self. Building a *Gestus* involves devising a repertoire of contradictory *Haltungen* (sing. *Haltung*) or comportments. That is, ways of relating towards something or someone that combine mental attitude and physical bearing.[8]

Puntila's first scene depicts the end-point of a two-day drinking binge involving Puntila and Judge Frederik. They are socializing in the Parkhotel, Tavasthus, a country pub set in a non-defined time period which is described in one rehearsal note as 1920.[9] While the Judge has succumbed to slumber, Puntila continues to order aquavit from the waiter and to engage Matti in a conversation. According to a commentary in a collection of notes belonging to dramaturg Isot Kilian, master–servant relations were quickly foregrounded through the opening *Arrangement* involving Puntila and the waiter. For example, the waiter was depicted as exhausted, buckled over and frozen into a servant *Haltung* gone wrong, a serviette laxly hanging from a drooping hand rather than over a formally bent arm. Puntila tapped gently on a bottle with a ring on his finger and in a friendly manner asked to be told the day of the week. Jolted out of his position, the waiter imprudently insisted on the correctness of his answer rather than concurring with Puntila's thoughts on the matter. Through this behaviour the actor and directorial team demonstrated a contradiction – that the waiter's long hours of service had led to a waning of his capability to serve. This contradiction caused Puntila to take a long walk in a threatening manner towards the servant. Through a firm demand for a drink, Puntila reasserted his authority. His pleasure in this reassertion was indicated by a proud look at the diamond on his pinky finger. Mechanically the waiter moved to carry out the order, showing his dependency. But in the very next moment he created a contradictory *Haltung* by turning and glancing at Puntila with animosity, protest and disdain. Puntila, deftly sensing the attitude expressed behind his back, turned and met the disdain with a threatening gaze. When the waiter re-entered with the drink, now fully conscious again of his employment relationship, Puntila expressed his satisfaction that the social order had been preserved by introducing the waiter to his new friend, Matti.[10]

In the following sequence between landowner and chauffeur, Puntila was presented as seeking to overcome the loneliness and isolation that ensued from his love of power by pursuing Matti's friendship. Shortly before the premiere, co-director Erich Engel commented that the courting of Matti is Puntila's *Grundgestus* (fundamental *Gestus*) in this scene.[11] Puntila's attempt to position himself in a friendly relationship with Matti was to be met with some resistance. For example, when Puntila invited Matti to sit down at the large table, positioned centre stage, and then moved himself into the chair next to Matti, the chauffeur created a distance by turning his chair towards the front of the table and slightly away from his boss. Later, when Matti told his story about seeing ghosts on Mr Pappmann's estate, attributing the strange developments and departure of workers to the inadequate food, Puntila's own *Haltung* shifted from friendliness to class-based wariness. Throughout the narration Puntila was to be silent and carefully scrutinizing. He then behaved in a friendly manner, but he made it clear that this attitude would last only as long as Matti served his master well.[12] Puntila's amusing behaviour, nevertheless, momentarily won Matti over to a tentative receptiveness. That is, at least until Puntila landed Matti with the job of dragging the Judge out of the hotel, a task made more laborious by Puntila's frequent verbal interruptions. In order to complete the task, Matti ultimately had to push Puntila to one side.[13] The body-hauling was one of the many pieces of business during the staging that showed the connections between the master's pleasure and the servants' toil. One effect of the changeable nature of the *Haltungen* in this scene was the development of a sense of how social division strongly impedes humane behaviour and friendship.

For the first Berlin production, Brecht sharpened the presentation of the master and his entourage as parasitic phenomena through a form of realist stylization that involved heightening physiognomic deformations by means of masks. By 'masks' I mean here alterations achieved through make-up and prosthetics that change not only the face and head, but other parts of the body too. For example, Leonard Steckel as Puntila wore what Brecht has described as an unattractive bald head and used make-up to create dissipated and base characteristics.[14] During rehearsal Brecht suggested the addition of a few strands of hair in order to create an appearance like that of Ghengis Khan,[15] Emperor of the Mongol Empire and a notoriously brutal conqueror. One of the goals of this mask work was to overcome the tendency Brecht had witnessed during the Zurich production for the audience to receive the character as a naturally likeable person who had a few nasty impulses when sober, and to associate that negative behaviour merely with his being hung-over.[16] Another aim was to communicate how this ruler would like to get out of his own skin.[17] These new bodily features were designed to help

Steckel indicate that Puntila's charm when he is drunk is also dangerous, and to liken the landowner's social approaches to those of a crocodile.[18]

In the 1952 production, the casting of the short and slight Curt Bois as Puntila has been interpreted as an attempt to combat the impression that Puntila was a naturally vigorous and strong force.[19] According to the film of a 1953 *Puntila* performance at the BE made by Hans-Jürgen Syberberg,[20] Bois' Puntila also sported a type of deformation, in this case oversized buttocks which perhaps suggested, among other things, the result of much leisurely sitting around. According to Brecht's commentary on the first BE production, other members of the upper stratum – the Attaché, the Parson, the Parson's wife and the Lawyer – wore grotesque masks and behaved in a majestic and silly way.[21]

By contrast, Eva, Matti, the women from Kurgela and the estate servants did not wear masks and moved in an everyday manner.[22] In the case of Puntila's daughter, her lack of mask conveyed a sense that she had not yet fully mastered her social role or become fixed within it.[23] Rather than parasitic, the working classes were presented as productive. Reviewer Luft claims that life in the servants' rooms was depicted as natural or artless.[24] In the case of the Kurgela women – Bootleg Emma, the chemist's assistant, the milk-maid and the telephonist – a note on the 1948 Zurich production refers to a plan to enhance the breasts and hips of these characters in order to reinforce their natural sensuality and fecundity and to create a contrast to the sterility of the upper classes.[25] In his own commentary on the Zurich production, Brecht explains that the depiction of the women as attractive was designed to demonstrate that their expulsion from Puntila Hall was due solely to low social standing.[26] In the first Berlin production, the women's faces were given a rustic look that included an invitingly warm golden skin tone.[27]

In a 1951 response to the question of whether the work with masks had fallen into the realm of symbolism, Brecht argued that rather than striving for hidden meaning, his theatre instead took a position on reality and exaggerated significant traits to be found within it.[28] Brecht's comment here is in line with the type of socialist realist approach he was theorizing shortly before the first writing phase for *Puntila* (1940–1), an approach typified by an overt support for 'the class that has in readiness the broadest solutions for the most urgent difficulties besetting human society'.[29] Brecht's brand of realism was also committed to achieving a unity between naturalness and stylization. Naturalness for Brecht involved paying attention to socio-historically specific particulars and remaining connected to carefully observed and contradictory phenomenal reality, often through literal representation such as imitation. Stylization involved the artistic intensification of the 'natural' in order to demonstrate what is socially important in the *Fabel*.[30] This intensification was often achieved through forms of defamiliarizing non-literal representation such as, in the case of this play, selection, isolation and magnification.[31]

Brecht's version of realist stylization is evident in the set designs for the *Puntila* productions. Teo Otto's set for the Zurich production consisted of carefully selected and isolated individual elements, such as the slaughtered pig in the kitchen scene that hung on a scaffold made out of crimson wood beams and a metal bar.[32] The set piece, which reappeared in later productions, both provided a realist representation of the food prepared for the engagement party in the next scene and pointed to the excessively consumptive and destructive nature of capitalism's socially elite. Such items were set against a permanent wall made out of birch bark,[33] pointing to the beauty of the rural Finnish landscape and conjuring up the trees in the forest that Puntila owns and profits from thanks to his devouring sawmill. In the 1949 design for the Scene 2 entrance to Puntila manor, the relatively bare stage was framed by a backdrop that presented three wall-mounted narrow skulls, placed in a triangular formation[34] and pinned onto trophy hangings that resembled eagles in full flight. This deathly bird-of-prey imagery recalled the recreational pastimes of the landowning set and again suggested a capacity for destruction.

Realist stylization was evident in the approach to acting, as exemplified in the imperious and silly movements of Puntila's legal, diplomatic and religious entourage that imitated the confidence of socially privileged people from their milieu. These movements also comically made that behaviour strange, showing it as not the product of innate merits but social position. For Brecht, a realist theatre-maker needed to avoid the pitfalls of those forms of stylization where 'the representation of human behaviour becomes schematic and nonspecific',[35] or of a symbolist approach that showed humans as driven by eternal basic drives.[36] Both approaches fail to present the world as amenable to progressive intervention.

The realist stylization in the Berlin productions exposed the workings of capitalist industry and/or the master–servant dialectic and, therefore, ensured that the theatre took a positon on reality. However, the mask work and presentation of behaviour in particular also contributed to what David Barnett has described as a loading of 'the dialectic in favour of the oppressed underdog'.[37] Such an approach to representation displays how Brecht's approach to realism and contradiction was both guided *and* limited by his Marxist worldview. For example, the contrast between grotesque and deformed upper-class characters and more ordinary and attractive workers invited a reading of the socially elite, perhaps with the exception of Eva, as irreversibly rigid and sterile, locked into behaviour patterns determined by their privileged status. While such a reading is in line with Brecht's critique of non-productive and exploitative behaviour in class-based society, it conflicts with aspects of his Marxist-inspired vision that humans are distinguished by the way they can use their consciousness to change themselves, even the bourgeoisie.

A Marxist mapping of social inscription across thinking bodies

For Marx, the human species was distinguished by the way it could consciously create and control the means of subsistence and in so doing change itself and the natural and social worlds.[38] However, humans were also conditioned 'by the social form which exists before they do, which they do not create, which is the product of the preceding generation'.[39] The *Puntila* productions in Berlin certainly illuminated the human potential to change self and world – particularly through, for instance, the portrayal of Puntila's capacity for different behaviour when drunk, Eva's contradictory *Haltungen* (discussed below), and Matti's actions at the finale. However, they also (and perhaps more assiduously) devoted attention to showing how human behaviour was socially and economically determined. Brecht's capacity to illuminate how behaviour and inter-human relations embody both dialectical contradiction and social determination are among his most significant contributions to directing. In the following discussions, the analysis turns more fully to how Brecht guided actors to show that the physical appearance, actions and beliefs of characters and groups are shaped by material, historical and social circumstances as well as by class and gender ideology.

The portrayal of Eino Sillaka, the Attaché, vividly illuminates how Brecht and his team portrayed the way a body and its behaviour is inscribed by the nature of its work and socio-economic position. As a member of an ambassador's staff, an attaché must perfect the art of diplomatic conduct and be able to operate in the realm of supposedly refined society. For the first BE production, Eino performed hackneyed gestures associated with upper-class dress code such as the adjusting of a cravat and the polishing of fingernails.[40] During rehearsals for the second BE production, the directorial team and actor crafted striking comical postures that displayed his 'professional' skill set and its limited nature. For example, when making his first appearance at the opening of Scene 2, the Attaché was to stand at the head of the stairs in Puntila's entrance hall as if leaning lightly against a wall with a cup of tea in his left hand.[41] The incongruous stance is an example of what Brecht called *Verfremdungseffekte* (defamiliarization, distantiation or estrangement effects), a term often abbreviated in English as V-effects. Here 'effects' refers both to artistic devices and the desired (though not necessarily achieved) impact of the devices on the audience's perceptions. The aim of V-effects is to generate insights into concealed or overly familiar social phenomena by both making them visible and appear strange, thereby removing 'the stamp of familiarity that protects them against intervention today'.[42] Functioning as a V-effect, the Attache's stance made his behaviour as a diplomat appear striking, revealing that he had become caught in habitualized behaviour that was not always appropriate for his situation.

According to Syberberg's film footage, the team also made the Attaché's attempts to secure marriage into Puntila's family appear strange. They did so by unfolding them as amusingly strenuous in a manner that drew attention to the impact of his economic situation: Eino has a large number of debts to pay and marrying Eva is one solution to that problem. For example, in the episode where sober Puntila and the Attaché stroll outside with their cigars, discussing the Attaché's merits and progress as a diplomat as well as his ability to convince the Minister to attend the engagement party, Eino moved in perfect line with his would-be benefactor, stepping and making turns in synchrony (Figure 6.1). Later at the party, where drunk Puntila decides Eino's lack of humour is one of the many features that makes him an unworthy son-in-law who must now be physically removed from his house, the Attaché tries to ignore the physical attack and minimize the possibility of a social scandal. The Attaché's final exit is a comic routine that reveals a body ridiculously locked within polite rituals of farewell. A would-be master of social tactics, the Attaché bows before each of the three gentlemen present (Judge, Parson and Lawyer) and, as he bends, Puntila swiftly boots his backside from behind.[43] It is only at the third bow that Eino realizes it is better to exit than bend yet again.

Brecht also paid close attention to how individual members of the working class, including female household servants, were shaped by their role in the mode of production and social position. In his notes on the Zurich production, Brecht points admiringly to the efforts of the actor playing the

FIGURE 6.1 *Curt Bois as Puntila walking in synchrony with Wolf Kaiser as the Attaché, with Regine Lutz as Eva peeking out from the sauna, c. 1952 (Photographer not known. Akademie der Künste, BBA Theaterdoku 2260/016).*

parlourmaid Fina for making her a memorable figure by showing that she works late into the night on washing and the lugging of butter, and that she falls asleep exhausted at the engagement table.[44] During the 1949 rehearsals Fina's fundamental *Haltung* was described as compliant and very keen. This attitude was expressed in her tendency to take Puntila's perspective, such as when she looks reproachfully at Matti after Puntila has accused him of laziness. Her *Haltung* was also described as sluggish and her movement as slow with shuffling steps, as if she did not wish to expend much energy.[45] Overall her submissive comportment contained a contradictory tension between a desire to serve and a compromised ability to do so thanks to factors such as service-induced fatigue.

Across the *Puntila* productions in Zurich and Berlin, *groups* were also shown as bound to the well-rehearsed and ritualistic behaviour of their social class and as shaped by work and social relations. During a rehearsal in 1949 of the conversation that opens the engagement party scene, the Parson, Judge and Lawyer were asked to remain a tightly-knit trio and the actor playing the Judge was cautioned not to move away when telling his joke.[46] During rehearsals for the 1952 production, the actors playing these characters were also guided to demonstrate how well versed these men were in the art of speaking by playing the conversation as light and flowing.[47] The socially constructed rather than spontaneous nature of their behaviour was emphasized through the separation of actions usually performed simultaneously, such as the stirring of spoons in cups *before* rather than during speaking. This separation rather than simultaneity of actions, a recurrent feature in Brecht's stagings, directed the spectator's gaze from point to point and encouraged analytical scrutiny and comparison. During rehearsals for *Winterschlacht* (Battle in Winter) that premiered in 1955, Brecht reputedly described this approach as 'hardly understood in the theatre' and compared it to a new type of magician's trick: 'don't put everything under one hat; on the contrary, always pull out a new rabbit from the hat'.[48] Both the farm workers and household servants were also depicted as involved in socialized behaviour, born of class position, and through clear gestural pieces of business. In the company of their masters the farmhands were to take off their caps and to put them back on once the masters had departed.[49] In the case of a scene that was too long, Brecht refused to cut the cap-doffing routine. As Barnett puts it: 'He was not prepared to sacrifice the ritualized sign of class division for the sake of a quicker running time.'[50]

Showing gender identity as socially constructed and changeable

During the *Puntila* productions, the attention to, firstly, the way human behaviour consists of rehearsed acts and appearances that are performed for specific audiences, and, secondly, to how these performances are shaped by modes of work, economic status and training, tended to engender a sense that identity was a changeable construct made by humans rather than something given at birth. Moreover, Brecht and his collaborators paid attention to how behaviour and belief was shaped not only by class but also by gender division and enculturation. This focus can be related to Brecht's interest in Karl Marx and Friedrich Engels's commentary on the oppression of women and its link to the sexual division of labour, an interest expressed in both his theoretical and creative writings.[51] In *The Origin of the Family, Private Property and the State* (1884), Engels claims that women's role as bearers of children led to their being designated to household work while men were responsible for gathering, hunting and cultivation. He attributes the oppression of women to early economic changes, such as the development of profitable herding methods, which led to the usurpation of the household means of subsistence by the male-controlled sphere of production.[52] Early Marxist commentary on the so-called 'woman question' has been criticized for its anthropologically inaccurate description of the division of labour in the family and assumption that this division was 'natural'. It has also been criticized for its heterosexual bias and its contribution to a narrative of history that is exclusively oriented around production, the supposedly male sphere of activity.[53] However, for all its blind spots, the Marxist attention to women's oppression and emancipation did open the eyes of activists and artists such as Brecht to many of the operations of patriarchy as well as to the intersections between class and gender politics.

That the numerous versions of the *Puntila* playtext all attend to gender identity and inequality between the sexes can also be explained by the inputs of the Finnish author Hella Wuolijoki and Brecht's lover-collaborator Margarete Steffin. Brecht, his family and colleagues such as Steffin were hosted by Wuolijoki in the early 1940s while in exile in Finland, and it was during this period that Brecht became enthused by her talent for storytelling. Wuolijocki had established herself as both a successful businesswoman and a leading Finnish playwright. During their discussions, Wuolijocki introduced Brecht to her unpublished comedy *Sahanpuruprinsessa* (Sawdust Princess) that addressed concerns and themes of interest to him. These included ways to develop a new form of *Volksstück* ('folk play' or 'play of and for the people') and the impossibility of goodness and happiness in class-based societies. Wuolijocki's theatre and film scripts contained the seeds of many of the characters, plot events and tales that would figure in *Puntila*. While her comedy was not characterized by a thoroughgoing commitment to forging Marxist dialectical drama,[54] it did offer clear challenges to the status quo, particularly through its centralization of the landowner's daughter, Eva, and portrayal of this protagonist as an energetic modern woman who capably runs the estate and saw mill, especially when her father is on his drinking sprees.

Brecht suggested to his hostess that they adapt the comedy for an upcoming national competition in Finland, to which Wuolijocki agreed. To this end she and Steffin worked on a German translation and adaptation of the text, followed by an intensive revision process in which Brecht played the lead role. While Wuolijocki ultimately expressed great satisfaction with the competition piece, she was understandably shocked by Brecht's decision to present German-language publications of the text as written after sources by Wuolijoki rather than as a co-authored work.[55] Brecht and the society of his day were still on a steep learning curve when it came to appropriately recognizing the creative labour of women and co-workers. Brecht himself acknowledged a similar learning process when he observed in a journal entry from January 1941 that Steffin had criticized his interest in Confucius on the grounds that the philosopher's attitude towards 'the woman question' was reactionary.[56]

In the adaptation led by Brecht, Eva is by contrast far from a feminist heroine. As Alisa Solomon has argued, Brecht did not usually offer his audience the possibility of identification with model protagonists in a traditional dramatic show-and-tell manner but challenged social arrangements through epic process.[57] In contrast to the sawdust princess, Brecht's Eva has been brought up in a manner that leaves her ill-equipped to control her economic future through any means other than marriage. Brecht's interest in bringing attention to Eva's precarious situation as the daughter who could so easily be disinherited was embodied in his approval of the way Steckel played Puntila's response to Eva's removal of his alcohol: Puntila's outburst recalled the eruptions of Shakespeare's King Lear. Furthermore, in the *Theaterarbeit* outline of the play's *Fabel*, the Puntila of Scene 2 is likened to a new King Lear and described as casting out his unnatural child.[58] In the BE productions, Eva was presented in her opening scene, where she waits for the overdue return of her father, as the bored product of a convent girls' school education in Brussels. In one iteration of the scene, Eva, seated on the bottom step of the entry hall staircase, thumbed through an old novel and chewed on chocolates that she picked out with firm grip from a tall and glamorous candy box.[59] In all of her scenes, attention was devoted to the way Eva spends considerable time performing clichéd gender roles. Eva's manner was dominated by her attempt to *copy* from cliché phrases to the vamp-postures she had seen in the movies. When Eva's feminine behaviour was overtly shown to be (tenuously) acquired through rehearsal rather than innate and stable, the BE staging called attention to what Judith Butler has referred to as the 'performative' nature of gender identity. That is, the way 'the illusion of an abiding gendered self' is created through a '*stylized repetition of acts*' including 'bodily gestures, movements and enactments'[60] that over time congeal 'to produce the appearance of substance, of a natural sort of being'.[61]

Due to her youth and inexperience, Eva did not always fully realize her various roles, and this inadequate copying can be read in some senses as a subversive repetition of gender acts. The treatment of Eva's cigarette-smoking by actor Regine Lutz in the scene where Eva tries to impress Matti with her sophisticated sexuality is a case in point. Due to Lutz's difficulties as a non-smoker with the cigarette, the team working on the 1952 production experimented with having Eva enter only with the overly-long holder,[62] an approach that would have heightened the fumbling nature of her attempts to become a sophisticated lady of society. According to some production photos, however, it appears that the cigarette was ultimately included (Figure 6.2). Here and elsewhere, the experimentation with inadequate mimicry suggests Brecht's interest also in drawing attention to Eva's malleability and openness to change.

On some occasions her failure to perform a role was attributed to her privileged upbringing, most notably during the engagement party scene. Here, after the Attaché has been booted out, Puntila declares Eva will marry his chauffeur and, at Eva's behest, Matti gives her a mock test to see whether she can adequately perform the role of a chauffeur's wife. According to the

FIGURE 6.2 *Regine Lutz as Eva with Erwin Geschonneck as Matti, c. 1952 (Hainer Hill. Akademie der Künste, BBA Theaterdoku 2260/50).*

playtext used in the BE productions, Eva fails to competently respond to the scenarios that Matti puts before her, such as darning her husband's sock or appropriately receiving and serving him when he returns from a hard day's work. In response to her humorous display of how she would berate the messenger who interrupts Matti's peace-and-quiet at home in order to let him know Puntila must be fetched from the station, Matti playfully slaps Eva on her backside. This gesture makes Eva both speechless and furious.[63] During a rehearsal of this episode, Lutz suggested that she move away from the heartfelt girly tone she had hitherto emphasized in the party scene and cultivate more a sense of the landowner's daughter. This suggestion was greeted as a helpful way to build the contradictions that would clarify the reason for the reversal in her behaviour. Previously her turnabout seemed to be caused primarily by the bodily experience of shock.[64] The addition of the mistress-of-the-estate tone would help explain the turnabout as primarily caused by her assumptions about how a gentleman should treat a lady and her desire to reassert her social superiority.

In a number of scenes Eva's capacity for change was also conveyed by the tension between the vamp *Haltung* of the woman who seeks to overcome her boredom and social isolation by seducing Matti – an echo of Puntila's earlier wooing of Matti in the country pub – and the egotistical woman who asserts her status as ruling-class mistress of the estate. Rehearsal notes from 1949 suggest that while her egoism was presented as the product of her upbringing, her behaviour was treated as explicable rather than excusable.[65] As an intelligent being, she was capable of behaving otherwise. Her relative intelligence was made apparent in her opening scene with the Attaché where he bores her with a speech about his sensitivity to scandal. When playing the role, Regine Lutz suggested that she could depict Eva's boredom by reading a novel during their conversation, and punctuate her astonishment at his capacity for stupidity by putting down her book and staring at him in silent amazement at the end of his monologue.[66] Here a sense of Eva's potential for alternative behaviour was achieved through the application of what Brecht called performing the 'not-but': Lutz demonstrated that Eva was *not* to be seen simply as a pampered and bored young woman, *but* as a reasonably intelligent person capable of criticizing her own class. The capacity for this type of insight, as well as the contradictory nature of her comportments – inexperienced seductress vs domineering mistress-of-the-manor – created parallels with her drunk/sober father and also suggested the more open and vulnerable nature of her unstable identity due to her age and gender.

In a reflection on her own theatre work, Lutz criticizes Eva as the only unsuccessful female figure created by Brecht, describing her as an incomprehensible conglomeration of multiple individual bits recalling various characters. While Lutz struggled with what she regarded as the character's volatility and lack of a fundamental *Gestus*,[67] it could be argued that these very traits generated a type of gender critique that focused on the performative, in-process and precarious nature of Eva's identity.

Showing sex–gender relations as primarily determined by economic forces

In addition to illuminating gender formation and enculturation, as a director Brecht also addressed the nature of relations between the sexes. While this work usefully unfolded the way these relations are impacted by class division and economic circumstances, it was also limited by a tendency to position class struggle as a more important conflict than that between men and women. In the portrayal of Eva's relationship with Matti, focus was given to the impact of their respective locations in the ruling and working class. A case in point is the 1949 rehearsals of the dialogue between Eva and Matti where she asks him to help her prompt the Attaché to call off the marriage. Matti comes up with amusing suggestions as to how they can fool Eino into thinking Eva is on intimate terms with Matti, and she ultimately agrees to playact a scene of hanky-panky with the chauffeur in the bath hut. Brecht explained that in this scene the dialogue was underpinned by a socio-economic contradiction: while the 'haves' always want something from the 'have-nots', they do not themselves want to give anything in return. Thus, Eva was to be portrayed, like her father, as insisting on her pleasure but avoiding any consequences. In accordance with his servant function, Matti was to offer his capacity for ingenuity in an unquestioning way – this form of service was also what he was paid for. While he could have some fun as a young man unsettling Eva's self-assured behaviour, he was to avoid suggesting genuine erotic tensions but to project the attitude that he would even sleep with Eva, if that was an order.[68] Master–servant relations were similarly highlighted in the 1949 rehearsals for the kitchen scene. Eva gives Matti her film-star vamp performance, then invites him to an evening expedition to gather crayfish for the engagement party the following day, directs him to drive her to the station so she can flee to Brussels for a few weeks and finally declares she would prefer to marry him rather than Eino. Here Eva was to be presented as using the chauffeur for her amusement. It has been noted that Eva's appearance as a constellation of piquant eroticism recalls the behaviour of the eponymous protagonist in Strindberg's *Miss Julie*, while the kitchen encounter echoes the finale in that same play.[69] However, unlike the valet Jean, Matti was played as wary and wearily servile, repeatedly protective of his opportunity to read the newspaper on his night off.[70] In both BE stagings of cross-class flirtation, economic positions were prioritized as the dominant determinant of the female–male relationship and other determinants, such as patriarchy and sexual desire, were given less attention and weight.

In the case of Eva and Eino, the economic necessity of the marriage was depicted as emasculating for the Attaché during the 1951 rehearsals. In the scene where Eino and Puntila stroll outside with their cigarettes, eventually becoming aware of the 'scandalous' scene in the bath hut, the Attaché initially ignored the situation. However, when Puntila began chastising both parties, Eino was to appear caught in a desperate situation: should he continue to be tactful in order to ensure her dowry, or should he appear manly in order to appeal to Eva?[71] Ultimately, he pursues the tactful course of action, attempting twice to offer Eva the bouquet of white roses he has gathered for her. Eva was to look angrily at the Attaché and only snatch the bouquet on the second offering, concealing her expression from her father. Brecht observed that at this point her father, thanks to his lack of tact and propriety, was her only hope. For this reason Eva was to keep her awareness of guilt alive and play the concerned party, bowing her head in the roses.[72]

The depiction of relations between Matti and the parlourmaid Fina at the opening of the farm kitchen scene, immediately prior to Eva's seductive vamp entrance, offered a rare exposure of patriarchy as an exploitative system underpinned by its own master–servant dynamic. More interestingly, it showed that this dynamic was parallel to, but also partially independent of, class division. In the opening Matti is found reading the paper, enjoying being off-duty. Fina enters to let him know Eva wants a word and comments on his relationship with the mistress. Matti invites Fina to go with him to the river, and after she rejects the offer he presents himself as a more economically viable option than the schoolteacher she has shown interest in. Matti beckons Fina over and she sits on his knee, only for both of them to be interrupted by the entry of the Judge and Lawyer from the steam bath. This opening was treated by the production team as a counter-scene to the earlier bath-hut episode and as a genuine '*in flagrante*' moment.[73] When Erwin Geschonneck played Matti in the 1951 rehearsals, at the moment when Matti beckons Fina, without otherwise changing his face or *Haltung*, he lightly tapped his thigh twice. The tapping was to be performed with the *Gestus*: 'You won't be summoned twice.' Fina was to respond by walking across to him, stiffly and with small unintended steps, as if heading to meet her fate. Matti was described as a Casanova towards whom Fina was propelled by forces beyond her control.[74] Matti's treatment of the parlourmaid, and his later dialogue with Eva in the same scene, helped establish him as master of the kitchen domain and rooster of the henhouse. The tapping *Gestus* made the relationship strange, drawing attention to the master–servant dynamic underpinning Matti's patronizing chauvinism and Fina's automatic acquiescence, thus highlighting patriarchal rather than class-based exploitation. Arguably, the interaction also suggested that Fina was partly in the grip of some sort of heterosexual desire, thereby giving credit to a range of behavioural determinants in addition to economic forces. Having opened up the possibility that a gender-based master–servant dynamic could occur for reasons in addition to class division, the '*in flagrante*' episode ended with a firm return to a critique of the destructive impact of capitalist society on intimacy and pleasure. In a 1949 rehearsal, Geschonneck, was instructed to make Matti's displeasure at the intrusive entrance of the Judge and Lawyer very clear. As a form of explanation for this staging choice, Brecht quipped that capitalists repeatedly disturbed things. It was also noted that Matti himself regarded capitalism as destructive to all human relations.[75]

Brecht's final production: A history lesson about ruling-class and patriarchal authority

Brecht's directorial work for what became his final production, *Leben des Galilei*, was again characterized by an interpretive approach that focused on the destructive impact of a hierarchical class-based society. However, in accordance with this history play's centralization of a struggle between the groundbreaking Renaissance scientist, Galileo (1564–1642), and the ruling-class authority of feudal Italy, the Roman Catholic church, this staging gave particular attention to the impact of ideology. That is, ideology understood as both the ways of thinking associated with the members of an economic class and the ways of thinking that bolster the ruling class. Galileo's challenge to geocentrism, the theory which positions the earth as the centre of the universe around which all other celestial bodies revolve, is presented as bringing him into conflict with the clergy in all three versions Brecht wrote for the stage. For the church, Aristotle and Ptolemy's geocentric models were reconcilable with the Bible's teachings of the universe and their own organization of the social order. In the third version of the playtext, the one used for the BE production, Galileo's scientific discoveries were shown as threatening to the clergy not simply because they cast doubt on the church's validity as an authority but also because his contributions as an engineer and physicist had the potential to accelerate the pace of industrialization within Italy and thereby assist the rise of the bourgeoisie.[76]

According to Marxist historical materialism, the bourgeoisie would ultimately replace the aristocratic landowners and their clerical helpmates, whose rights to leadership and property were ideologically justified as sanctioned by God. In the BE version of the *Fabel*, considerable emphasis was given to Galileo's failure both to resist the authority of his day and to take up the offer of protection from a representative of the north Italian manufacturers, who proclaim their eagerness to support new scientific research. Galileo's decision to turn down that offer due to a naïve belief that reason would triumph over doctrinal powers was to be read as leaving science in the hands of an oppressive authority. It would also slow down the development of capitalist society, the next step in the liberation of humankind from competition for resources. As the following discussion will make clear, Brecht went on to sharpen the presentation of Galileo's failure as a socially progressive scientist by the way he depicted his failure as a parent to his daughter, Virginia. In so doing, Brecht sought to create a *Fabel* that would also denounce patriarchal behaviour as complicit with the ruling class and as a contributor to the retardation of social progress.

In a study of Brecht's dramaturgy, one of his directorial assistants, Käthe Rülicke-Weiler, observes that in *Life of Galileo* Brecht the playwright does not use V-effects, such as chorus, reports or direct address to the audience in order to comment on Galileo's behaviour and to give insight into social mechanisms. Rather, this commentary comes through the protagonist when he seeks to account for his actions and through the comments and attitudes of other characters.[77] What the rehearsal documentation for Brecht's work at the BE confirms is that he did in certain productions use the type of overt V-effects listed by Rülicke-Weiler that have become trademarks for his theatre. These include the half curtain that Brecht mentions in his notes for the Zurich *Puntila*,[78] which, through partially exposing what goes on 'behind the scenes', draws attention to how illusionist theatre conceals theatre's nature as collective and creative labour. However, the rehearsal documentation for Brecht's final productions makes apparent that the majority of the defamiliarizing commentary was achieved through creating socially encoded representations of human behaviour. As the following discussion clarifies, aesthetic techniques that Brecht frequently used to generate social commentary included strategies also featured in *Puntila*: responsiveness as a playwright-director to the social and political context of the audience; a dialectical foregrounding of contradiction and human changeability; and an epic showing of socially significant *Haltungen* in accordance with the *Fabel*.

Brecht's interest in forging a theatre practice that responded to changes in the social world through changes in its aesthetic strategies is embodied in the three versions of the playtext. Version one, written with assistance from Steffin in 1938 to 1939, during Brecht's exile in Denmark, emerged in a time of deep political crisis, one marked by the progress of Fascism in Spain and Germany, and the end of the Great Terror in the USSR (1936–8). Not surprisingly, given this reactionary context, the depiction of a struggle between a dissident scientist and a theocracy, where the scientist is forced to recant his theories, yet manages to secretly continue his work and find an avenue for its broader dissemination, has been interpreted as offering a model for intellectuals caught in the Third Reich.[79] However, in April 1944 Brecht expressed his dismay at the interpretation that Galileo recanted in order to carry on his work, and insisted instead that Galileo had 'let the people down' by removing science to 'the domain of experts, apolitical, isolated'.[80] By contrast, version two, an English-language text written in exile in California between 1944 and 1947 involving a fruitful collaboration with the actor Charles Laughton, stressed 'Galileo's criminal evolution after the recantation' and 'bourgeois science's fall from grace at the beginning of its rise – its surrender of scientific knowledge to the rulers'.[81] This change was instigated not only by the reception of the first version but, most significantly, by the dropping of the first atom bomb on Hiroshima on 6 August 1945.

Completed between 1953 and 1955 in a collaboration with Elisabeth Hauptmann and Benno Besson with input from Ruth Berlau,[82] the third version of *Galileo* addressed an audience caught in a tense Cold War situation. By this point both the USA and the USSR had developed the hydrogen bomb and the American physicist J. Robert Oppenheimer, one of the fathers of the first atomic bomb who went on to be an opponent of the H-bomb, was declared a security risk and fired from the University of Minnesota for communist associations. Brecht and his BE team responded to this situation through a further heightening of a critique of the scientist who serves the ruling class rather than the progress of humankind. As in the second version, this playtext pointed to the similarities between Galileo's predicament and that of the scientist in a capitalist system.[83] However, some Western reviewers of the BE production, betraying certain Cold-War sensibilities themselves, chose to read the feudal church as an analogue for the GDR's politburo.[84]

When rehearsals began in December 1955, Ernst Busch was cast in the role of Galileo. Just as he had done when working with Laughton, Brecht sought to develop the contradiction between the scientist who both assists and impedes social progress. Brecht's work with Busch and Regine Lutz on Galileo's scenes with his daughter illuminate not only one of the ways Brecht sought to build the negative side of the scientist's relation to progress, but also how he showed patriarchy as a contributing factor in Galileo's failure to bring science to the people (Figure 6.3). This demonstration is

FIGURE 6.3 *Brecht rehearsing with Ernst Bush as Galileo and Regine Lutz as Virginia, 1956 (Gerda Goedhart. Suhrkamp Verlag and Akademie der Künste, BBA-FA 12/010.01).*

nowhere clearer than in the rehearsals for Scene 3 which, like many of the rehearsals during Brecht's three-month period as director, were recorded on tape. These recordings offer a vivid picture of an experimental method that proceeded through a rigorous testing out of the most suitable comportments and gestures for the unfolding of the *Fabel*.

One of the episodes that came in for particular testing during Scene 3 involved the dialogue between father and daughter. This takes place shortly after Galileo, working deep into the night at the telescope with his friend Sagredo, has discovered the missing evidence for Copernican theories about the heliocentric nature of the universe. Galileo calls with excitement to his housekeeper, Frau Sarti, to fetch her son Andrea in order to share his discoveries with one of his favourite pupils. After she exits, Virginia enters, dressed for early morning mass. Following a brief dialogue about why both father and daughter are up so early, Virginia asks: 'Can I have a look?' Galileo replies: 'What for?' and when she does not know what to say, he comments: 'It's not a toy.'[85] He then moves on to a discussion of a likely move to Florence where Galileo hopes to secure the Grand Duke as his patron. Following the approach taken in the American productions, Brecht sought to use this brief scene to indicate how far Galileo 'might be blamed for Virginia's subsequent behaviour as a spy for the Inquisition. He does not take her interest in the telescope seriously and sends her off to matins'.[86]

According to various rehearsal notes and recordings, a number of approaches to performance were tested out. One note-taker draws attention to two contrasting approaches. In the first, a teenage Virginia was played as having a childlike interest in the telescope, an interest Galileo ignores due to his belief that his daughter is unintelligent. Instead of addressing her interest and looking into her eyes he talks over her to Sagredo, leaving her standing unnoticed. He then sends her away because he does not want to have her witness a letter to the Grand Duke that he himself regards as obsequious. The note-taker observes that in this version, Galileo does not take his daughter's human interest in him and his work activity seriously. This staging speaks against him. In the second version, Galileo finds her request unusual and checks to see whether it is genuine, looking the whole time into her eyes. He gives up when she can supply no answer. This is his last attempt to engage with her about his work. He will now focus instead on securing her dowry and marriage. Virginia leaves in a confused state, not having understood her father's behaviour. The note-taker concludes that this version confirms Virginia's lack of intelligence and that there is no point paying particular attention to her. This staging speaks for Galileo.[87]

The recordings for March 1956, the last month of rehearsals that Brecht was involved in, suggest that he was tending towards a dialectical synthesis of the aforementioned versions and one that stressed the patriarchal nature of Galileo's behaviour without losing a sense of his love of scientific enquiry and capacity to pass on his ideas. Lutz experimented with showing that her character was indeed interested, thanks to natural curiosity and that she was wrongly dismissed and sent off to church with the end result that the church turns her into her father's jailer. Virginia's joy at the prospect of attending court in Florence was to be overshadowed by this rejection. Virginia thanked her father politely, but suggested an awareness that her dad was fobbing her off with the offer of Florence and that she would prefer to look through the telescope. Busch simultaneously sought to show that Galileo's question to his daughter was genuine, but that the scientist's interest too quickly cools and moves to a dismissive attitude. Significantly, Brecht concluded that at this point Galileo fails to win a '*Mitarbeiterin*' (female co-worker).[88] By not allowing Virginia to access an important instrument of knowledge, he also contributes to the maintenance of astronomy as a preserve of an exclusive(ly male) few. When directing the scene, Brecht intimated that Galileo's exclusionary behaviour was also patriarchal. For example, he drew Lutz's attention to the contrast between the willingness to wake Andrea up and the dismissal of the daughter. He also directed Busch to play the action as a person who regards Virginia as superficial, a girl.[89]

According to a reflection on Busch's Galileo by Rülicke-Weiler, the actor found it difficult to respond to Virginia's interest in the telescope in the way Laughton had done: Busch would have preferred she had not shown an interest at all. Apparently, Lutz helped ease the situation by merely playing at being interested.[90] Whether Brecht fully approved this *Arrangement* is unclear, but his work during the January rehearsals on the father-daughter relationship in the final scene certainly shows a critical interpretation of Galileo as underestimating Virginia's intelligence and capacity to learn. In this scene, a sight-impaired Galileo is depicted living in seclusion with Virginia as both his housekeeper and a spy for the Inquisition, an institution within the Catholic church charged with combatting heresy. Brecht and Busch discussed how high Galileo now ranked the capacities of his daughter to comprehend his statements and actions. Brecht stated that while the scientist had held his daughter for unintelligent, her intelligence had greatly developed under the tutelage of her confessor.[91] While this comment could be read as pointing to Virginia's susceptibility to religious indoctrination, a reflection by Rülicke-Weiler on Busch's approach to the final scene suggests that Brecht wanted to foreground that Virginia had become a serious opponent for her father; that he had underestimated her intelligence; and that he had raised a spy rather than a colleague.[92]

The creation of a searing portrayal of the changes in Virginia's comportments across the course of the play, and of the antagonistic relationship between father and daughter in the concluding scene was highly significant. It demonstrated Brecht's interest in showing the way the thinking body was responsive rather than impervious to its social circumstances, and how that body and its interactions with others are inscribed by ideology and power structures. After the telescope incident, and the moment in which Galileo's heretical pursuit of science brings an end to her engagement to the landowner Ludovico, Virginia's *Haltung* in her next appearance was not only to suggest the passing of nearly a decade but also a stark contrast to the young fiancé. Faded and hollowed out as she waits with Galileo in the Medici palace to be admitted by the Grand Duke, she was also to sit rigidly and very straight, a type of sitting Brecht indicated would contribute to the character cracking or breaking down.[93] This posture fell away in the play's final scene where Virginia was presented as dominated by the *Gestus* of devotion to God and a lack of interest in the sensual world. Brecht developed this *Gestus* by helping Lutz to create a display of self-denial and puritanical repression. Unkemptness and dirtiness, corporeal laziness, sloppy consonants and a shuffling gait in flat-soled shoes, each step taken only for God, were combined with sullen moroseness and open contempt towards her father's sinful carnality and greed.[94] Although Brecht closely attended to Virginia's development of unattractive qualities in this scene, he also agreed with Lutz that it was important to build in moments that engendered sympathy for a woman whose life Galileo had ruined.[95] While Virginia could be played in this scene as accepting her new role of protector and companion with no regret or bitterness,[96] such a sentimental interpretation was a far cry from Brecht's realist approach.

Galileo's dictation to Virginia of his weekly letter to the archbishop in this scene was to be played as a cat-and-mouse game, with Lutz letting the audience know that her character was being tested and subjected to mockery. Brecht instructed Lutz to play Virginia as initially bearing the provocations with Christian mildness, such as when Galileo tries to avoid the letter-writing by making the claim that he does not feel well, and then moving to communicate all that she has suppressed.[97] In turn, the portrayal of Virginia was accompanied by experiments with playing Galileo as a childish old man controlled by his daughter, or as an intellectually strong father who is mean to his daughter. When asked about the pros and cons of these contradictory versions, Brecht replied that they were two layers of the same person. However, he declared his interest in the idea that Galileo's possession of his brainpower in this final scene made his wrongdoing even worse because it demonstrated he was capable of analysing it.[98] Overall the experimentation with the *Haltungen* of father and daughter both in the telescope and final scenes show how acquiescence to ruling-class power and ideology, including patriarchy, makes its own contribution to the curtailment of scientific enquiry and the perpetuation of an inhumane antagonistic society.

Brecht now

Brecht's directorial work at the BE was committed to helping forge what he hoped would become a creative, egalitarian and peaceful communist society. To this end he co-devised types of *Fabel* that sought to attune post-war audiences to the operations of problematic economic and political structures, and to their impact on thinking bodies, interpersonal relations and the material world. Brecht's *Fabel*, unfolded through vividly defamiliarizing

Arrangements and *Gests*, also demonstrated that these seemingly stable structures could be overturned. One of the main ways they did so was through presenting identity as historically specific, contradictory and performative, a mutable social construct rather than a given and fixed essence. Through the depiction of class-based oppositions and the treatment of characters as an unstable unity of contradictions, Brecht and his team also invited audiences to perceive, be astonished by and moved to resolve negative social behaviour and relations. In a late capitalist context where a utopian society no longer appears to be on the horizon, what can Brecht's work as a director offer to contemporary theatre-makers? Our historical moment is marked by the dissolution of institutionalized state communism, ubiquitous capitalism, ongoing social divisions, terrorism and warfare, intensified global warming and forced migration. The pervasiveness of these conditions often engender a sense that change is beyond our grasp. Yet, it could be argued that in such a context Brecht's capacity to find striking theatrical means to surprise his audience about the way we construct, are inscribed by, and resist destructive socio-economic systems continues to provide a provocative model for directors seeking to unveil decisive elements in material reality today.

Admittedly, there are aspects of the interpretive framework that guided Brecht's BE work that now require revision. These include the faith in the historical materialist metanarrative of proletarian revolution. The untenability of this faith informed Einar Schleef's staging of *Puntila* at the BE in 1996. Schleef challenged Brecht's loading of the master–servant dialectic in favour of Matti, the superior and oppressed underdog, through the portrayal of a group of Matti figures who dutifully served in a manner recalling Nazi obedience: '"Matti" was no longer Puntila's opponent, but traced a brutal masculine arc across class boundaries in which the worker was not imbued with an implicit immunity to his "class enemy", but could be canalised for violent action.'[99] Here the removal of the macho proletarian figure as the vehicle of resistance did not constitute an abandonment of the Brechtian concern with how 'the most wretched can still offer resistance', but a recalibration of the narrative of defiance.[100]

It is the very dialectical nature of Brecht's theatre techniques that somewhat ironically implies 'the redundancy of aspects of his theories in new contexts'.[101] In the final part of his career, Brecht acknowledged that his key 1948 treatise, the 'Short Organon for the Theatre', had been characterized by a 'possibly over-impatient and over-exclusive concern with the "principal side of the contradiction"'.[102] Brecht footnotes this comment with a reference to Mao Tse-Tung's idea that while the 'principal side' is the major determinant, as in the example of the opposition between economic foundation and superstructure, the dominant position is not to be regarded as a fixed state because each of the positions transform themselves in to each other.[103] Brecht's stage craft at the BE also displayed an over-exclusive emphasis on the principal side when, for example, it prioritized the demonstration of the socially determined nature of humans over their capacity to act as agents of change. The repeated portrayal of the Attaché as a mindless monochrome character, locked within the posture of the diplomat until he is conditioned by Puntila's boot to respond otherwise, is a case in point. And while Brecht's dialectical 'not-but' holds the potential to present the spectator with the type of palimpsestic 'rough sketches that indicate traces of other movements and features all around the fully worked-out character',[104] on the BE stage this rich evocation of fluid and complex life was often congealed into a tightly choreographed and legible grid of socially significant oppositions.[105] Brecht's lucid dialectical stagings, designed to facilitate the audience's capacity to judge, have been found wanting as a vehicle for responding to the complexity and epistemological uncertainty of contemporary reality.

In response to these perceived shortcomings, post-Brechtian directors have reached for new ways of working with components of a dialectic. These ways include: 'removing the reference system for decoding the signs onstage'; replacing denotative signs with imagery that arouses connotations and associations; and an emphasis on 'pointing to moments of social interest rather than on interpreting them'.[106] However, as Lara Stevens notes in her study of the adaptation of Brecht's aesthetics by recent playwrights, Brecht's emphasis on 'dialectics in theatre as the basis for a revolution in consciousness or sceptical thinking' remains potent.[107] In a context where capitalism is arguably more widespread, complex and interactive, and hence better equipped to conceal its nature and alternatives than hitherto, Brecht's project to make interconnections and mutually dependent processes in flux more comprehensible than they are in literally mimetic realism or everyday life, has a new urgency.

It could be argued that Brecht's emphasis on economic determination limited the capacity of his staging to deal with a crucial aspect of interconnectivity: the interaction of multiple determinants of human actions. The kitchen flirtation scene between Matti and Eva is one of numerous instances in which Brecht's *Fabel* prioritized economic position as the dominant determinant of a relationship with other possible determinants, such as psycho-sexual forces, being given short shrift. However, by contrast, the encounter between Matti and Fina opens up a broader spectrum of interdependent causal factors. At its best, Brecht's theatre is an excellent model for engagement with the interconnection of diverse social and material processes. Brecht's focus on economic class as the primary site of oppression is also an element in need of revision but one that proves readily adaptable to sites he left relatively unexplored such as race, sexuality and disability. In the increasingly globalized economy that has emerged since the early 1990s, where economic disparities deepen, but class tends to be underplayed, and Western post-feminists proclaim the achievement of gender equality while gender pay-gaps remain, Brecht's theatre work provides a timely reminder of how to apply complex seeing to our modes of production and reproduction. To this end he models for us 'the wit of contradictory circumstances' that fosters 'enjoyment of the liveliness of people, things and processes' and heightens both 'the art of living and the joy of living'.[108]

NOTES

Introduction to the Series

1   Simon Shepherd, *Direction* (Basingstoke: Palgrave Macmillan, 2012).

2   P.P. Howe, *The Repertory Theatre: A Record & a Criticism* (London: Martin Secker, 1910).

3   Alexander Dean, *Little Theatre Organization and Management: For Community, University and School* (New York: Appleton, 1926), 297–8.

4   Constance D'Arcy Mackay, *The Little Theatre in the United States* (New York: H. Holt, 1917).

5   William Lyon Phelps, *The Twentieth Century Theatre: Observations on the Contemporary English and American Stage* (New York: Macmillan, 1920); Hiram Kelly Moderwell, *Theatre of Today* (New York: Dodd, Mead & Co., 1914, 1923); Dean, *Little Theatre Organization and Management*.

Introduction to Volume 2

1   See Jonathan Pitches, *Vsevolod Meyerhold* (London: Routledge, 2003), 52.

2   Anthony Jackson, *Theatre, Education and the Making of Meanings. Art or Instrument?* (Manchester: Manchester University Press, 2007), 73.

3   See Bertolt Brecht, 'Kritik der *Poetik* des Aristoteles', in *Grosse kommentierte Berliner und Frankfurter Ausgabe*, vol. 22, ed. Werner Hecht, Jan Knopf, Werner Mittenzwei and Hans-Detlef Müller (Berlin and Frankfurt am Main: Aufbau and Suhrkamp, 1993), 171–2. The essay has not yet been translated into English.

4   See Meyerhold, 'The Reconstruction of the Theatre', in *Meyerhold on Theatre*, revised edition, ed. Edward Braun (London: Methuen, 1991), 253–74, here p. 267.

5   See Piscator, *The Political Theatre*, ed. Hugh Rorrison (London: Methuen, 1980), 16.

6   See Brecht, *Buying Brass*, in Brecht, *Brecht on Performance*, ed. Tom Kuhn, Steve Giles and Marc Silberman (London: Bloomsbury, 2014), 113–16.

7   Brecht, 'Stanislawski – Wachtangow – Meyerhold', in Brecht, *Grosse kommentierte Ausgabe*, 285–6, here p. 285. The translation is mine.

Chapter 1

1   Vsevolod Meyerhold, *Stat'i, Pis'ma, Rechi, Besed'i. 1891–1917*, ed. A.V. Fevral'ski (Moscow: Iskusstvo, 1968), 85. All translations from the Russian are our own unless otherwise stated.

2   Ibid., 74–7 and 88–92.

3   Simon Shepherd's *Direction* (Basingstoke: Palgrave Macmillan, 2012) presents a useful overview of how contested, complex and privileged the role of the director remains in contemporary performance practice.

4   See Peter Boenisch, *Directing Scenes and Senses: The thinking of regie* (Manchester: Manchester University Press, 2015) who eloquently argues that directing in the theatre appeared as early as 1771.

5   See Gerasimov in S.V. Vladimirov, Y.K. Gerasimov, N.V. Zaitsev, L.P. Klimova and M.N. Lyubimurov, *U Istokov Rezhissurui: Ocherki iz istorii russkoi rezhissurui kontsa XIX – nachala XX veka* (Leningrad: Leningradski Gosudarstvennuii Institut Teatra, Muzuiki i Kinematografii, 1976), 7, or J. Douglas Clayton, *Pierrot in Petrograd: Commedia dell'Arte/Balagan in Twentieth-Century Russian Theatre and Drama* (Montreal: McGill-Queen's University Press, 1993), 44.

6   Shepherd, *Direction*, 11.

7   See Bryan Brown, *A History of the Theatre Laboratory* (London: Routledge, 2018).

8   In the Autumn these courses were divided into two formal institutions which shortly thereafter were incorporated into the Russian State Institute for the Performing Arts.

9   The Russian plural would be *rezhisserui* but for ease of comprehension we have anglicized the term.

10 Laurence Senelick, *Historical Dictionary of Russian Theatre* (Lanham: Rowman & Littlefield, 2015), 111.

11 See Nikolai Volkov, *Meierkhol'd. Tom I (1874–1908)* (Moscow: Academia, 1929), 76–8.

12 The term 'emploi' is a character type dependent upon the actor's physical and vocal features as well as their mental capabilities and personal traits.

13 See Laurence Senelick, *Stanislavsky: A Life in Letters* (London: Routledge, 2014), 200.

14 Briusov, in Bert Cardullo and Robert Knopf, eds, *Theater of the Avant-Garde, 1890–1950: A Critical Anthology* (New Haven, CT: Yale University Press, 2001), 76.

15 See Michael Duane Johnson, 'On the Paths of the Soul: Stanisław Przybyszewski and the Russian Stage. The Cases of Vera Komissarzhevskaia and Vsevolod Meierkhol'd' (PhD Thesis, University of Kansas, 2008), 47 fn. 145.

16 Dassia N. Posner, *The Director's Prism: E. T. A. Hoffmann and the Russian Theatrical Avant-Garde* (Evanston, IL: Northwestern University Press, 2016), 2, emphasis added.

17 Meyerhold in Edward Braun, *Meyerhold: A Revolution in Theatre* (London: Methuen Drama, 1988), 18.

18 See Vsevolod Meyerhold, *Meyerhold on Theatre*, ed. Edward Braun (London: Bloomsbury Methuen Drama, 2016), 27–44.

19 Wagner in Raymond Furness, *Wagner and Literature* (Manchester: Manchester University Press, 1982), 13.

20 For more on mutuality, see Alison Hodge, 'Wlodzimierz Staniewski: Gardzienice and the Naturalised Actor', in *Actor Training*, ed. Alison Hodge (London: Routledge, 2010), 268–87.

21 Meyerhold, *Stat'i, Pis'ma, Rechi, Besed'i. 1891–1917*, 76.

22 Konstantin Rudnitsky, *Meyerhold, the Director*, trans. George Petrov (Ann Arbor, MI: Ardis, 1981), 82.

23 Shepherd, *Direction*, 9.

24 Ol'ga A. Zhukova, 'The Philosophy of New Spirituality: The Creative Manifesto of Nikolai Berdyaev', *Russian Studies in Philosophy* 53, no. 4 (2015): 276–90.

25 See Meyerhold in Michael Green, *The Russian Symbolist Theater: An Anthology of Plays and Critical Texts* (Ann Arbor, MI: Ardis, 1986), 130.

26 Remizov in Claude Schumacher, *Naturalism and Symbolism in European Theatre 1850–1918* (Cambridge: Cambridge University Press, 1996), 230.

27 Braun, *Meyerhold: A Revolution in Theatre*, 21.

28 Such a notion of the *rezhisser* is reiterated by Polish laboratory theatre director Jerzy Grotowski when he highlights the role of directing as the organizer of two ensembles: the actors and the spectators in *Towards a Poor Theatre* (New York: Routledge, 2002), 157.

29 'Theatre of Searches' is a translation of *teatr iskanii*, which is translated variously in English. See Meyerhold, *Stat'i, Pis'ma, Rechi, Besed'i. 1891–1917*, 110.

30 *Avtor Spektaklya* is the term Meyerhold used on the poster for his role in *The Government Inspector*. It can be translated as 'author of the spectacle' or 'production'. See Laurence Senelick, 'Theatre', in *The Cambridge Companion to Russian Culture*, ed. Nicholas Rzhevsky (Cambridge: Cambridge University Press: 2012), 296.

31 See Kathryn Mederos Syssoyeva, 'Revolution in the Theatre I: Meyerhold, Stanislavsky and Collective Creation, Russia, 1905', in *A History of Collective Creation*, eds Kathryn Mederos Syssoyeva and Scott Proudfit (Basingstoke: Palgrave Macmillan, 2013), 49–54.

32 For more understanding of how these circles operated as incubators for Russian philosophy and culture, and particularly the development of Russian theatre, see Brown, *A History of the Theatre Laboratory*.

33 Posner, *The Director's Prism*, 6.

34 For ease of comprehension we have chosen to refer to this Studio as Dr Dapertutto's Studio. See also Marjorie L. Hoover, 'A Mejerxol'd Method? – *Love for Three Oranges* (1914–1916)', *The Slavic and East European Journal* 13, no. 1 (1969): 23–41.

35 Vsevolod Meyerhold, *Lektsii. 1918–1919*, ed. O.M. Fel'dman (Moscow: OGI, 2000), 207.

36 Ibid.

37 Ibid., 27.

38 Ibid., 74.

39 See John Caughie, *Theories of Authorship: A Reader* (London: Routledge, 2005), 9.

40 Meyerhold, *Lektsii. 1918–1919*, 74.

41 Avra Sidiropoulou, *Authoring Performance: The Director in Contemporary Theatre* (Basingstoke: Palgrave Macmillian, 2011), 1.

42 Posner, *The Director's Prism*, 12.

43 Ibid., 11.

44 Meyerhold, *Lekstii. 1918–1919*, 48.

45 Ibid., 47.

46 Ibid., 78.

47 Meyerhold in L.D. Vendrovskaya and A.V. Fevral'ski, eds, *Tvorcheskoe Nasledie V.E. Meierkhol'da* (Moscow: VTO, 1978), 55–6.

48 Meyerhold, *Lektsii. 1918–1919*, 48.

49 Ibid., 49.

50 See J.L. Styan, *Max Reinhardt* (Cambridge: Cambridge University Press, 1982), 120, for a full discussion of its contents.

51 Vendrovskaya and Fevral'ski, *Tvorcheskoe Nasledie V.E. Meierkhol'da*, 89.

52 See E.L. Garin, *S Meierkhol'dom* (Moscow: Isskustvo, 1974), 78 and 104. See also Robert Leach, *Vsevolod Meyerhold* (Cambridge: Cambridge University Press, 1989), 126.

53 See Marjorie L. Hoover, *Meyerhold: The Art of Conscious Theatre* (Amherst: University of Massachusetts Press, 1974), 67, and Leach, *Vsevolod Meyerhold*, 126.

54 For an in-depth historical and contemporary understanding of *mise en scène*, see Patrice Pavis, *La Mise en Scène Contemporaine: Staging Theatre Today*, trans. Joel Anderson (London: Routledge, 2013).

55 Meyerhold, *Lektsii. 1918–1919*, 48.

56 See Daniel Spoto, *The Art of Alfred Hitchcock: Fifty Years of His Motion Pictures* (New York: Hopkinson and Blake Publishers, 1976), 384.

57 See Amy S. Green, *The Revisionist Stage: American Directors Reinvent the Classics* (Cambridge: Cambridge University Press, 1994), 21–2.

58 Vendrovskaya and Fevral'ski, *Tvorcheskoe Nasledie V.E. Meierkhol'da*, 93.

59 Julia Listengarten, *Russian Tragifarce: Its Cultural and Political Roots* (London: Associated University Presses, 2000), 39.

60 N.V. Petrov in L.D. Vendrovskaya, ed., *Vstrechi S Meierkhol'dom* (Moscow: VTO, 1967), 159–60.

61 Meyerhold, *Stat'i, Pis'ma, Rechi, Besed'i.1917–1939*, 444–5.

62 Katie Mitchell, *The Director's Craft* (London: Routledge, 2008), 230 and 15.

63 Meyerhold, *Lektsii. 1918–1919*, 48–9.

64 Vendrovskaya and Fevral'ski, *Tvorcheskoe Nasledie V.E. Meierkhol'da*, 89.

65 Meyerhold, *Lektsii. 1918–1919*, 49.

66 See Jonathan Pitches, *Vsevolod Meyerhold* (London: Routledge, 2003), 77–110, for a fuller understanding of this seminal production.

67 See Robert Robertson, *Eisenstein and the Audiovisual: The Montage of Music, Image and Sound in Cinema* (London: Tauris Academic Studies, 2009), 60–1.

68 Meyerhold in ibid., 53.

69 Posner, *The Director's Prism*, 17.

70 Robertson, *Eisenstein and the Audiovisual*, 53.

71 See Pitches, *Vsevolod Meyerhold*, 26 and 111–54, and Robert Leach, 'Meyerhold and Biomechanics', in Alison Hodge, ed., *Actor Training*, 26–42.

72 *Balagan* is a complex term that can be translated as 'farce' or 'the fairground show'. Similar to the *commedia dell'arte*, it is provocative and scandalous, encompassing a Bakhtinian sense of the carnivalesque. See Clayton, *Pierrot in Petrograd*, 54–61 and 159–204.

73 Meyerhold, *Lektsii. 1918–1919*, 39.

74 Leach, *Vsevolod Meyerhold*, 137.

75 Vendrovskaya and Fevral'ski, *Tvorcheskoe Nasledie V.E. Meierkhol'da*, 94.

76 Robertson, *Eisenstein and the Audiovisual*, 55.

77 See Richard Stourac and Kathleen McCreery, *Theatre as a Weapon: Workers' Theatre in the Soviet Union, Germany and Britain, 1917–1934* (London: Routledge, 1986), 20.

78 Posner, *The Director's Prism*, 35.

79 Meyerhold, *Lektsii. 1918–1919*, 19–20.

80 Meyerhold, *Stat'i, Pis'ma, Rechi, Besed'i. 1917–1939*, 448–9.

81 Mikhail Sadovsky in Vendrovskaya, ed., *Vstrechi S Meierkhol'dom* (Moscow: VTO, 1967), 510.

82 See Shepherd, *Direction*, 26.

83 Meyerhold, *Lekstii. 1918–1919*, 47–8.

84 Vendrovskaya and Fevral'ski, *Tvorcheskoe Nasledie V.E. Meierkhol'da*, 87.

85 See Brown, *A History of the Theatre Laboratory*.

86 Meyerhold, *Lektsii. 1918–1919*, 19.

87 See David Roesner, *Musicality in Theatre: Music as Model, Method and Metaphor in Theatre-Making* (Abingdon: Ashgate, 2014), 91–4, for a useful explanation of how Meyerhold's aesthetic of the grotesque was unique and informed by his sense of musicality. See Robertson, *Eisenstein and the Audiovisual*, for a fuller account of Meyerhold's impact on film.

88 See Leach, *Vsevolod Meyerhold*, 103 and 116.

89 Ibid., 74 and 126–37. See also Rudnitsky, *Meyerhold, the Director*, 148–56.

Chapter 2

1   Vsevolod Meyerhold, 'The Reconstruction of the Theatre', 1930, in *Meyerhold on Theatre*, ed. and trans. Edward Braun (London: Methuen, 1998), 256.

2   See Braun, *Meyerhold on Theatre*, 240. Braun cites Ilya Ehrenburg's recollections of performances of Meyerhold's production of *The Government Inspector* in Paris during this tour, which were attended by, among others, Pablo Picasso, Louis Jouvert, Charles Dullin and Jean Cocteau.

3   Meyerhold's reference to the revolution as his 'second birth' can be found in Aleksandr Gladkov, *Meyerhold Speaks, Meyerhold Rehearses* (Amsterdam: Harwood Academic Publishers, 1997), 93. Robert Leach discusses the meeting for artists called by the new Bolshevik government in Leach, *Vsevolod Meyerhold*, 13.

4   Braun dedicates a chapter to Meyerhold's work on October in the Theatre in *Meyerhold on Theatre*, 159–82.

5   For more on Socialist Realism, particularly in the context of Russian theatre, see Anatoly Smeliansky, *The Russian Theatre after Stalin*, trans. Patrick Miles (Cambridge: Cambridge University Press, 1999) or Inna Solovyova, 'The Theatre and Socialist Realism, 1929–1953', in *A History of Russian Theatre*, eds Robert Leach and Victor Borovsky (Cambridge: Cambridge University Press, 1999), 325–57.

6   Braun's article 'Meyerhold: the Final Act' (*New Theatre Quarterly 9*, no. 33 [1993]) outlines the circumstances around Meyerhold's death.

7   Braun, *Meyerhold on Theatre*, 274. The New Economic Policy (NEP) and the Five Year Plans were early- to mid-twentieth-century Soviet economic policies introduced by leaders Lenin and Stalin, respectively. NEP was a limited concession to capitalism in Soviet economics, allowing some individuals to accumulate a little personal wealth through free trade. Stalin's Five Year Plans reversed this policy, actively punishing those who had benefited. The Five Year Plans aimed for rapid industrial growth in the Soviet Union and were accompanied by a brutal policy of collectivization in farming, leading to enforced famine across the Russian countryside.

8   See Marjorie L. Hoover, *Meyerhold and his Set Designers* (New York: Peter Lang, 1988) or Alla Mikhailova, *Meyerhold and Set Designers* (Moscow: Galart, 1995).

9   See, for example, Edward Braun, *Meyerhold: A Revolution in Theatre* (London: Methuen, 1998); Leach, *Vsevolod Meyerhold*; Rudnitsky, *Meyerhold the Director*. Many images from Meyerhold's productions are available online through the Global Performing Arts Database (www.glopad.org).

10 Meyerhold, 'The Naturalistic Theatre and the Theatre of Mood' (1908), in Braun, *Meyerhold on Theatre*, 32.

11 Mikhailova, *Meyerhold and Set Designers*, 51.

12 Ibid., 64.

13 In *Meyerhold and Set Designers*, Alla Mikhailova brings together records and images from Meyerhold's productions. A number of Russian terms

are recorded for Meyerhold's designers, including *khudozhnik* (artist), *khudozhnik-konstruktor* (artist-designer or artist-engineer), and *oformlenie* (design, appearance or composition). I am using the term 'designer-realiser' to indicate one variant of Meyerhold's working relationship with designers, where the ideas for the staging are generated by Meyerhold but brought into being through collaboration with the artist, whose role is practically and creatively to bring the design to life.

14 Meyerhold, 'The Naturalistic Theatre and the Theatre of Mood', 31.

15 Meyerhold, in Gladkov, *Meyerhold Speaks, Meyerhold Rehearses*, 116.

16 Vsevolod Meyerhold, 'First Attempts at a Stylized Theatre' (1907), in Braun, *Meyerhold on Theatre*, 49.

17 Vsevolod Meyerhold, 'The Fairground Booth' (1913), in Braun, *Meyerhold on Theatre*, 122.

18 Vsevolod Meyerhold, 'Tristan and Isolde' (1910), in Braun, *Meyerhold on Theatre*, 82.

19 For further reading on Meyerhold's biomechanics, see the section 'Biomechanics' in Braun, *Meyerhold on Theatre*, 197–204. For additional critical commentary and source material, see Mel Gordon and Alma Law, *Meyerhold, Eisenstein and Biomechanics: Actor Training in Revolutionary Russia* (Jefferson, NC: MacFarland, 1996). Jonathan Pitches provides a practical introduction to Meyerhold's system in *Vsevolod Meyerhold* (London: Routledge, 2003).

20 Stephen Bann's book *The Traditions of Constructivism* (New York: Da Capo Press, 1974) brings together key documents and commentary on the constructivist movement.

21 See Gvozdev in Braun, *Meyerhold: A Revolution in Theatre*, 180. More on *The Magnanimous Cuckold* can be found in Alma H. Law, 'Meyerhold's *The Magnanimous Cuckold*', *The Drama Review* 26, no. 1 (1982): 61–86, or Nick Worrall, 'Meyerhold's production of the *Magnificent* [sic] *Cuckold*', *The Drama Review* 17, no. 1 (1973): 14–34.

22 I have written about this effect in my article 'Surfaces, Depths and Hypercubes: Meyerholdian Scenography and the Fourth Dimension', *Theatre and Performance Design* 1, no. 3 (2015): 204–19.

23 Meyerhold, 'The Reconstruction of the Theatre', 254.

24 Anne Ubersfeld, *Reading Theatre* (Toronto: University of Toronto Press, 1999), 94.

25 Rudnitsky, *Meyerhold the Director*, 239.

26 It should be noted that the notion of curved space was particularly prevalent in early twentieth-century mathematics, for example, in the work of Henri Poincaré, who argued against the popular mathematical understanding of space as a uniform and flat surface. In Poincaré's model of curved space, Euclid's parallel postulate, a foundation stone of modern geometry, does not function and many extant geometrical rules had to be reconsidered. The use of curves in Meyerhold's *mise en scène* thus finds a contextual counterpoint in Poincaré's work. Other relevant reference points can be found in Albert

Einstein's Theories of Relativity, his collaborations with Hermann Minkowski and the development of curved space-time.

27   Meyerhold, 'On the staging of Verhaeren's *The Dawn*' (1920), in Braun, *Meyerhold on Theatre*, 173.

28   Gay McAuley, 'A Taxonomy of Spatial Function', in *Theatre and Performance Design: A Reader in Scenography*, eds Jane Collins and Andrew Nisbet (London and New York: Routledge, 2010), 90.

29   Ibid.

30   Ibid.

31   Meyerhold, 'The Naturalistic Theatre and the Theatre of Mood', 25.

32   Ibid.

33   Meyerhold, 'The Reconstruction of the Theatre', 256.

34   This figure is based on Robert Leach's list of Meyerhold's productions (see Leach, *Vsevolod Meyerhold*, 194–204). In the first six years of his career, Meyerhold toured to eleven regions in the Russian provinces, indicating that he had a strong grasp of the need to adapt his productions to different venues. During his career post-1917, in addition to productions at his own theatre, he also contributed to work at other venues, including the Theatre of the Revolution (where he was also artistic director), the Stanislavsky State Opera Theatre and the Kamerny Theatre (all located in Moscow).

35   It should be noted that, although Meyerhold was invited to join the Moscow Art Theatre's new Studio project in 1905 as artistic director and rehearsed four productions there, the Studio was closed before these productions opened and the work remained unfinished. The official reason for the closure was political unrest and the failed attempt at Revolution in Russia in 1905, although there were also significant artistic differences between Meyerhold and Stanislavsky. For more detail on Meyerhold's experiences at the Art Theatre Studio, see Braun, *Meyerhold: A Revolution in Theatre*, 27–44, or Leach, *Vsevolod Meyerhold*, 4–6.

36   Leach, *Vsevolod Meyerhold*, 21.

37   See Mikhail Barkhin and Sergei Vakhtangov, 'A Theater for Meyerhold', *Theatre Quarterly* 2, no. 7 (1972): 69–73. After the abandonment of the part-completed new Meyerhold Theatre project, the site was reassigned as the Tchaikovsky Concert Hall. This building, which still stands on Moscow's Mayakovsky Square, gives some small indication of Meyerhold's intentions for his new theatre.

38   Meyerhold, 'The Reconstruction of the Theatre', 255.

39   See http://en.alexandrinsky.ru/articles/about/history (accessed 23 August 2016).

40   Edward Braun explains that the placement of Varmalov on the proscenium was certainly in part a pragmatic solution by Meyerhold, in response to issues caused by the actor himself: 'The mountainous Sganarelle of Konstantin Varmalov was the one stationary figure in the entire production; not only did his bulk and a severe heart condition limit his mobility, but with his incorrigibly bad memory he was left helpless with the removal

of the downstage prompter's box which the construction of the forestage necessitated.' Braun goes on to explain that the solution of two screens concealing prompters solved the problem of Varmalov's lines, and that the actor 'was permitted to spend most of the play happily ensconced on a stool adjacent to one screen or the other and the entire *mise-en-scène* was adapted to accommodate him'. Braun, *Meyerhold: A Revolution in Theatre*, 107.

41 Vsevolod Meyerhold, 'Dom Juan' (1913), in Braun, *Meyerhold on Theatre*, 99. Molière's play *Tartuffe* (1664) was premiered less than a year before *Don Juan* (1665), and caused controversy with the church over its representation of religious hypocrisy, leading to threats of excommunication for spectators at its performances.

42 It should be noted that, in Edward Braun's words, Meyerhold appears to 'have read into Molière's theatre what he himself wished to find' (Braun, *Meyerhold: A Revolution in Theatre*, 103), and his understanding of the playwright is not necessarily accurate as his work is understood today.

43 Rudnitsky, *Meyerhold the Director*, 149.

44 Ibid., 150.

45 The Russian Soviet Federative Socialist Republic (RSFSR) became the Union of Soviet Socialist Republics (USSR) in 1922.

46 Ibid., 269.

47 Meyerhold, 'On the Staging of Verhaeren's *The Dawn*', 170.

48 Leach, *Vsevolod Meyerhold*, 36–7.

49 Meyerhold, 'The Reconstruction of the Theatre', 255.

50 Leach, *Vsevolod Meyerhold*, 39.

51 Gail Lenhoff, 'The Theatre of Okhlopkov', *The Drama Review* 17, no. 1 (1973): 93.

52 Ibid. Lenhoff's work on Nikolai Okhlopkov indicates that Meyerhold's configuration of the stage space was relatively conservative in terms of the actor–audience relationship. Having trained under Meyerhold, Okhlopkov spoke of his frustration at Meyerhold's persistent separation of spectator and performer: on leaving the Meyerhold Theatre, Lenhoff records, Okhlopkov noted that 'the temptation of swinging my legs over the edge of the stage and having a talk with the spectator [...] proved irresistible' (Lenhoff, 'The Theatre of Okhlopkov', 93). At his own theatre, the Realistic Theatre, Okhlopkov experimented with the actor–audience relationship by creating a new configuration of the theatre space for each production, combining raised platforms with audiences placed onto or behind the stage, and proto-immersive environments such as his work on Alexander Serafimovich's *Zhelezhyi Potok* (*The Iron Flood*, 1934): see Lenhoff, 'The Theatre of Okhlopkov', 90–104, or Nick Worrall, *Modernism to Realism on the Soviet Stage* (Cambridge: Cambridge University Press, 1989), 140–96.

53 Vsevolod Meyerhold, 'Inaugural Speech to the Company of the R.S.F.S.R. Theatre No. 1' (1920), in Braun, *Meyerhold on Theatre*, 170.

54 Vsevolod Meyerhold, 'First Attempts at a Stylized Theatre' (1907), in Braun, *Meyerhold on Theatre*, 50.

55 Ibid.

56 Ibid., 51–2.

57 Ibid., 50.

58 In his assessment of Meyerhold's practice, written after a visit to his theatre in the 1930s, Houghton describes Meyerhold's actors as 'rubber balls', who exist only to be bounced by the director, that is, that Meyerhold developed a rehearsal environment in which actors are called to be nothing but responsive to Meyerhold's demands and not to demonstrate creativity in their own right. Norris Houghton, *Moscow Rehearsals* (London: George Allen and Unwin, 1938), 120.

59 Meyerhold, 'The Reconstruction of the Theatre', 253.

60 Ibid.

61 Ibid.

62 Karel Brušák, 'Imaginary Action Space in Drama' (1936), in *Drama und Theater. Theorie – Methode-Geschichte*, eds H. Schmid and K. Hedwig (Munich: Otto Sagner, 1992), 147.

63 McAuley, 'A Taxonomy of Spatial Function', 92.

64 Meyerhold, 'The Naturalistic Theatre and the Theatre of Mood', 28.

65 It should be noted that one of the production's episodes (entitled 'After Penza') took place on a unique, larger truck that incorporated a staircase: see Nick Worrall, 'Meyerhold directs Gogol's *Government Inspector*', *Theatre Quarterly* 2, no. 7 (1972): 75–95.

66 Meyerhold, 'The Reconstruction of the Theatre', 257.

67 Meyerhold also associates this kinetic model with attempts to 'cinefy' the stage, responding to the technological developments of film, and classes *The Government Inspector* as one of 'a number of victories' that he has scored 'over cinema' (in Meyerhold, 'The Reconstruction of the Theatre', 258).

68 Rudnitsky, *Meyerhold the Director*, 394. Images of Meyerhold's production of *The Government Inspector* can be found online at http://www.glopad.org/pi/en/record/piece/497 (accessed 18 October 2016).

69 Brušák, 'Imaginary Action Space in Drama', 148.

70 I have written elsewhere about the relationship between these fragmented spaces and the notion of collage, a popular device in early twentieth-century avant-garde visual art. See Amy Skinner, *Meyerhold and the Cubists: Perspectives in Painting and Performance* (Bristol: Intellect, 2015).

71 Hoover, *Meyerhold and his Set Designers*, 51.

72 Brušák, 'Imaginary Action Space in Drama', 148.

Chapter 3

1 Piscator, *The Political Theatre*, 9.

2 See Hans-Jörg Grell, 'Erwin Piscator 1893–1966', in *'Leben ist immer ein Anfang!' Erwin Piscator 1893–1966*, ed. Ullrich Amlung in collaboration with the Akademie der Künste Berlin (Marburg: Jonas Verlag, 1993), 12.

3   Piscator, *The Political Theatre*, 9.

4   Program, 'Tribute to Erwin Piscator', 4 June 1967, Box 131, Folder 7, Erwin Piscator Papers 1930–71, Southern Illinois University Special Collections Research Center. This pamphlet was published in English.

5   See Piscator, *The Political Theatre*, 7.

6   See ibid., 10. On the public enthusiasm for the war, see also Modris Eksteins, *Rites of Spring: The Great War and the Birth of the Modern Age* (New York: Houghton Mifflin, 1989).

7   See Piscator, *The Political Theatre*, 13.

8   Ibid., 13–14.

9   Ibid., 15.

10   Ibid., 17.

11   Ibid., 19.

12   Ibid., 20.

13   See ibid., 21.

14   See Helen Boak, *Women in the Weimar Republic* (Manchester: Manchester University Press, 2013), 20.

15   See Katie Sutton, '"We Too Deserve a Place in the Sun": The Politics of Transvestite Identity in Weimar Germany', *German Studies Review* 35, no. 2 (2012): 335–54.

16   See Bernd Widdig, 'Cultural Dimensions of Inflation in Weimar Germany', *German Politics & Society* 32 (1994): 11.

17   See ibid., 12.

18   Piscator, *The Political Theatre*, 9.

19   See Minou Arjomand, 'Performing Catastrophe: Erwin Piscator's Documentary Theatre', *Modern Drama* 59, no. 1 (2016): 49–74.

20   Karl Marx, 'Theses on Feuerbach', in *The Marx-Engels Reader*, ed. Robert C. Tucker (New York: Norton, 1978), 145.

21   See C.D. Innes, *Erwin Piscator's Political Theatre: The Development of Modern German Drama* (Cambridge: Cambridge University Press, 1972), 3.

22   See Piscator, *The Political Theatre*, 40.

23   See Peter Bürger, *Theory of the Avant-Garde*, trans. Michael Shaw (Minneapolis: University of Minnesota Press, 1984).

24   See ibid., 79.

25   See Michael Schwaiger, 'Einbruch der Wirklichkeit: Das Theater Bertolt Brechts und Erwin Piscators', in *Bertolt Brecht und Erwin Piscator: Experimentelles Theater im Berlin der Zwangierjahre*, ed. Michael Schwaiger (Vienna: Christian Brandstätter, 2004), 12.

26   See ibid., 10.

27   See Brecht, *Brecht on Performance*, 60.

28   Piscator, *The Political Theatre*, 39.

29   See ibid., 40.

30   See John Willett, *The Theatre of Erwin Piscator* (New York: Holmes and Meier, 1979), 101.

31   Kurt Pinthus, *8-Uhr Abendblatt*, Berlin, 4 April 1930, quoted in Innes, *Erwin Piscator's Political Theatre*, 137.

32   See Willett, *The Theatre of Erwin Piscator*, 51.

33   Piscator, *The Political Theatre*, 32.

34   Ibid., 33.

35   Piscator, *The Political Theatre*, 45.

36   See Willett, *The Theatre of Erwin Piscator*, 62.

37   See Innes, *Erwin Piscator's Political Theatre*, 68.

38   See Willett, *The Theatre of Erwin Piscator*, 63.

39   See ibid., 71.

40   See Innes, *Erwin Piscator's Political Theatre*, 70.

41   See Erika Fischer-Lichte, *The Routledge Introduction to Theatre and Performance Studies*, eds Minou Arjomand and Ramona Mosse, trans. Minou Arjomand (New York and London: Routledge, 2014).

42   Piscator, *The Political Theatre*, 96–7.

43   My translation. Erwin Piscator, 'Bühne der Gegenwart und Zukunft', in *Schriften 2*, ed. Ludwig Hoffmann (East Berlin: Henschel, 1968), 36.

44   Ibid., 37.

45   Schwaiger, 'Einbruch der Wirklichkeit', 11.

46   See Thomas Tode, 'Wir Sprengen die Guckkastenbühne', in *Erwin Piscator and Bertolt Brecht*, 21.

47   Piscator, *The Political Theatre*, 75.

48   Brecht, *Brecht on Performance*, 60.

49   Piscator, *The Political Theatre*, 93.

50   See Willett, *The Theatre of Erwin Piscator*, 95.

51   See Innes, *Erwin Piscator's Political Theatre*, 77.

52   Piscator, *The Political Theatre*, 91.

53   See ibid., 19.

54   See Tode, 'Wir Sprengen die Guckkastenbühne', 16.

55   Piscator, *The Political Theatre*, 94.

56   See Tode, 'Wir Sprengen die Guckkastenbühne', 17.

57   See ibid., 27.

58   See ibid., 20.

59   See Julius Richter, 'Wegen technischer Schwierigkeiten…', in Schwaiger, ed., *Bertolt Brecht und Erwin Piscator*, 35–7.

60   See Lothar Schirmer, 'Theater Film – Theater – Technik – Theater: Die politischen Bühnenlandschaften des Erwin Piscator in den Zwanziger Jahren', in Amlung, ed., *'Leben ist immer ein Anfang!'*, 43.

61   See Willett, *The Theatre of Erwin Piscator*, 58.

62   See ibid., 103.

63   Walter Benjamin, *Illuminations*, ed. Hannah Arendt, trans. Harry Zohn (New York: Schocken, 1969), 84.

64   It is unclear how many performances featured this ending, it proved so controversial that it was ultimately cut. Schirmer, 'Theater Film – Theater – Technik – Theater', 44.

65   Georg Simmel, 'The Metropolis and Mental Life', in *The Sociology of Georg Simmel*, ed. and trans. Kurt H. Wolff (New York and London: Free Press, 1950), 410.

66   Brecht, *Brecht on Performance*, 115.

67   See Simmel, 'The Metropolis and Mental Life', 409.

68   See Schirmer, 'Theater Film – Theater – Technik – Theater', 43.

69   See Grell, 'Erwin Piscator 1893–1966', 16.

70   Ibid., 18.

71   See Innes, *Erwin Piscator's Political Theatre*, 75.

72   Quoted in Willett, *The Theatre of Erwin Piscator*, 55.

73   See Theodor Adorno et al., *Aesthetics and Politics* (New York: Verso, 2007).

74   See Willett, *The Theatre of Erwin Piscator*, 122.

75   Ibid.

76   Ibid., 66–8.

77   My translation. Bertolt Brecht, BFA 13, 307–8.

78   Benjamin, *Illuminations*, 241.

79   Ibid., 242.

Chapter 4

1   Erwin Piscator to Boleslaw Barlog, n.d. [April 1955], in Erwin Piscator, *Briefe. Volume 3.2: Bundesrepublik Deutschland, 1955–1959*, ed. Peter Diezel (Berlin: B&S Siebenhaar, 2011), 38. All translations from the German are mine unless otherwise acknowledged.

2   Barry B. Witham, *A Sustainable Theatre: Jasper Deeter at Hedgerow* (New York: Palgrave Macmillan, 2013), 64. Piscator's stage adaptation of Dreiser's novel is available in print: Paul Green and Erwin Piscator, *The 'Lost' Group Theatre Plays. Volume 3. The House of Connelly, Johnny Johnson, & Case of Clyde Griffiths*, ed. The ReGroup Theatre Company (New York: CreateSpace, 2013).

3   Witham, *A Sustainable Theatre*, 66.

4   Ibid., 67. When Piscator managed to attend a performance of the show later on-site, when the Hedgerow revived the original production in the 1947/48

season, the outrageous, steadfast production made him 'freeze in his seat'. Experiencing Deeter's production was an overwhelming re-encounter with his earlier work. It confronted Piscator with the ferocity of political criticism that had characterized much of his work during the 1920s. He felt that he had mostly relinquished this aspect of his theatre when he had resumed directing in 1940.

5 Witham, *A Sustainable Theatre*, 67.

6 X. Theodore Barber, 'Drama with a Pointer: The Group Theatre's Production of Piscator's Case of Clyde Griffiths', *TDR* 28, no. 4 (1984): 61–72.

7 Erwin Piscator, *Theater, Film, Politik. Ausgewählte Schriften*, ed. Ludwig Hoffmann (Berlin: Henschel, 1980), 162.

8 Erwin Piscator to Albert S. Shcherbakov (draft), 21 November 1935, in Erwin Piscator, *Die Briefe. Volume 1: Berlin – Moskau (1909–1936)*, ed. Peter Diezel (Berlin: Bostelmann und Siebenhaar, 2005), 393.

9 Hermann Haarmann, 'Abschied von Europa: "Ein bedeutendes Kunstwerk…" Erwin Piscators Spielfilm *Der Aufstand der Fischer*', in *Exil in der Sowjetunion 1933–1945*, eds Hermann Haarmann and Christoph Hesse (Marburg: Tectum, 2010), 121–31, 127–9.

10 During his years in France (1936–8), he had planned a touring company of German-speaking actors in the United States, collaborated with Austrian-born film producer (and future Hollywood legend) Sam Spiegel on a Mexican national theatre project and initiated a film distribution company.

11 Leon Askin with C. Melvin Davidson, *Quietude and Quest: Protagonists and Antagonists in the Theatre, on and off Stage as seen Through the Eyes of Leon Askin* (Riverside, CA: Ariadne Press, 1989), 184.

12 Alexander Granach to Lotte Lieven, 14 June 1938, in Alexander Granach, *Du mein liebes Stück Heimat. Briefe an Lotte Lieven aus dem Exil*, eds Angelika Wittlich and Hilde Recher (Augsburg: Ölbaum, 2008), 211.

13 Ilka Saal, 'Broadway and the Depoliticization of Epic Theatre: The Case of Erwin Piscator', in *Brecht. Broadway and United States Theatre*, ed. J. Chris Westgate (Newcastle: Cambridge Scholars, 2007), 45–71, 54.

14 Maria Ley-Piscator, *The Piscator Experiment. The Political Theatre* (New York: James H. Heineman, 1967), 47.

15 Erwin Piscator to Alvin S. Johnson, 22 May 1939, in Erwin Piscator, *Briefe. Volume 2.2: New York 1939–1945*, ed. Peter Diezel (Berlin: B&S Siebenhaar, 2009), 105.

16 Erwin Piscator to Paul Tillich, n.d. [June/July 1965], in Erwin Piscator, *Briefe. Volume 3.3: Bundesrepublik Deutschland, 1960–1966*, ed. Peter Diezel (Berlin: B&S Siebenhaar, 2011), 671.

17 Judith Malina, *The Piscator Notebook* (London: Routledge, Chapman & Hall, 2012), 10.

18 Askin, *Quietude and Quest*, 216.

19 Don Craig, *Washington Daily News*, 11 March 1940, quoted in Thomas George Evans, *Piscator in the American* Theatre. *New York, 1939–1951* (Ann Arbor: University of Wisconsin Press, 1968), 120.

20   Askin, *Quietude and Quest*, 217.

21   Nelson B. Bell, *Washington Post*, 15 March 1940, quoted in Evans, *Piscator in the American Theatre*, 119.

22   Erwin Piscator to Antonie Piscator, 23 March 1940, in Piscator, *Briefe*. Volume 2.2, 169.

23   Evans, *Piscator in the American Theatre*, 118.

24   *Washington News*, 10 June 1940, quoted in ibid., 130.

25   Day Tuttle to Thomas G. Evans, 7 July 1967, quoted in Evans, *Piscator in the American Theatre*, 122.

26   *Washington Post*, 15 July 1940, quoted in Evans, *Piscator in the American Theatre*, 130.

27   *Washington Post*, 2 September 1940, quoted in Evans, *Piscator in the American Theatre*, 130.

28   Maria Ley-Piscator, *Der Tanz im Spiegel. Mein Leben mit Erwin Piscator* (Reinbek bei Hamburg: Wunderlich, 1989), 275.

29   *The Evening Star*, Washington, 25 November 1940.

30   *Washington Post*, 9 December 1940, quoted in Evans, *Piscator in the American Theatre*, 132.

31   Ley-Piscator, *The Piscator Experiment*, 104.

32   Evans, *Piscator in the American Theatre*, 124.

33   Ibid., 125.

34   Erwin Piscator, *The Political Theatre* (New York: Avon, 1978), 198.

35   'Minutes of the Inaugural Assembly of the Studio', in Piscator, *The Political Theatre*, 199.

36   John Willett, *The Theatre of Erwin Piscator. Half a Century of Politics in the Theatre* (London: Eyre Methuen, 1978), 155.

37   Ley-Piscator, *The Piscator Experiment*, 99–100.

38   Harry Belafonte and Michael Shnayerson, *My Song. A Memoir* (New York: Alfred A. Knopf, 2011), 66.

39   Malina, *The Piscator Notebook*, 11.

40   Erwin Piscator, 'Objective Acting', in *Actors on Acting: The Theories, Techniques, and Practices of the Great Actors of All Times as Told in their Own Words*, eds Toby Cole and Helen Krich Chinoy (New York: Crown, 1949), 285–91.

41   Ibid., 291.

42   Ibid., 286.

43   Ibid., 289.

44   Willett, *The Theatre of Erwin Piscator*, 156.

45   Quoted in Ley-Piscator, *The Piscator Experiment*, 150.

46   Peter M. Rutkoff, 'Politics on Stage. Piscator and the Dramatic Workshop', in *New School: A History of the New School for Social Research*, eds Peter M. Rutkoff and William B. Scott (New York: Macmillan, 1986), 172–95, 195.

47 *War and Peace* (programme), Studio Theatre, 20 May 1942, quoted in Ley-Piscator, *The Piscator Experiment*, 190.

48 *New York Times*, 8 December 1940, quoted in Ley-Piscator, *The Piscator Experiment*, 160.

49 *New York News*, 16 December 1940, quoted in Evans, *Piscator in the American Theatre*, 172.

50 Arthur Pollock, *Brooklyn Eagle*, 24 May 1942, quoted in Evans, *Piscator in the American Theatre*, 227.

51 Burns Mantle, *New York News*, 13 March 1942, quoted in Evans, *Piscator in the American Theatre*, 209.

52 Piscator's attempts to direct Paul Osborne's play *The Innocent Voyage* in October 1943 at the Guild Theatre (to replace a proposed production of Brecht's *Schweik in the Second World War*) and Irving Kaye Davis's contemplative retirement drama *The Last Stop* in the Ethel Barrymore Theatre in September 1944 were abandoned during rehearsals due to disagreements with the theatre director, producer or author. Thea Kirfel-Lenk, *Erwin Piscator im Exil in den USA 1939–1951. Eine Darstellung seiner antifaschistischen Theaterarbeit am Dramatic Workshop der New School for Social Research* (Berlin: Henschel, 1984), 189–90.

53 Erwin Piscator to Alvin S. Johnson, n.d. (*c.* February 1944), in Piscator, *Briefe*, Volume 2.2, 369–70.

54 Rutkoff, 'Politics on Stage', 189.

55 Ibid., 190.

56 Erwin Piscator to unknown recipient, 21 February 1946, in Piscator, *Briefe*, Volume 2.3, 34.

57 Ley-Piscator, *Der Tanz im Spiegel*, 293.

58 Willett, *The Theatre of Erwin Piscator*, 159.

59 Malina, *The Piscator Notebook*, 127.

60 Erwin Piscator, Diary 23, p. 52 (December 1960).

61 Erwin Piscator, 'The American Theatre: A Note or Two on Playwrights, the Box Office, and the Ideal', *New York Times*, 21 January 1940.

62 Malina, *The Piscator Notebook*, 109.

63 Ben Gazzara, *In the Moment: My Life as an Actor* (New York: Carrol & Graff, 2004), 47–8.

64 Rutkoff, *Politics on Stage*, 191.

65 *New York Times*, 18 April 1947, quoted in Evans, *Piscator in the American Theatre*, 298.

66 *New York Herald Tribune*, 16 February 1949, quoted in Evans, *Piscator in the American Theatre*, 325.

67 Kirfel-Lenk, *Erwin Piscator im Exil*, 211–12.

68 'Even War doesn't hinder Red Front. School Officials, VA, back party line, workshop', *The Tablet. A Catholic Weekly* (Brooklyn), 25 August 1951. Reprint of an anonymous contribution from 'Counterattack (Facts to Combat Communism)', 10 August 1951.

69 Tape recording of an interview with Piscator by Kurt Joachim Fischer, April
    1964, Special Collections Research Center (SCRC) of the Morris Library at
    Southern Illinois University Carbondale (SIU), Aleida Montijn Papers.

70 Adalbert Schultz-Norden to Erwin Piscator, 8 May 1948 and 10 June 1948, in
    Piscator, *Briefe*. Volume 2.3, 179.

71 On Piscator's return to West Germany, his wife, refusing to live in the nation
    that provoked the war, had to take over the management of the Dramatic
    Workshop. In later years, she sold the school to a long-time collaborator, the
    film and theatre agent Saul C. Colin.

72 Klaus Wannemacher, *Erwin Piscators Theater gegen das Schweigen. Politisches
    Theater zwischen den Fronten des Kalten Kriegs* (Tübingen: Max Niemeyer,
    2004), 23; and Günther Rühle, *Theater in Deutschland 1945–1966. Seine
    Ereignisse – seine Menschen* (Frankfurt am Main: S. Fischer, 2014), 407–8.

73 Erwin Piscator to Fritz Kortner, 24 April 1951, in Piscator, *Briefe,* Volume 2.3,
    259–60.

74 This was perhaps a clear-sighted move, given the deep-rooted mistrust of GDR
    government officials towards him: during a meeting in January 1952, the
    Central Committee Secretariat of the SED addressed the topic of extending
    an official invitation to Piscator to work in the GDR. The discussion resulted
    in the recommendation not to enter into negotiations due to Piscator's alleged
    inclination to adopt 'American existentialist' drama.

75 Gerhard Jacoby to Erwin Piscator, 25 July 1950, quoted in Wannemacher,
    Erwin Piscators Theater, 22–3.

76 Marita Krauss, *Heimkehr in ein fremdes Land. Geschichte der Remigration
    nach 1945* (Munich: C. H. Beck, 2001), 90–2.

77 Erwin Piscator, Diary 2, p. 12 (1952), quoted in Wannemacher, *Erwin
    Piscators Theater*, 232.

78 Barbara Elling, 'Theater as the Conscience of Society: Erwin Piscator's
    "Interim Achievement"', in *Playing for Stakes: German-Language Drama in
    Social Context*, eds Anna K. Kuhn and Barbara D. Wright (Oxford/Providence:
    Berg Publishers, 1994), 101–18, 113.

79 Wannemacher, *Erwin Piscators Theater*, 51–2.

80 See Arjomand, 'Performing Catastrophe', 49–74, 53–6.

81 An English version of the stage adaptation was published later as Leo Tolstoy,
    War and Peace, adapted for the stage by Alfred Neumann, Erwin Piscator and
    Guntram Prüfer. English adaptation by Robert David MacDonald (London:
    Macgibbon & Kee, 1963).

82 Erwin Piscator to Klaus Juncker, 19 April 1958, in Piscator, *Briefe,* Volume
    3.2, 518.

83 Rühle, *Theater in Deutschland 1945–1966*, 546–7.

84 Erwin Piscator, 'Auseinandersetzung mit der Kritik anlässlich der Aufführung
    von "Krieg und Frieden"', in *Erwin Piscator. Eine Arbeitsbiographie in 2
    Bänden, Vol. 2, Moskau – Paris – New York – Berlin 1931–1966*, eds Knut
    Boeser and Renata Vatková (Berlin: Edition Hentrich, 1986), 156–64, 159.

85 Friedrich Luft, 'Frieden ist besser als Krieg: Genügt das für ein Drama?', *Die Welt*, 22 March 1955.

86 Friedrich Luft, 'Die Irrtümer des Erwin Piscator', *Süddeutsche Zeitung*, 23 March 1955.

87 Erwin Piscator to Käthe Hamburger, 27 April 1955, in *Piscator, Briefe*. Volume 3.2, 56.

88 According to the Rowohlt Verlag, the stage adaptation by Prüfer, Piscator and Neumann has been produced in sixteen countries (and in cities such as Vienna, Oslo, London, Warsaw, New York and Tel Aviv). Radio versions of the adaptation were broadcast by several German radio stations as well as Genf Radio and Basel Funk. It has been presented on TV in the GDR (1958), the UK (1963) and the Netherlands (1966). Different translations exist.

89 Piscator, 'Auseinandersetzung mit der Kritik', 158.

90 Erwin Piscator to Boleslaw Barlog, n.d. [April 1955], in Piscator, *Briefe*. Volume 3.2, 38.

91 For a detailed comparison of Piscator's early and late aesthetic approaches see Wannemacher, *Erwin Piscators Theater*, 225–65.

92 Piscator, *Theater, Film, Politik*, 352–76, 355.

93 Leo Tolstoy, *Krieg und Frieden* (War and Peace), Schiller-Theater, Berlin, 20 March 1955; William Faulkner, *Requiem für eine Nonne* (Requiem for a Nun), Schloßpark Theater Berlin, 10 November 1955; Bertolt Brecht, *Flüchtlingsgespräche* (Refugee Conversations), Munich Kammerspiele, 15 February 1962.

94 Gotthold E. Lessing, *Nathan the Wise*, Schauspielhaus Marburg, 14 May 1952 (thrust stage); Friedrich Schiller, *Die Räuber* (The Robbers), Nationaltheater Mannheim, 13 January 1957 (traverse stage); Arthur Miller, *The Crucible*, Nationaltheater Mannheim, 20 September 1954 (thrust stage), Max Frisch, *The Fire Raisers*, Nationaltheater Mannheim, 22 May 1959 (theatre in the round).

95 Leo Tolstoy, *War and Peace*; Georg Büchner, *Dantons Tod* (Danton's Death), Schiller-Theater Berlin, 4 May 1956.

96 Friedrich Schiller, *The Robbers*; Richard Strauss, *Salome*, Teatro Comunale Firenze, 31 May 1964; Gerhart Hauptmann, *Fuhrmann Henschel* (Drayman Henschel), Freie Volksbühne Berlin, 1 April 1965.

97 Diary 10, p. 65 (5 October 1953), quoted in Wannemacher, *Erwin Piscators Theater*, 257.

98 For example, Jean-Paul Sartre, *Im Räderwerk* (In the Mesh), Städtische Bühnen Frankfurt am Main, 27 September 1953; Leo Tolstoy, *War and Peace*; Friedrich Schiller, *The Robbers*.

99 Diary 16, p. 138 (18 January 1957), quoted in Wannemacher, *Erwin Piscators Theater*, 257.

100 For example, Boris Blacher, *Rosamunde Floris*, Städtische Oper Berlin, 21 September 1960, and Richard Strauss, *Salome*, Teatro Comunale Firenze, 31 May 1964.

101 Diary 14, p. 119 (April/May 1955), quoted in Wannemacher, Erwin Piscators Theater, 243.

102 Helmuth de Haas, 'Piscator bereitete einen grandiosen Abend', *Die Welt*, 7 March 1958.

103 Werner Tamms, 'Im Haus der Verdammten', *Westdeutsche Allgemeine Zeitung*, 14 January 1958.

104 Theodor W. Adorno, 'Was bedeutet: Aufarbeitung der Vergangenheit?', in *Eingriffe. Neun kritische Modelle*, ed. Adorno (Frankfurt am Main: Suhrkamp, 1963), 125–46.

105 Among Piscator's world premieres during the 1950s and 1960s were Günther Weisenborn, *Göttingen Cantata*, Liederhalle Stuttgart, 18 May 1958; Hans Henny Jahnn, *The Dusty Rainbow*, Städtische Bühnen Frankfurt am Main, 17 March 1961; Bertolt Brecht, *Refugee Conversations*; Rolf Hochhuth, *Der Stellvertreter* (The Deputy), Theater am Kurfürstendamm, 20 February 1963; Heinar Kipphardt, *In der Sache J. Robert Oppenheimer* (In the Matter of J. Robert Oppenheimer), Freie Volksbühne Berlin, 11 October 1964; Peter Weiss, *Die Ermittlung* (The Investigation), Freie Volksbühne Berlin, 19 October 1965; and Hans Hellmut Kirst, *Aufstand der Offiziere* (The Officers' Uprising), Freie Volksbühne Berlin, 2 March 1966.

106 Ley-Piscator, *Der Tanz im Spiegel*, 326.

107 For more information on the Volksbühne Berlin, see Minou Arjomand's chapter in this volume.

108 Rolf Hochhuth to Heinrich Maria Ledig-Rowohlt, 3 March 1962, in Piscator, *Briefe*. Volume 3.3, 391.

109 Heinrich Maria Ledig-Rowohlt to Erwin Piscator, 8 March 1962, quoted in Wannemacher, *Erwin Piscators Theater*, 158.

110 Willett, *The Theatre of Erwin Piscator*, 179.

111 Birgit Lahann, *Hochhuth – Der Störenfried* (Bonn: J.H.W. Dietz Nachf, 2016), 44–5.

112 Willy H. Thiem, 'Die Fehlbarkeit des Papstes oder der unteilbare Christus', *Die Abendpost*, 22 February 1963.

113 Piscator, *Eine Arbeitsbiographie in 2 Bänden*, Volume 2, 201.

114 For example, in September 1963 in Basel, in December 1963 in Paris (346 performances), in January 1964 in Vienna and in February 1964 in New York City (316 performances).

115 Lahann, *Hochhuth – Der Störenfried*, 60.

116 Bertolt Brecht, 'Gespräche mit jungen Intellektuellen', in Bertolt Brecht, *Schriften 3. Schriften 1942–1956*, eds Werner Hecht, Jan Knopf, Werner Mittenzwei and Klaus Detlef Müller (Berlin and Weimar, Frankfurt am Main: Aufbau and Suhrkamp, 1993), 97–103, 101.

117 'Auschwitz auf dem Theater? Ein Podiumsgespräch im Württembergischen Staatstheater Stuttgart am 24. Oktober 1965 aus Anlass der Erstaufführung der *Ermittlung*', in *Deutsche Nachkriegsliteratur und der Holocaust*, eds Stephan Braese, Holger Gehle, Doron Kiesel and Hanno Loewy (Frankfurt am Main: Campus, 1998), 71–97, 75–6.

118 Piscator, *Theater, Film, Politik*, 412.

119 'Drei Fragen an fünf Intendanten', *Die Zeit*, 29 October 1965, 20.

120 Walter Jens, '*Die Ermittlung* in Westberlin', *Die Zeit*, 29 October 1965.

121 Wannemacher, *Erwin Piscators Theater*, 156–7.

122 Particularly Gerhart Hauptmann's *Atreus Tetralogy* (1962), Rolf Hochhuth's *The Deputy* (1963), Heinar Kipphardt's *In the Matter of J. Robert Oppenheimer* (1964), and Peter Weiss's *The Investigation* (1965).

123 Rühle, *Theater in Deutschland 1945–1966*, 1093.

124 Piscator, *The Political Theatre*, 66.

125 Markus Moninger, 'Auschwitz erinnern: *Merchant*-Inszenierungen im Nachkriegsdeutschland', in *Das Theater der anderen. Alterität und Theater zwischen Antike und Gegenwart*, ed. Christopher Balme (Tübingen, Basel: Francke, 2001), 229–48.

126 Erwin Piscator to Maria Ley, 22 February 1963, Erwin-Piscator-Center, Archiv der Akademie der Künste.

Chapter 5

1 Heinrich Scheuffelhut, quoted in Werner Frisch and K.W. Obermeier, *Brecht in Augsburg. Errinnerungen, Dokumente, Texts, Fotos* (Berlin and Weimar: Aufbau, 1986), 43. All translations from the German are mine unless otherwise acknowledged.

2 See Werner Hecht, *Brecht Chronik* (Frankfurt am Main: Suhrkamp, 1997), 139.

3 Asja Lacis, quoted and translated in Stephen Parker, *Bertolt Brecht: A Literary Life* (London: Bloomsbury: 2014), 212.

4 Edward Braun, *The Director and the Stage: From Naturalism to Grotowski* (London: Methuen, 1982), 164.

5 Bruce Gaston, 'Brecht's Pastiche History Play: Renaissance Drama and Modernist Theatre in *Leben Eduards Des Zweiten Von England*', *German Life and Letters* 56, no. 4 (2003): 344–62, 360.

6 See Manfred Pfister, 'Vor- und Nachgeschichte der Tragödie *Eduard II.* von Marlowe über Brecht und Feuchtwanger bis zu Ihering und Kerr', in *Großbritannien und Deutschland. Europäische Aspekte der politisch-kulturellen Beziehungen beider Länder in Geschichte und Gegenwart. Festschrift für John W. Bourke*, ed. Ortwin Kuhn (Munich: Goldmann, 1974), 395.

7 Bernhard Reich, *Im Wettlauf mit der Zeit* (Berlin: Henschel, 1970), 262.

8 John Fuegi, *Bertolt Brecht: Chaos, According to Plan* (Cambridge: Cambridge University Press, 1987), 56.

9 Ibid., 185.

10 Herbert Ihering, quoted in Hecht, *Brecht Chronik*, 303.

11 Bertolt Brecht, 'Notes to the 1937 Edition' [of *Man Equals Man*], in Brecht, *Collected Plays*, vol. 2, ed. John Willett and Ralph Manheim (London: Bloomsbury, 1994), 269.

12 Ibid., 270.

13 See Laura Bradley, *Brecht and Political Theatre: 'The Mother' On Stage* (Oxford: Oxford University Press, 2006), 30.

14 Ibid.

15 Carl Weber, 'The Actor and Brecht, or: The Truth Is Concrete', *Brecht Yearbook* 13 (1984): 63–74, 71.

16 Karl Marx, 'Theses on Feuerbach', written in 1845, https://www.marxists.org/archive/marx/works/1845/theses/theses.htm (accessed 15 August 2016).

17 Margaret Eddershaw, 'Actors on Brecht', in *The Cambridge Companion to Brecht*, eds Peter Thomson and Glendyr Sacks, 2nd edition (Cambridge: Cambridge University Press, 2006), 286.

18 Meg Mumford, 'Showing the Gestus: A Study of Acting in Brecht's Theatre' (Unpublished PhD Thesis, University of Bristol, 1997), 22.

19 John, *Chaos, According to Plan*, xiii.

20 Meg Mumford, *Bertolt Brecht* (Abingdon: Routledge, 2009), 49–50.

21 Ruth Berlau, in Hans Bunge, *Brechts Lai-Tu. Erinnerungen und Notate von Ruth Berlau* (Darmstadt: Luchterhand, 1985), 288.

22 After two years with the BE, the actor Regine Lutz confessed to her parents that 'dialectics are still a mystery to me' (Lutz to her Parents, 26 December 1951, Bertolt Brecht Archive (henceforth BBA) Lutz file 'Briefe ab Feb 1951 bis Nov 1954'). Ekkehard Schall, on the other hand, represents one of the great Brechtian actors who confronted the philosophical underpinnings of Brecht's theatre and speaks eloquently and incisively about them in his book *The Craft of Theatre* (London: Methuen, 2008). He is, however, more the exception than the rule.

23 See The Editors, 'General Introduction', in Brecht, *Brecht on Theatre*, ed. Marc Silberman, Steve Giles and Tom Kuhn, 3rd edition (London: Bloomsbury, 2014), 4–5 for a fuller discussion.

24 '*Der Zerbrochene* [*sic*] *Krug*', undated, p. 3 (1), Berliner Ensemble Archive (henceforth BEA) File 7.

25 Ibid.

26 Ibid., 2.

27 'Probe *Zerbrochener Krug* 3. 1. 52', undated, p. 6 (1), BEA File 7.

28 Ibid.

29 'Probe *Zerbrochener Krug* 12. 1. 52 Probenhaus', undated, p. 6 (6), BEA File 7.

30 '*Der Zerbrochene* [*sic*] *Krug*', undated, p. 3 (3), BEA File 7.

31 See Lutz to her parents, 4 November 1951, BBA Lutz files 'Briefe ab Feb. 1951 bis Nov. 1954'.

32 Manfred Wekwerth, *Schriften: Arbeit mit Brecht*, 2nd revised and expanded edition (Berlin: Henschel, 1975), 111.

33 Käthe Reichel, in Christa Neubert-Herwig, 'Wir waren damals wirklich Mitarbeiter', in *Benno Besson: Theater spielen in acht Ländern. Texte – Dokumente – Gespräche*, ed. Neubert-Herwig (Berlin: Alexander, 1998), 33.

34 For more detailed information on how Brecht rehearsed, see David Barnett, *Brecht in Practice: Theatre, Theory and Performance* (London: Bloomsbury, 2014), 137–53.

35 Berliner Ensemble and Helene Weigel, eds, *Theaterarbeit: 6 Aufführungen des Berliner Ensembles* (Dresden: VVV Dresdner Verlag, 1952), 434.

36 Bertolt Brecht, 'The Popular and the Realistic', in Brecht, *Brecht on Theatre*, 203.

37 '*Der Zerbrochene [sic] Krug*', undated, pp. 3 (1), BEA File 7.

38 Untitled, n.d., n.p., BEA File 7.

39 Brecht, in '*Der Zerbrochene [sic] Krug*', undated, n.p., BEA File 7.

40 Anon., 'Probe *Zerbrochener Krug* 31. 12. 51', undated, p. 5 (4), ibid.

41 Ibid., p. 2.

42 See Lutz to her parents, 6 January 1952, BBA Lutz files 'Briefe ab Feb. 1951 bis Nov. 1954'.

43 See Hansheinrich [sic], '*Der zerbrochene Krug*', *Berliner-Montag*, 29 January 1952, and Henryk Keisch, '*Der zerbrochene Krug*', *Neues Deutschland*, 5 February 1952.

44 However, he, too, incurred the wrath of the fickle SED in the months after the premiere of the play through his record company Lied der Zeit.

45 'Fehler, die die Fabel verwischen', n.d., n.p., Ernst Busch Archive, Akademie der Künste, Berlin, no catalogue number. All subsequent references to this material will appear as 'EBA'. None of the documents have a catalogue number.

46 'Einige Eingriffe Brechts in die Inszenierung des *Glockenspiel*', n.d., n.p., ibid.

47 See '*Glockenspiel des Kreml*', n.d., n.p., ibid.

48 Brecht, '[Die Auswahl der einzelnen Elemente]', in Brecht, *Große kommentierte Berliner und Frankfurter Ausgabe*, vol. 22, ed. Werner Hecht, Jan Knopf, Werner Mittenzwei and Klaus-Detlef Müller (Berlin and Frankfurt am Main: Aufbau and Suhrkamp, 1993), 253. References to this edition will henceforth appear as 'BFA' followed by a volume and page number.

49 'Einige Eingriffe Brechts in die Inszenierung des *Glockenspiel*', n.d., n.p., EBA.

50 'Fehler, die die Fabel verwischen', n.d., n.p., ibid.

51 Hans Ulrich Eylau, '*Das Glockenspiel des Kreml*', *Berliner Zeitung*, 28 March 1952.

52 See Brecht to Johannes R. Becher, 2 February 1954, in Brecht, *Letters 1913– 1956*, ed. John Willett (London: Methuen, 1990), 527.

53 See Brecht to Emil Burian, 20 September 1954, ibid., 532.

54 Johannes R. Becher, quoted in Amy Lynn Wlodarski, *Musical Witness and Holocaust Representation* (Cambridge: Cambridge University Press, 2015), 210.

55 Brecht, *Buying Brass*, in Brecht, *Brecht on Performance*, ed. Steve Giles, Tom Kuhn and Marc Silberman (London: Bloomsbury, 2014), 35.

56 Brecht, *Bertolt Brecht's Me-ti: Book of Interventions in the Flow of Things*, ed. Antony Tatlow (London: Bloomsbury, 2016), 47.

57 Brecht, 'Dialektische Betrachtung der *Winterschlacht*', BFA 24: 446.

58 Brecht, '[Hamlets Zögern als Vernunft]', BFA 22: 611.

59 Burian, quoted in 'Notate *Winterschlacht*', n.d., pencil note 'Burian', p. 15, BEA File 18.

60 Ibid., p. 4.

61 Heinz Kahlau, 'Notate *Winterschlacht*', n.d., p. 35 (29), BEA File 18.

62 Regine Lutz to her parents, 28 November 1954, BBA Lutz file 'Briefe ab Feb. 1951 bis Nov.1954'.

63 Brecht, in Kahlau, 'Notate *Winterschlacht*', p. 6, BEA File 18.

64 See Käthe Rülicke, 'Historisierende Lesarten von J.R. Bechers *Winterschlacht*', *notate* 1 (1988): 18–19, 18.

65 Brecht, 'Schwierigkeiten, denen Burians Konzeption in Berlin begegnet', BFA 24: 449.

66 Brecht, in Kahlau, 'Notate *Winterschlacht*', p. 8, BEA File 18.

67 Anon., 'Zur *Winterschlacht*', n.d., BBA 940/13.

68 Brecht, 'Letter to the Actor Playing Young Hörder in *Winter Battle*', in Brecht, *Brecht on Theatre*, 300–3, 301.

69 Brecht, 'Schwierigkeiten', 449.

70 See Kahlau, 'Notate *Winterschlacht*', p. 14.

71 Brecht, quoted in 'Notate *Winterschlacht*', n.d., p. 14 (3–4).

72 Brecht, quoted in Käthe Rülicke, 'Szenenanalyse IV. Akt (Erschiessung Karl Hörders)', 26 November 1954, BBA 1076/07.

73 Kahlau, '*Winterschlacht* – Notate', n.d., n.p., BEA File 18.

74 Anonymous to Kurt Palm, 13 November 1954, ibid.

75 See, for example, Heinz Hofmann, 'Denkzettel für neue Uralstürmer', *National-Zeitung*, 16 January 1955, and Ernst Kluft, 'Tragödie eines "unbekannten Soldaten"', *Neue Zeit*, 18 January 1955.

76 See, for example, W.B., 'Lautes Prusten im Parkett', *Die Welt*, 22 January 1955.

77 See Brecht, 'Short List of the Most Frequent, Common and Boring Misconceptions about Epic Theatre', in Brecht, *Brecht on Theatre*, 131–2, 131.

78 Brecht, 'Über rationellen und emotionellen Standpunkt', BFA 22: 501.

79 Brecht, 'Short Organon for the Theatre', in Brecht, *Brecht on Theatre*, 229–55, 254 and 255.

80 Brecht, 'Will man Schweres bewältigen, muss man es sich leicht machen', BFA 23 168–9.

81 See Brecht, 'On humour', in Brecht, *Me-ti*, 81.

82 See Pusch, Hagen and Kellner, 'Protokoll über die durchführte Finanzrevision für den Zeitraum vom 1.1.1954–31.7.1955', 10 September 1955, Bundesarchiv, DR1/18169, p. 8 (3); and Weigel, Giersch, Neumann and Kellner, 'Protokoll über die durchführte Revision des Haushalts- und Finanzwirtschaft. Zeitraum 1.1.58–31.12.1960', 5 April 1961, Bundesarchiv, DR1/18164, p. 25 (4).

Chapter 6

1 See Hans Peter Neureuter, ed., Brechts 'Herr Puntila und sein Knecht Matti' (Frankfurt am Main: Suhrkamp, 1987), 186.

2 See Brecht, 'Ist ein Stück wie Herr Puntila und sein Knecht Matti nach der Vertreibung der Gutsbesitzer bei uns noch aktuell?', 1951, BFA 24: 314.

3 Brecht, Mr. Puntila and his Man Matti, trans. John Willett (London: Eyre Methuen, 1977), 92.

4 Brecht, 9 December 1948, in Journals 1933–1945, ed. John Willett, trans. Hugh Rorrison (London: Methuen, 1993), 404–5.

5 Brecht, 'Das Typische', c. 1951, BFA 23: 141 and '[Notiz zum Typischen]', January 1956, BFA 23: 381.

6 See Meg Mumford, Bertolt Brecht (Abingdon and New York: Routledge, 2009), 109, 167; David Barnett, Brecht in Practice: Theatre, Theory and Performance (London and New York: Bloomsbury, 2015), 85–6, 90.

7 See Mumford, Bertolt Brecht, 54.

8 See Darko Suvin, 'Brecht: Bearing, Pedagogy, Productivity', Gestos 5, no. 10 (1990): 12; David Barnett, A History of the Berliner Ensemble (Cambridge: Cambridge University Press, 2015), 30.

9 See Anonymous, n.d., Bertolt Brecht Archive 509/67, henceforth BBA.

10 See Isot Killian notes file, undated, BBA 1824/45–6.

11 See Egon Monk et al. rehearsal notes, 19 September 1949, BBA 1598/08; Neureuter, ed., Brechts Puntila, 168.

12 See Monk et al. rehearsal notes, BBA 1598/08.

13 See Ruth Berlau notes on Puntila file, n.d., BBA 1950/114.

14 See Brecht, 'Steckels zwei Puntilas', 1951, BFA 24: 310.

15 See Egon Monk et al. rehearsal notes, BBA 1598/11, 14.

16 See Brecht, 'Steckels zwei Puntilas', 310.

17 See Monk et al. rehearsal notes, BBA 1598/11.

18 See Brecht, 'Steckels zwei Puntilas', 310.

19 See Hans Peter Neureuter, 'Herr Puntila und sein Knecht Matti', in Brecht Handbuch, vol. 1, ed. Jan Knopf (Stuttgart and Weimar: J.B. Metzler, 2001), 454.

20 See Hans Jürgen Syberberg, Syberberg filmt bei Brecht: 'Herr Puntila und sein Knecht Matti', 'Urfaust', 'Die Mutter' (Berlin: Alexander, 1993).

21 See Brecht, 'Die Masken', 1951, BFA 24: 313.

22 See ibid., 313.

23 See Klaus Detlef-Müller, editorial notes on *Herr Puntila und Sein Knecht Matti*, BFA 6: 470.

24 See Friedrich Luft, *Stimme der Kritik* (Berlin-West), 13 November 1949, in Neureuter, ed., *Brechts Puntila*, 182.

25 See Anon., n.d., notes on the Zurich premiere, BBA 566/7.

26 See Brecht, 'Notizen über die züricher Erstaufführung (1948)', BFA 24: 302.

27 See Brecht, 'Die Frauen von Kurgela', 1951, BFA 24: 311.

28 See Brecht, 'Die Masken', 313.

29 Brecht, 'The Popular and the Realistic', June 1938, in *Brecht on Theatre*, 203.

30 See Brecht, 'Short Organon for the Theatre', summer 1948, in *Brecht on Theatre*, 254; Brecht, '*Antigone* Model 1948', in *Brecht on Performance: 'Messingkauf' and Modelbooks*, eds Tom Kuhn, Steve Giles and Marc Silberman, trans. Charlotte Ryland et al. (London and New York: Bloomsbury, 2014), 169.

31 See Meg Mumford, 'Gestic Masks in Brecht's Theatre: A Testimony to the Contradictions and Parameters of a Realist Aesthetic', *The Brecht Yearbook* 26 (2001): 146–8, 122.

32 See Brecht, 'Notizen über die züricher Erstaufführung (1948)', BFA 24: 301.

33 See ibid.

34 See Barnett, *A History of the Berliner Ensemble*, 63.

35 Brecht, '*Antigone* Model 1948', 166.

36 See Brecht, '[Kennzeichen und Symbole]', autumn 1936, BFA 22.1: 263.

37 Barnett, *A History of the Berliner Ensemble*, 421.

38 See Karl Marx, *The German Ideology*, in Karl Marx, *Selected Writings*, ed. David McLellan (Oxford: Oxford University Press, 1977), 160.

39 Karl Marx, 'Letter to Annenkov', in Karl Marx, *Selected Writings*, 192.

40 See Monk et al. rehearsal notes, 20 September 1949, BBA 1598/22.

41 See Rehearsal notes for *Puntila* by Brecht's co-workers, 26 August 1951, BBA 1599/05.

42 Brecht, 'Short Organon for the Theatre', 242.

43 See ibid., 3 September 1951, BBA 1599/19.

44 See Brecht, 'Notizen über die züricher Erstaufführung (1948)', 300.

45 See Monk et al. rehearsal notes, 27 September 1949, BBA 1598/49–50.

46 See ibid., 27 October 1949, BBA 1598/70.

47 See Rehearsal notes for *Puntila* by Brecht's co-workers, 20 September 1951, BBA 1599/45.

48 Heinz Kahlau, 'Notate *Winterschlacht*', undated, BEA File 18, p. 25, in Barnett, *Brecht in Practice*, 102.

49 See Rehearsal notes for *Puntila* by Brecht's co-workers, 10 September 1951, BBA 1599/28.

50   Barnett, *Brecht in Practice*, 155.

51   See Meg Mumford, '"Dragging" Brecht's Gestus Onwards: A Feminist Challenge', in *Bertolt Brecht: Centenary Essays*, eds Steve Giles and Rodney Livingstone (Amsterdam: Rodopi, 1998), 244.

52   Frederick Engels, *The Origin of the Family, Private Property and the State*, trans. Alec West (London: Lawrence and Wishart, 1972), 117–20.

53   See, for example, Moira Maconachie, 'Engels, Sexual Divisions and the Family', in *Engels Revisited: New Feminist Essays*, eds, Janet Sayers, Mary Evans and Nanneke Redclift (London and New York: Tavistock, 1987), 105–6, 108–9.

54   See Margareta N. Deschner, 'Wuolijoki's and Brecht's Politization of the *Volksstück*', in *Bertolt Brecht: Political Theory and Literary Practice*, eds Betty Nance Weber and Hubert Heinen (Manchester: Manchester University Press, 1980), 122.

55   See ibid., 125–6.

56   Brecht, 14 January 1941, in *Journals 1934–1955*, 126.

57   See Alisa Solomon, 'Materialist Girl: *The Good Person of Szechwan* and Making Gender Strange', *Theater* 25, no. 2 (1994): 52–3.

58   See Brecht, 'Clownerie', 1951, BFA 24: 309; Berliner Ensemble, ed., *Theaterarbeit: 6 Aufführungen des Berliner Ensembles*, 2nd edition (Berlin: Henschelverlag Kunst und Gesellschaft, 1961), 9.

59   See Isot Killian notes file, BBA 1824/49.

60   Judith Butler, 'Performative Acts and Gender Constitution: An Essay in Phenomenology and Feminist Theory', *Theatre Journal* 40, no. 4 (1988): 519–20.

61   Judith Butler, *Gender Trouble: Feminism and the Subversion of Identity* (London and New York: Routledge, 1990), 33.

62   See Monk et al., BBA 1599/14.

63   See Brecht, *Mr. Puntila and his Man Matti*, 77.

64   See Rehearsal notes for *Puntila* by Brecht's co-workers, 18 October 1951, BBA 1599/82.

65   See Monk et al., 25 October 1949, BBA 1598/61.

66   See Rehearsal notes for *Puntila* by Brecht's co-workers, 26 August 1951, BBA 1599/5.

67   See Regine Lutz, *Schauspieler – der schönste Beruf: Einblicke in die Theaterarbeit* (Munich: Langen Müller, 1993), 248–9.

68   See Monk et al., 27 September 1949, BBA 1598/51.

69   See Neureuter, '*Herr Puntila und sein Knecht Matti*', 444, 447.

70   See Monk et al., 22 September and 26 October 1949, 1598/28, 64–6.

71   See Rehearsal notes for *Puntila* by Brecht's co-workers, 12 September 1951, BBA 1599/32.

72   See ibid., 5 October 1951, BBA 1599/70.

73   Ibid., 13 September 1951, BBA 1599/34.

74 See ibid.

75 See ibid., 22 September 1951, BBA 1599/28, 37.

76 See Brecht, letter 528 to Stefan S. Brecht, September–October 1946, in Brecht, *Letters*, ed. John Willett, trans. Ralph Manheim (New York: Routledge; London: Methuen, 1990), 416.

77 See Käthe Rülicke-Weiler, *Die Dramaturgie Brechts: Theater als Mittel der Veränderung* (Berlin: Henschelverlag Kunst und Gesellschaft, 1966), 126.

78 See Brecht, 'Notizen über die züricher Aufführung (1948)', BFA 24: 299.

79 Hugh Rorrison, 'Commentary', in Brecht, *Life of Galileo*, trans. John Willett (London: Methuen Student, 1986), xxi.

80 Brecht, 6 April 1944, in *Journals 1934–1955*, 308.

81 Brecht, 'The Analysis' from *Aufbau einer Rolle/Laughtons Galilei* (Berlin: Henschel, 1956), in Brecht, *Collected Plays*, vol. 5, eds John Willett and Ralph Manheim (London: Methuen Drama, 1995), 230.

82 See Rainer E. Zimmermann, '*Leben des Galilei*', in Knopf, ed., *Brecht Handbuch*, 359.

83 See Stephen Parker, 'Taoist Paradox and Socialist-Realist Aesthetics: Re-Grounding the Galileo Complex in the "Danish" *Leben des Galilei*. Brecht's Testimony from the "finsteren Zeiten"', *German Life and Letters* 69, no. 2 (2016): 197.

84 See Barnett, *A History of the Berliner Ensemble*, 156–7.

85 Brecht, *Life of Galileo*, in *Collected Plays*, vol. 5, 29.

86 Brecht, '[Rejection of Virginia]', from *Aufbau einer Rolle/Laughtons Galilei* (Berlin: Henschel, 1956), in Brecht, *Collected Plays: Five*, 218.

87 See Rehearsal notes for *Life of Galileo* by Brecht's co-workers, n.d., BBA 675/150.

88 See the transcription of tape-recordings of *Life of Galileo* rehearsals, 15 January and 16 March 1956, BBA 2187/215–16, 235 respectively.

89 Ibid., 215–16.

90 See notes taken by Käthe Rülicke for the section on Busch's Galilei for the 1958 *Life of Galileo* model book, BBA 609/112.

91 See the transcription of tape-recordings of *Life of Galileo* rehearsals, 20 January 1956, BBA 2191/162.

92 See notes by Käthe Rülicke, BBA 609/112.

93 See the transcription of tape-recordings of *Life of Galileo* rehearsals, 28 January 1956, BBA 2190/277.

94 See the transcription of tape-recordings of *Life of Galileo* rehearsals, 21 January 1956, BBA 2191/158–64.

95 See ibid., 163.

96 See Bernard Fenn, *Characterisation of Women in the Plays of Bertolt Brecht* (Frankfurt am Main: Peter Lang, 1982), 162.

97 See the transcription of tape-recordings of *Life of Galileo* rehearsals, 21 January 1956, BBA 2191/165.

98   See Käthe Rülicke's notes on her discussion with Brecht about Scene 13 on
      21 January 1956, BBA 2071/07.

99   David Barnett, 'Performing Dialectics in an Age of Uncertainty, or: Why
      Post-Brechtian ≠ Postdramatic', in *Postdramatic Theatre and the Political:
      International Perspectives on Contemporary Performance*, eds Karen Jürs-
      Munby, Jerome Carroll and Steve Giles (London and New York: Bloomsbury,
      2013), 58.

100   Ibid., 57.

101   Lara Stevens, *Anti-War Theatre After Brecht: Dialectical Aesthetics in the
      Twenty-First Century* (London: Palgrave Macmillan, 2016), 46.

102   Brecht, 'Appendices to the *Short Organon*', *c.* 1954 in *Brecht on Theatre*, 257.

103   Meg Mumford, 'Brecht on Acting for the 21st Century: Interrogating and Re-
      Inscribing the Fixed', *Communications from the International Brecht Society*
      29, nos 1–2 (2000): 49.

104   Brecht, 'Short Organon for the Theatre' (1948), in *Brecht on Theatre*, 241.

105   Mumford, 'Brecht on Acting for the 21st Century', 45.

106   David Barnett, 'Toward a Definition of Post-Brechtian Performance: The
      Example of *In the Jungle of the Cities* at the Berliner Ensemble, 1971',
      Modern Drama 54, no. 3 (2011): 344.

107   Stevens, *Anti-War Theatre After Brecht*, 21.

108   Brecht, 'Appendices to the Short Organon', 257.

BIBLIOGRAPHY

General

Adorno, Theodor W. 'Was bedeutet: Aufarbeitung der Vergangenheit?' In *Eingriffe. Neun kritische Modelle*, 125–46. Frankfurt am Main: Suhrkamp, 1963.

Adorno, Theodor, et al. *Aesthetics and Politics*. New York: Verso, 2007.

Anonymous. 'Auschwitz auf dem Theater? Ein Podiumsgespräch im Württembergischen Staatstheater Stuttgart am 24. Oktober 1965 aus Anlass der Erstaufführung der *Ermittlung*'. In *Deutsche Nachkriegsliteratur und der Holocaust*. Edited by Stephan Braese, Holger Gehle, Doron Kiesel and Hanno Loewy, 71–97. Frankfurt am Main: Campus, 1998.

Askin, Leon, and C. Melvin Davidson. *Quietude and Quest: Protagonists and Antagonists in the Theatre, on and off Stage as seen Through the Eyes of Leon Askin*. Riverside, CA: Ariadne Press, 1989.

Bann, Stephen. *The Traditions of Constructivism*. New York: Da Capo Press, 1974.

Belafonte, Harry, and Michael Shnayerson. *My Song. A Memoir*. New York: Alfred A. Knopf, 2011.

Benjamin, Walter. *Illuminations*. Edited by Hannah Arendt. Translated by Harry Zohn. New York: Schocken, 1969.

Boak, Helen. *Women in the Weimar Republic*. Manchester: Manchester University Press, 2013.

Boenisch, Peter M. *Directing Scenes and Senses: The Thinking of Regie*, Manchester: Manchester University Press, 2015.

Braun, Edward. *The Director and the Stage: From Naturalism to Grotowski*. London: Methuen, 1982.

Brown, Bryan. *A History of the Theatre Laboratory*. London: Routledge, 2018.

Brušák, Karel. 'Imaginary Action Space in Drama'. In *Drama und Theater. Theorie -Methode-Geschichte*. Edited by H. Schmid and K. Hedwig, 144–62. Munich: Otto Sagner, 1992. [Original in French in *Travaux* 6 (1936): 20–32.]

Bürger, Peter. *Theory of the Avant-Garde*. Translated by Michael Shaw. Minneapolis: University of Minnesota Press, 1984.

Butler, Judith. *Gender Trouble: Feminism and the Subversion of Identity*. London and New York: Routledge, 1990.

Cardullo, Bert and Robert Knopf. *Theater of the Avant-Garde, 1890–1950: A Critical Anthology*. New Haven, CT: Yale University Press, 2001.

Caughie, John. *Theories of Authorship: A Reader*, London: Routledge, 2005.

Clayton, J. Douglas. *Pierrot in Petrograd: Commedia dell'Arte/Balagan in Twentieth-Century Russian Theatre and Drama*. Montreal: McGill-Queen's University Press, 1993.

Engels, Frederick. *The Origin of the Family, Private Property and the State*. Translated by Alec West. London: Lawrence and Wishart, 1972.

Fischer-Lichte, Erika. *The Routledge Introduction to Theatre and Performance Studies*. Edited by Minou Arjomand and Ramona Mosse. New York and London: Routledge, 2014.

Furness, Raymond. *Wagner and Literature*. Manchester: Manchester University Press,1982.

Gazzara, Ben. *In the Moment: My Life as an Actor*. New York: Carrol & Graff, 2004.

Granach, Alexander. *Du mein liebes Stück Heimat. Briefe an Lotte Lieven aus dem Exil*. Edited by Angelika Wittlich and Hilde Recher. Augsburg: Ölbaum, 2008.

Green, Amy S. *The Revisionist Stage: American Directors Reinvent the Classics*. Cambridge: Cambridge University Press, 1994.

Green, Michael. *The Russian Symbolist Theater: An Anthology of Plays and Critical Texts*. Ann Arbor: Ardis, 1986.

Grotowski, Jerzy. *Towards a Poor Theatre*. New York: Routledge, 2002.

Hodge, Alison, ed. *Actor Training*. London: Routledge, 2010.

Hoover, Marjorie L. and O. M. Fel'dman, eds. *Lektsii. 1918–1919*. Moscow: OGI, 2000.

Hoover, Marjorie L. and A.V. Fevral'ski, eds. *Stat'i, Pis'ma, Rechi, Besed'i. 1891–1917 (Tom 1) & 1917–1939 (Tom 2)*. Moscow: Iskusstvo, 1968.

Houghton, Norris. *Moscow Rehearsals*. London: George Allen and Unwin, 1938.

Jackson, Anthony. *Theatre, Education and the Making of Meanings. Art or Instrument?* Manchester: Manchester University Press, 2007.

Krauss, Marita. *Heimkehr in ein fremdes Land. Geschichte der Remigration nach 1945*. Munich: C.H. Beck, 2001.

Lahann, Birgit. *Hochhuth – Der Störenfried*. Bonn: J.H.W. Dietz Nachf, 2016.

Lenhoff, Gail. 'The Theatre of Okhlopkov'. *The Drama Review* 17, no. 1 (1973): 90–104.

Listengarten, Julia. *Russian Tragifarce: Its Cultural and Political Roots*. London: Associated University Presses, 2000.

Lutz, Regine. *Schauspieler – der schönste Beruf: Einblicke in die Theaterarbeit*. Munich: Langen Müller, 1993.

Maconachie, Moira. 'Engels, Sexual Divisions and the Family'. In *Engels Revisitied: New Feminist Essays*. Edited by Janet Sayers, Mary Evans and Nanneke Redclift, 98–112. London and New York: Tavistock, 1987.

Marx, Karl. *Selected Writings*. Edited by David McLellan. Oxford: Oxford University Press, 1977.

Marx, Karl. 'Theses on Feuerbach'. *The Marx-Engels Reader*. Edited by Robert C. Tucker. New York: Norton, 1978.

McAuley, Gay. 'A Taxonomy of Spatial Function'. In *Theatre and Performance Design: A Reader in Scenography*. Edited by Jane Collins and Andrew Nisbet, 90–4. London and New York: Routledge, 2010.

Mitchell, Katie. *The Director's Craft*, London: Routledge, 2008.

Moninger, Markus. 'Auschwitz erinnern: *Merchant*-Inszenierungen im Nachkriegsdeutschland'. In *Das Theater der anderen. Alterität und Theater zwischen Antike und Gegenwart*. Edited by Christopher Balme, 229–48. Tübingen, Basel: Francke, 2001.

Neubert-Herwig, Christa. '"Wir waren damals wirklich Mitarbeiter"'. In Neubert-Herwig, *Benno Besson: Theater spielen in acht Ländern. Texte – Dokumente – Gespräche*, 33–6. Berlin: Alexander, 1998.

Pavis, Patrice. *La Mise en Scène Contemporaine: Staging Theatre Today*. Translated by Joel Anderson. London: Routledge, 2013.

Posner, Dassia N. *The Director's Prism: E. T. A. Hoffmann and the Russian Theatrical Avant-Garde*. Evanston, IL: Northwestern University Press, 2016.

Reich, Bernhard. *Im Wettlauf mit der Zeit*. Berlin: Henschel, 1970.

Robertson, Robert. *Eisenstein and the Audiovisual: The Montage of Music, Image and Sound in Cinema*. London: Tauris Academic Studies, 2009.

Roesner, David. *Musicality in Theatre: Music as Model, Method and Metaphor in Theatre-Making*. Surrey: Ashgate, 2014.

Rühle, Günther. *Theater in Deutschland 1945–1966. Seine Ereignisse – seine Menschen*. Frankfurt am Main: S. Fischer, 2014.

Rzhevsky, Nicholas, ed. *The Cambridge Companion to Russian Culture*. Cambridge: Cambridge University Press, 2012.

Schall, Ekkehard. *The Craft of Theatre*. London: Methuen, 2008.

Schumacher, Claude, ed. *Naturalism and Symbolism in European Theatre 1850–1918*, Cambridge: Cambridge University Press, 1996.

Senelick, Laurence. *Stanislavsky: A Life in Letters*. London: Routledge, 2014.

Senelick, Laurence. *Historical Dictionary of Russian Theatre*. Lanham: Rowman & Littlefield, 2015.

Shepherd, Simon. *Direction*. Basingstoke: Palgrave Macmillan, 2012.

Sidiropoulou, Avra. *Authoring Performance: The Director in Contemporary Theatre*. Basingstoke: Palgrave Macmillian, 2011.

Simmel, Georg. *The Sociology of Georg Simmel*. Edited and translated by Kurt H. Wolff. Glencoe, IL: Free Press, 1950.

Smeliansky, Anatoly. *The Russian Theatre after Stalin*. Cambridge: Cambridge University Press, 1999.

Solovyova, Inna. 'The Theatre and Socialist Realism, 1929–1953'. In *A History of Russian Theatre*. Edited by Robert Leach and Victor Borovsky, 325–57. Cambridge: Cambridge University Press, 1999.

Spoto, Daniel. *The Art of Alfred Hitchcock: Fifty Years of His Motion Pictures*. New York: Hopkinson and Blake Publishers, 1976.

Stourac, Richard and Kathleen McCreery. *Theatre as a Weapon: Workers' Theatre in the Soviet Union, Germany and Britain, 1917–1934*. London: Routledge, 1986.

Styan, J.L. *Max Reinhardt*. Cambridge: Cambridge University Press, 1982.

Sutton, Katie. '"We Too Deserve a Place in the Sun": The Politics of Transvestite Identity in Weimar Germany'. *German Studies Review* 35, no. 2 (2012): 335–54.

Ubersfeld, Anne. *Reading Theatre*. Translated by Frank Collins. Toronto: University of Toronto Press, 1999.

Vladimirov, S.V., Y.K. Gerasimov, N.V. Zaitsev, L.P. Klimova and M.N. Lyubimurov. *U Istokov Rezhissurui: Ocherki iz istorii russkoi rezhissurui kontsa XIX – nachala XX veka*. Leningrad: Leningradski Gosudarstvennuii Institut Teatra, Muzuiki i Kinematografii, 1976.

Widdig, Bernd. 'Cultural Dimensions of Inflation in Weimar Germany'. *German Politics & Society* 32 (1994): 10–27.

Witham, Barry B. *A Sustainable Theatre: Jasper Deeter at Hedgerow*. New York: Palgrave Macmillan, 2013.

Wlodarski, Amy Lynn. *Musical Witness and Holocaust Representation*. Cambridge: Cambridge University Press, 2015.

Worrall, Nick. *Modernism to Realism on the Soviet Stage: Tairov, Vakhtangov, Okhlopkov*. Cambridge: Cambridge University Press, 1989.

Zhukova, Ol'ga A. 'The Philosophy of New Spirituality: The Creative Manifesto of Nikolai Berdyaev'. *Russian Studies in Philosophy* 53, no. 4 (2015): 276–90.

Vsevolod Meyerhold

Barkhin, Mikhail and Sergei Vakhtangov. 'A Theatre for Meyerhold'. Translated by E. Braun. *Theatre Quarterly* 2, no. 7 (1972): 69–73.

Braun, Edward. *Meyerhold on Theatre*. London: Methuen, 1969, 1995, 1998.

Braun, Edward. 'Meyerhold: The Final Act'. *New Theatre Quarterly* 9, no. 33 (1993): 3–15.

Braun, Edward. *Meyerhold: A Revolution in Theatre*. London: Methuen, 1995, 1998.

Garin, E.L. *S Meierkhol'dom*. Moscow: Isskustvo, 1974.

Gladkov, Aleksandr. *Meyerhold Speaks, Meyerhold Rehearses*. Translated by A. Law. Amsterdam: Harwood Academic Press, 1997.

Hoover, Marjorie L. 'A Mejerxol'd Method? – *Love for Three Oranges* (1914–1916)'. *The Slavic and East European Journal* 13, no. 1 (1969): 23–41.

Hoover, Marjorie L. *Meyerhold: The Art of Conscious Theatre*. Amherst: University of Massachusetts Press, 1979.

Hoover, Marjorie L. *Meyerhold and his Set Designers*. New York: Peter Lang, 1988.

Hoover, Marjorie L. and Edward Braun, eds. *Meyerhold on Theatre*. London: Bloomsbury Methuen Drama, 2016.

Johnson, Michael Duane. *On the Paths of the Soul: Stanisław Przybyszewski and the Russian Stage. The Cases of Vera Komissarzhevskaia and Vsevolod Meierkhol'd*. Ann Arbor: ProQuest, 2008.

Law, Alma H. 'Meyerhold's *The Magnanimous Cuckold*'. *The Drama Review* 26, no. 1 (1982): 61–86.

Leach, Robert. *Vsevolod Meyerhold*. Cambridge: Cambridge University Press, 1989.

Meyerhold, Vsevolod. 'The Reconstruction of the Theatre'. In Meyerhold, *Meyerhold on Theatre*. Rev. edn. Edited by Edward Braun, 253–74. London: Methuen, 1991.

Mikhailova, Alla. *Meyerhold and Set Designers*. Translated by E. Bessmertnaya. Moscow: Galart, 1995.

Rudnitsky, Konstantin. *Meyerhold the Director*. Translated by George Petrov. Ann Arbor, MI: Ardis, 1981.

Skinner, Amy. 'Surfaces, Depths and Hypercubes: Meyerholdian Scenography and the Fourth Dimension'. *Theatre and Performance Design* 1, no. 3 (2015): 204–19.

Skinner, Amy. *Meyerhold and the Cubists: Perspectives in Painting and Performance*. Bristol: Intellect, 2015.

Syssoyeva, Kathryn Mederos. 'Revolution in the Theatre I: Meyerhold, Stanislavsky and collective creation, Russia, 1905'. In *A History of Collective Creation*.

Edited by Kathryn Mederos Syssoyeva and Scott Proudfit. Basingstoke: Palgrave Macmillan, 2013.

Vendrovskaya, L.D., ed. *Vstrechi S Meierkhol'dom*. Moscow: VTO, 1967.

Vendrovskaya, L.D. and A.V. Fevral'ski, eds. *Tvorcheskoe Nasledie V.E. Meierkhol'da*. Moscow: VTO, 1978.

Volkov, Nikolai. *Meierkhol'd. Tom I (1874–1908)*. Moscow: Academia, 1929.

Worrall, Nick. 'Meyerhold Directs Gogol's *Government Inspector*'. *Theatre Quarterly* 2, no. 7 (1972): 75–95.

Worrall, Nick. 'Meyerhold's Production of the *Magnificent Cuckold*'. *The Drama Review* 17, no. 1 (1973): 14–34.

Erwin Piscator

Amlung, Ullrich, ed. '*Leben is immer ein Anfang!' Erwin Piscator 1893–1966*. Marburg: Jonas Verlag, 1993.

Arjomand, Minou. 'Performing Catastrophe: Erwin Piscator's Documentary Theatre'. *Modern Drama* 59, no. 1 (2016): 49–74.

Barber, X. Theodore. 'Drama with a Pointer: The Group Theatre's Production of Piscator's Case of Clyde Griffiths'. *TDR* 28, no. 4 (1984): 61–72.

Boeser, Knut and Renata Vatková, eds. *Erwin Piscator. Eine Arbeitsbiographie in 2 Bänden, vol. 2, Moskau – Paris – New York – Berlin 1931–1966*. Berlin: Edition Hentrich, 1986.

Elling, Barbara. 'Theater as the Conscience of Society: Erwin Piscator's "Interim Achievement"'. In *Playing for Stakes: German-Language Drama in Social Context. Essays in Honor of Herbert Lederer*. Edited by Anna K. Kuhn and Barbara D. Wright, 101–18. Oxford and Providence, RI: Berg Publishers, 1994.

Evans, Thomas George. *Piscator in the American* Theatre. *New York, 1939–1951*. Ann Arbor, MI: University of Wisconsin Press, 1968.

Haarmann, Hermann. 'Abschied von Europa: "Ein bedeutendendes Kunstwerk" Erwin Piscators Spielfilm *Der Aufstand der Fischer*'. In *Exil in der Sowjetunion 1933–1945*. Edited by Hermann Haarmann and Christoph Hesse. Marburg: Tectum, 2010.

Innes, C.D. *Erwin Piscator's Political Theatre: The Development of Modern German Drama*. Cambridge: Cambridge University Press, 1972.

Kirfel-Lenk, Thea. *Erwin Piscator im Exil in den USA 1939–1951. Eine Darstellung seiner antifaschistischen Theaterarbeit am Dramatic Workshop der New School for Social Research*. Berlin: Henschel, 1984.

Ley-Piscator, Maria. *Der Tanz im Spiegel. Mein Leben mit Erwin Piscator*. Reinbek bei Hamburg: Wunderlich, 1989.

Ley-Piscator, Maria. *The Piscator Experiment. The Political Theatre*. New York: James H. Heineman, 1967.

Malina, Judith. *The Piscator Notebook*. London: Routledge Chapman & Hall, 2012.

Piscator, Erwin. 'Objective Acting'. In *Actors on Acting: The Theories, Techniques, and Practices of the Great Actors of All Times as Told in their Own Words*. Edited by Toby Cole and Helen Krich Chinoy, 285–91. New York: Crown, 1949.

Piscator, Erwin. *Schriften 2*. Edited by Ludwig Hoffmann. East Berlin: Henschel, 1968.

Piscator, Erwin. *The Political Theatre*. Edited and translated by Hugh Rorrison. New York: Avon, 1978.

Piscator, Erwin. *Theater, Film, Politik. Ausgewählte Schriften*. Edited by Ludwig Hoffmann. Berlin: Henschel, 1980.

Piscator, Erwin. *The Political Theatre*. Edited and translated by Hugh Rorrison. London: Methuen, 1980.

Piscator, Erwin. *Die Briefe*, vol. 1: Berlin – Moskau (1909–1936). Edited by Peter Diezel. Berlin: Bostelmann und Siebenhaar, 2005.

Piscator, Erwin. *Briefe*, vol. 2.2: New York 1939–1945. Edited by Peter Diezel. Berlin: B&S Siebenhaar, 2009.

Piscator, Erwin. *Briefe*, vol. 2.3: New York 1945–1951. Edited by Peter Diezel. Berlin: B&S Siebenhaar, 2009.

Piscator, Erwin. *Briefe*, vol. 3.2: Bundesrepublik Deutschland, 1955–1959. Edited by Peter Diezel. Berlin: B&S Siebenhaar, 2011.

Piscator, Erwin. *Briefe*, vol. 3.3: Bundesrepublik Deutschland, 1960–1966. Edited by Peter Diezel. Berlin: B&S Siebenhaar, 2011.

Pitches, Jonathan. *Vsevolod Meyerhold*. London: Routledge, 2003.

Rutkoff, Peter M. 'Politics on Stage. Piscator and the Dramatic Workshop'. In Peter M. Rutkoff and William B. Scott, *New School: a History of the New School for Social Research*, 172–95. New York: Macmillan, 1986.

Saal, Ilka. 'Broadway and the Depoliticization of Epic Theatre: The Case of Erwin Piscator'. In *Brecht. Broadway and United States Theatre*. Edited by J. Chris Westgate, 45–71. Newcastle: Cambridge Scholars, 2007.

Tolstoy, Leo. *War and Peace*. Adapted for the stage by Alfred Neumann, Erwin Piscator and Guntram Prüfer. English adaptation by Robert David MacDonald. London: Macgibbon & Kee, 1963.

Wannemacher, Klaus. *Erwin Piscators Theater gegen das Schweigen. Politisches Theater zwischen den Fronten des Kalten Kriegs*. Tübingen: Max Niemeyer, 2004.

Willett, John. *The Theatre of Erwin Piscator: Half a Century of Politics in the Theatre*. London: Eyre Methuen, 1978.

Willett, John. *The Theatre of Erwin Piscator*. New York: Holmes and Meier, 1979.

Bertolt Brecht

Barnett, David. 'Toward a Definition of Post-Brechtian Performance: The Example of *In the Jungle of the Cities* at the Berliner Ensemble, 1971'. *Modern Drama* 54, no. 3 (2011): 333–56.

Barnett, David. 'Performing Dialectics in an Age of Uncertainty, or: Why Post-Brechtian ≠ Postdramatic'. In *Postdramatic Theatre and the Political: International Perspectives on Contemporary Performance*. Edited by Karen Jürs-Munby, Jerome Carroll and Steve Giles, 47–66. London and New York: Bloomsbury, 2013.

Barnett, David. *Brecht in Practice: Theatre, Theory and Performance*. London: Bloomsbury, 2014.

Barnett, David. *A History of the Berliner Ensemble*. Cambridge: Cambridge University Press, 2015.

Berliner Ensemble and Helene Weigel, eds. *Theaterarbeit: 6 Aufführungen des Berliner Ensembles*. Dresden: VVV Dresdner Verlag, 1952.

Berliner, Ensemble and Helene Weigel, eds. *Theaterarbeit: 6 Aufführungen des Berliner Ensembles*. 2nd edn. Berlin: Henschelverlag Kunst und Gesellschaft, 1961.

Bradley, Laura. *Brecht and Political Theatre: 'The Mother' On Stage*. Oxford: Oxford University Press, 2006.

Brecht, Bertolt. *Mr. Puntila and his Man Matti*. Translated by John Willett. London: Eyre Methuen, 1977.

Brecht, Bertolt. *Life of Galileo*. Translated by John Willett. London: Methuen Student, 1986.

Brecht, Bertolt. *Große kommentierte Berliner und Frankfurter Ausgabe*, abbreviated to BFA, 30 vols. Edited by Werner Hecht, Jan Knopf, Werner Mittenzwei and Klaus-Detlef Müller. Berlin and Frankfurt am Main: Aufbau und Suhrkamp, 1988–2000. [= complete Works in German].

Brecht, Bertolt. *Letters 1913–1956*. Edited by John Willett. Translated by Ralph Manheim London: Methuen, 1990.

Brecht, Bertolt. 'Der Theater-Kommunist'. In BFA 13, 307–8.

Brecht, Bertolt. 'Gespräche mit jungen Intellektuellen'. In Brecht, *Schriften 3. Schriften 1942–1956*, 97–103. Berlin, Weimar and Frankfurt am Main: Aufbau and Suhrkamp, 1993.

Brecht, Bertolt. *Journals 1933–1945*. Edited by John Willett. Translated by Hugh Rorrison. London: Methuen, 1993.

Brecht, Bertolt. '[Kritik der *Poetik* des Aristoteles]'. In Brecht, BFA 22, 171–2'. Edited by Werner Hecht, Jan Knopf, Werner Mittenzwei and Hans-Detlef Müller, 171–2. Berlin and Frankfurt am Main: Aufbau and Suhrkamp, 1993.

Brecht, Bertolt. *Collected Plays*, vol. 2. Edited by John Willett and Ralph Manheim. London: Bloomsbury, 1994.

Brecht, Bertolt. *Collected Plays: Five*. Edited by John Willett and Ralph Manheim. London: Methuen Drama, 1995.

Brecht, Bertolt. *Brecht on Performance: Messingkauf and Modelbooks*. Edited by Tom Kuhn, Steve Giles and Marc Silberman. Translated by Charlotte Ryland, Romy Fursland, Steve Giles, Tom Kuhn and John Willet. London: Bloomsbury, 2014.

Brecht, Bertolt. *Brecht on Theatre*. 3rd edn. Edited by Marc Silberman, Steve Giles and Tom Kuhn. London: Bloomsbury, 2014.

Brecht, Bertolt. *Bertolt Brecht's Me-ti: Book of Interventions in the Flow of Things*. Edited by Antony Tatlow. London: Bloomsbury, 2016.

Bunge, Hans. *Brechts Lai-Tu. Erinnerungen und Notate von Ruth Berlau*. Darmstadt: Luchterhand, 1985.

Butler, Judith. 'Performative Acts and Gender Constitution: An Essay in Phenomenology and Feminist Theory'. *Theatre Journal* 40, no. 4 (1988): 519–31.

Deschner, Margareta N. 'Wuolijoki's and Brecht's Politization of the *Volksstück*'. In *Bertolt Brecht: Political Theory and Literary Practice*. Edited by Betty Nance Weber and Hubert Heinen, 115–28. Manchester: Manchester University Press, 1980.

Eddershaw, Margaret. 'Actors on Brecht'. In *The Cambridge Companion to Brecht*. 2nd edn. Edited by Peter Thomson and Glendyr Sacks, 278–96. Cambridge: Cambridge University Press, 2006.

Eylau, Hans Ulrich. '*Das Glockenspiel des Kreml*'. *Berliner Zeitung*, 28 March 1952.

Fenn, Bernard. *Characterisation of Women in the Plays of Bertolt Brecht*. Frankfurt am Main: Peter Lang, 1982.

Frisch, Werner and K.W. Obermeier. *Brecht in Augsburg. Errinnerungen, Dokumente, Texts, Fotos*. Berlin and Weimar: Aufbau, 1986.

Fuegi, John. *Bertolt Brecht: Chaos, According to Plan*. Cambridge: Cambridge University Press, 1987.

Gaston, Bruce. 'Brecht's Pastiche History Play: Renaissance Drama and Modernist Theatre in *Leben Eduards Des Zweiten Von England*'. *German Life and Letters* 56, no. 4 (2003): 344–62.

Hecht, Werner. *Brecht Chronik*. Frankfurt am Main: Suhrkamp, 1997.

Hofmann, Heinz. 'Denkzettel für neue Uralstürmer'. *National-Zeitung*, 16 January 1955.

Kluft, Ernst. 'Tragödie eines 'unbekannten "Soldaten"'. *Neue Zeit*, 18 January 1955.

Mumford, Meg. 'Showing the Gestus: A Study of Acting in Brecht's Theatre' (Unpublished PhD Thesis, University of Bristol, 1997).

Mumford, Meg. '"Dragging" Brecht's Gestus Onwards: A Feminist Challenge'. In *Bertolt Brecht: Centenary Essays*. Edited by Steve Giles and Rodney Livingstone, 240–57. Amsterdam: Rodopi, 1998.

Mumford, Meg. 'Brecht on Acting for the 21st Century: Interrogating and Re-Inscribing the Fixed'. *Communications from the International Brecht Society* 29, nos 1–2 (2000): 44–9.

Mumford, Meg. 'Gestic Masks in Brecht's Theatre: A Testimony to the Contradictions and Parameters of a Realist Aesthetic'. *The Brecht Yearbook*, 26 (2001): 143–71.

Mumford, Meg. *Bertolt Brecht*. Abingdon and New York: Routledge, 2009.

Neureuter, Hans Peter, ed. *Brechts 'Herr Puntila und sein Knecht Matti'*. Frankfurt am Main: Suhrkamp, 1987.

Neureuter, Hans Peter. '*Herr Puntila und sein Knecht Matti*'. In *Brecht Handbuch*, vol. 1. Edited by Jan Knopf, 440–56. Stuttgart and Weimar: J.B. Metzler, 2001.

Parker, Stephen. *Bertolt Brecht: A Literary Life*. London: Bloomsbury: 2014.

Parker, Stephen. 'Taoist Paradox and Socialist-Realist Diadactics: Re-Grounding the Galileo Complex in the "Danish" *Leben des Galilei*. Brecht's Testimony from the "finsteren Zeiten"'. *German Life and Letters* 69, no. 2 (2016): 192–212.

Pfister, Manfred. 'Vor- und Nachgeschichte der Tragödie *Eduard II*. von Marlowe über Brecht und Feuchtwanger bis zu Ihering und Kerr'. In *Großbritannien und Deutschland. Europäische Aspekte der politisch-kulturelle Beziehungen beider Länder in Geschichte und Gegenwart. Festschrift für John W. Bourke*. Edited by Ortwin Kuhn, 372–440. Goldmann: Munich 1974.

Rülicke, Käthe. 'Historisierende Lesarten von J.R. Bechers *Winterschlacht*'. *Notate* 1 (1988).

Rülicke-Weiler, Käthe. *Die Dramaturgie Brechts: Theater als Mittel der Veränderung*. Berlin: Henschelverlag Kunst und Gesellschaft, 1966.

Schwaiger, Michael, ed. *Bertolt Brecht und Erwin Piscator: Experimentelles Theater im Berlin der Zwangierjahre*. Vienna: Christian Brandstätter, 2004.

Solomon, Alisa. 'Materialist Girl: "The Good Person of Szechwan" and Making Gender Strange'. *Theater* 25, no. 2 (1994): 42–55.

Stevens, Lara. *Anti-War Theatre After Brecht: Dialectical Aesthetics in the Twenty-First Century*. London: Palgrave Macmillan, 2016.

Suvin, Darko. 'Brecht: Bearing, Pedagogy, Productivity'. *Gestos* 5, no. 10 (1990): 11–28.

Weber, Carl. 'The Actor and Brecht, or: The Truth Is Concrete'. *The Brecht Yearbook* 13 (1984): 63–74.

Wekwerth, Manfred. *Schriften: Arbeit mit Brecht*. 2nd rev. and expanded edn. Berlin: Henschel, 1975.

Zimmermann, Rainer E. '*Leben des Galilei*'. In *Brecht Handbuch*, vol. 1. Edited by Jan Knopf, 357–79. Stuttgart and Weimar: J.B. Metzler, 2001.

INDEX